Linds

Straightforward

Elementary Student's Book

MACMILLAN

Reading	Listening	Speaking	Writing (in the Workbook)
Dialogues: the first day at a new job		Guided dialogue: introductions	
	A phone call to a language school	Making a phone call to a language school **Did you know?** The world of social networks	Completing a form
	Dialogues about possessions	Game: *What's this in English?*	
An email from a tour company	Dialogues at a welcome party	Roleplay: offering and responding at a welcome party	
The Expat Files: an article about Britons living abroad	A Briton talking about living abroad	Talking about life as an expat	
	A radio interview about men, women and friendship	Talking about things you do with your friends	A personal e-message
An Englishman's home: an article about a man who lives with his parents		**Did you know?** The family in Britain	
	A phone call describing people arriving at the airport	Communication activity: describing famous faces past and present	
Houseswap: a website describing houses		Game: *Class Houseswap*	
	A documentary about the White House	Giving a short presentation of your home **Did you know?** 10 Downing Street	Giving directions
A dialogue about a new flat		Communication activity: finding differences between two rooms	
	Dialogues at the information desk of a shopping mall	Roleplay: giving directions in a building	
MetroNaps: an article about a nap service		Communication activity: talking about daily routines	
An interview about Nothing Day	Dialogues about special days	Talking about adding an extra national holiday to the calendar	
	A radio phone-in about housework	Survey: life and work at home	Phone messages
	Three phone dialogues	Roleplay: phone calls **Did you know?** Phone facts: Canada and the US	
High-speed trains: an article about fast trains		Talking about languages	
	People talking about holiday photos	Talking about holiday photos **Did you know?** Top destinations for Canadian tourists	Describing a holiday
A dialogue about holiday preparations		Talking about things to take on holiday	
Two advertisements for hotels	Dialogues at a hotel	Talking about a past holiday Roleplay: at a hotel	

4

Reading	Listening	Speaking	Writing (in the Workbook)
Blogs about celebrations		Talking about celebrations	
	Actor! Author! A TV quiz programme	Communication activity: films Game: *Actor! Author!* **Did you know?** The Big Read: favourite books	A card for a special occasion
Crying – good for your health: an article about men and crying		Game: *The Dialogue Game*	
	Dialogues about likes and dislikes	Talking about things to do in London Talking about likes and dislikes	
	Exposed: A TV programme about diets	Inventing your own 'miracle' diet	
An article about rice		Communication activity: food	
	Dialogues about eating habits	Dialogue: complaining about food	A dish for you
Eating out: a survey	A dialogue in a restaurant	Survey: eating out Guided dialogue at a restaurant **Did you know?** Restaurants by numbers – in the US	
Fear of flying: an article about flying		Questionnaire and talking about travel	
	A traffic report on the radio	Game: *In Traffic* **Did you know?** London's Congestion Charge	An invitation
Tracy Dick P.I.: detective story		Communication activity: a normal day and a special day	
	Dialogues about crossing a city	Dialogue: suggesting things to do	
A website about first impressions		Talking about making a good impression	
Health: an article about sitting at work	Exercise instructions	Survey: health Giving exercise instructions	
	An interview about how people remember faces	Memory test **Did you know?** Faces on coins	Giving advice
	Dialogues about feeling ill	Roleplay: not feeling well	
An article about strange laws		Making classroom 'laws' **Did you know?** Banning smoking in India	
	People talk about life in the capital city of their country	Talking about living in the capital Communication activity: moving to another city	A city guide
Best of the best: an extract from a guide book about Cape Town		Talking and giving advice about the best things to do in a city	
	A dialogue in a souvenir shop	Roleplay: in a souvenir shop	
	Behind the scenes: a TV programme about jobs	Talking about work Game: *Guess The Job* **Did you know?** The NHS	
An article about the future of work		Talking about your future working life	A job for the summer
16 before 60: an article about healthy living	People talk about future plans	Talking about plans for the future	
Signs in the workplace	Dialogues in the workplace	Dialogue: invitations	
The music fans: an article about people who love music		Talking about music and musicians you like	
	Interviews about speaking in public	Questionnaire about speaking in public **Did you know?** Person of the Year	Thanks
English in your life: brochure for a language school		A short presentation	
	Dialogues at the end of an event	Game: *Travel with English*	

Basics 1

INTERNATIONAL ENGLISH

1 Look at the international English words in the photos. Which ones do you know?

2 🔘 **1.1** Listen and point to the words you hear.

3 🔘 **1.2** Listen and repeat.

NUMBERS 1–10

1 🔘 **1.3** Read and listen to the numbers.

1	2	3	4	5	6	7	8	9	10

2 🔘 **1.3** Listen and repeat.

3 🔘 **1.4** Listen and write the number you hear.

___ ___ ___ ___ ___ ___

4 Work in pairs, A and B. Turn to page 137.

INTRODUCTIONS 1

1 🔘 **1.5** Read and listen to the dialogue.

Woman: Hello.
Frank: Hi.
Woman: What's your name?
Frank: My name's Frank.
Woman: Nice to meet you.
Frank: Nice to meet you.

2 🔘 **1.5** Listen and repeat.

3 🔘 **1.6** Listen to two dialogues. Match the dialogues to the pictures.

A ____

B ____

4 Practise the dialogue from exercise 1.

ALPHABET

1 🔘 **1.7** Read and listen to the alphabet.

A B C D E F G H I J K L M N O P Q R S T U V W X Y Z

2 🔘 **1.7** Listen and repeat.

3 🔘 **1.8** Look at the circles. Listen to the sound and the letters.

/eɪ/ A, H, J

/iː/ B, C, D, E, G, P

/e/ F, L, M, N, S

/aɪ/ I

/əʊ/ O

/ɑː/ R

/uː/ Q, U

4 Write the letters from the box in the correct circles.

K   T   V   W   X   Y   Z

5 🔘 **1.9** Listen to the recording to check your answers. Repeat the letters.

6 🔘 **1.10** Listen and write the letters you hear.

1 _____   2 _____   3 _____   4 _____   5 _____

INTRODUCTIONS 2

1 Put the dialogue in the correct order.

☐ Hi. My name's Simon. What's your name?
☐ L-I-N-D-S-A-Y.
☐ Oh. How do you spell that?
☐ My name's Lindsay.
☐ Hello.

2 🔘 **1.11** Listen and check.

3 Work in groups. Ask other people to spell their name.

What's your name?
My name's Viktor.
How do you spell that?
V-I-K-T-O-R.

Basics 2

CLASSROOM ENGLISH 1

1 Match the pictures to the verbs in the box.

| write listen to open close look at read talk |

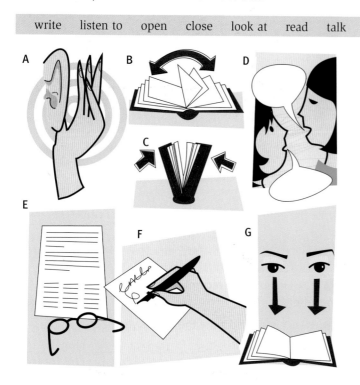

2 🔘 **1.12** Listen to the recording and write a word from exercise 1 in the space.

1 _____ your books. 5 _____ the picture.
2 _____ your books. 6 _____ the text.
3 _____ the words. 7 _____ the CD.
4 _____ to a partner.

3 🔘 **1.12** Listen again and check.

COLOURS

1 Match the words in the box to the colours.

| red white green brown blue black yellow |

2 🔘 **1.13** Listen and repeat.

DAYS OF THE WEEK

1 🔘 **1.14** Listen to the days of the week and complete the words.

2 🔘 **1.15** Listen and repeat.

3 🔘 **1.16** Listen to five dialogues. <u>Underline</u> the day of the week you hear.

1 *Monday / Sunday*   4 *Saturday / Sunday*
2 *Tuesday / Thursday*   5 *Friday / Thursday*
3 *Friday / Saturday*

NUMBERS 11–100

1 Match the words to the numbers.

eleven	14
twelve	11
thirteen	20
fourteen	15
fifteen	17
sixteen	19
seventeen	13
eighteen	12
nineteen	18
twenty	16

2 🔘 **1.17** Listen and repeat.

3 Write the numbers for these words.

twenty-one   _21_   seventy-five   ____
thirty-three _33_   eighty-eight   ____
forty-seven   ____   ninety-one   ____
fifty-nine   ____   one hundred   ____
sixty-one   ____

Things around you

1 🔘 **1.18** Look at the photos and listen to the words.

an ID card	an earring	an apple	coins
keys	photos	a pen	sweets

Sandra, Pete and G____ h

2 🔘 **1.19** Read and listen to the words. What things are in your classroom? Tick (✓) or cross (✗) the boxes.

☐ a TV   ☐ a door   ☐ a CD player
☐ a board   ☐ a window

3 🔘 **1.20** Listen to words from exercises 1 and 2. Point to the object on the page or in the class and say the word.

4 Work in pairs. What things do you have with you today? Ask your partner. Use the picture and the words to help you.

Do you have an ID card? Yes.
Do you have photos? No.
Do you have an apple? Yes.
Do you have a pen? Yes.

Grammar: *a/an*, plurals

> With singular nouns, use the article *a/an*.
> **an** + vowel
>   *an* apple
>   *an* ID card
>
> **a** + **consonant**
>   *a* TV
>   *a* pen
>
> To make nouns plural = noun + *s/es/ies*
>   *sweets*
>   *sandwiches*

> ❯ See Language Reference page 40

1 Make the words plural.

1 wallet _____
2 bus _____
3 taxi _____
4 hotel _____
5 mobile phone _____
6 sandwich _____

2 Write *a*, *an* or nothing.

1 __ ID card   5 __ airport
2 __ bus   6 __ key
3 __ apples   7 __ hotels
4 __ taxis   8 __ hospital

Classroom English 2

1 🔘 **1.21** Listen and complete the questions and sentences with a word from the box.

say	mean	don't

1 What does *apple* _____?
2 How do you _____ *merci* in English?
3 I _____ know.
4 I _____ understand.

2 Look at the words and pictures on pages 8 and 9. Work in pairs and ask your partner questions.

What does ... mean?
How do you say ... in English?

GRAMMAR TERMS

The words in bold are grammar terms used in *Straightforward* Elementary. What are they in your language?

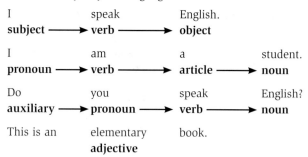

I	speak	English.
subject →	**verb** →	**object**

I	am	a	student.
pronoun →	**verb** →	**article** →	**noun**

Do	you	speak	English?
auxiliary →	**pronoun** →	**verb** →	**noun**

This is an	elementary	book.
	adjective	

PRONUNCIATION

Vowel sounds

i:	ɪ	ʊ	u:
eat	it	book	new
tree	six	pull	school
e	ə	ɜː	ɔː
very	American	her	born
any	mother	bird	awful
æ	ʌ	ɑː	ɒ
back	up	car	what
apple	does	after	on

ɪə	eɪ	ʊə	əʊ
here	face	Europe	no
ear	ate	tour	open
ɔɪ	eə	aɪ	aʊ
boy	their	hi	house
noisy	airport	eye	down

Consonant sounds

p	b	t	d	tʃ	dʒ
stop	bar	ten	desk	cheese	June
parents	job	light	red	teach	orange
k	g	f	v	θ	ð
can	go	father	very	think	the
look	bag	laugh	live	fourth	mother
s	z	ʃ	ʒ	m	n
see	zoo	she	television	make	never
rice	has	information	usually	name	ten
ŋ	h	l	r	w	j
English	hello	like	read	water	yes
sing	hand	ill	practise	where	year

A/an, plurals

Use *a* and *an* in front of singular nouns.

Use *a* with a consonant.

a TV
a pen
a door

Use *an* with a vowel.

an apple
an ID card
an earring

To make nouns plural add *-s*, *-es*, *-ies*.

-s

pen	pens
door	doors
apple	apples

-es

sandwich	sandwiches
bus	buses

-ies

dictionary	dictionaries
baby	babies

Do not use *a/an* with plural nouns.
Not ~~a doors~~

WORD LIST

International words

airport *n* ***	/ˈeəpɔːt/
bus *n* ***	/bʌs/
football *n* **	/ˈfʊtbɔːl/
hotel *n* ***	/həʊˈtel/
hospital *n* ***	/ˈhɒspɪt(ə)l/
pizza *n* *	/ˈpiːtsə/
police *n* ***	/pəˈliːs/
station *n*	/ˈsteɪʃ(ə)n/
taxi *n* ***	/ˈtæksi/
train *n*	/treɪn/

Numbers

one ***	/wʌn/
two ***	/tuː/
three	/θriː/
four	/fɔː(r)/
five	/faɪv/
six	/sɪks/
seven	/ˈsev(ə)n/
eight	/eɪt/
nine	/naɪn/
ten	/ten/
eleven	/ɪˈlev(ə)n/
twelve	/twelv/
thirteen	/ˌθɜː(r)ˈtiːn/
fourteen	/ˌfɔː(r)ˈtiːn/
fifteen	/fɪfˈtiːn/
sixteen	/ˌsɪksˈtiːn/
seventeen	/ˌsev(ə)nˈtiːn/
eighteen	/eɪˈtiːn/
nineteen	/ˌnaɪnˈtiːn/
twenty	/ˈtwenti/
thirty	/ˈθɜː(r)ti/
forty	/ˈfɔː(r)ti/
fifty	/ˈfɪfti/
sixty	/ˈsɪksti/
seventy	/ˈsev(ə)nti/
eighty	/ˈeɪti/
ninety	/ˈnaɪnti/
one hundred	/wʌn ˈhʌndrəd/

Classroom English

book *n* ***	/bʊk/
CD *n* **	/siː ˈdiː/
close *v* ***	/kləʊz/
listen to *v* ***	/ˈlɪs(ə)n/
look at *v* ***	/ˈlʊk ət/
open *v* ***	/ˈəʊpən/
partner *n* ***	/ˈpɑː(r)tnə(r)/
picture *n* ***	/ˈpɪktʃə(r)/
read *v* ***	/riːd/
talk *v* ***	/tɔːk/
text *n* ***	/tekst/
word *n* ***	/wɜː(r)d/
write *v* ***	/raɪt/

Days of the week

Monday ***	/ˈmʌndeɪ/
Tuesday ***	/ˈtʃuːzdeɪ/
Wednesday ***	/ˈwenzdeɪ/
Thursday ***	/ˈθɜː(r)zdeɪ/
Friday ***	/ˈfraɪdeɪ/
Saturday ***	/ˈsætə(r)deɪ/
Sunday ***	/ˈsʌndeɪ/

Colours

black *adj* ***	/blæk/
blue *adj* ***	/bluː/
brown *adj* ***	/braʊn/
green *adj* ***	/griːn/
grey *adj* ***	/greɪ/
red *adj* ***	/red/
white *adj* ***	/waɪt/
yellow *adj* ***	/ˈjeləʊ/

Things around you

apple *n* ***	/ˈæp(ə)l/
board *n* ***	/bɔː(r)d/
CD player *n*	/ˌsiː ˈdiː ˈpleɪə(r)/
coin *n* ***	/kɔɪn/
door *n* ***	/dɔː(r)/
earring *n* *	/ˈɪərɪŋ/
ID card *n*	/aɪ ˈdiː kɑːd/
key *n* ***	/kiː/
mobile phone *n* **	/məʊbaɪl ˈfəʊn/
pen *n* **	/pen/
photo *n* **	/ˈfəʊtəʊ/
sweet *n* *	/swiːt/
TV *n* ***	/ˌtiː ˈviː/
wallet *n*	/ˈwɒlɪt/
window *n* ***	/ˈwɪndəʊ/

Abbreviations

n	noun	*sth*	something
v	verb	*C*	countable
adj	adjective	*U*	uncountable
adv	adverb	*pl*	plural
sb	somebody	*s*	singular
***	the most common and basic words		
**	very common words		
*	fairly common words		

1A The new person

READING & LISTENING

1 Read the text.

It's Monday. This is Alyssa.
She's new. It's her first day at work.

2 Match the dialogues 1–4 to the pictures A–D.

1 B

Alyssa:	Hello.
Charles:	Good morning.
Alyssa:	My name's Alyssa.
Charles:	You're new. Hello, I'm Charles. I'm the manager.

2 C

Charles:	Good morning, Julian.
Julian:	Good morning, Charles.
Charles:	Julian, this is Alison. She's new.
Julian:	Nice to meet you, Alison.
Alyssa:	I'm not Alison.
Julian:	What?
Alyssa:	My name isn't Alison. It's Alyssa.
Julian:	Nice to meet you, Alyssa.
Charles:	Sorry.

3 D

Baasim:	Alyssa!
Alyssa:	Hello, Baasim!
Baasim:	How are you?
Alyssa:	I'm fine, thanks. How are you?
Baasim:	Fine. Good to see you. Goodbye.
Alyssa:	Yeah, bye.

4 A

Margaret:	She's new.
Carlo:	What's her name?
Margaret:	Alyssa.
Carlo:	Alyssa? How do you spell that?
Margaret:	I don't know.

> ### Useful language
>
> *Good morning:* < 12:00 pm
> *Good afternoon:* 12:00 pm – 6:00 pm
> *Good evening:* > 6:00 pm

3 🔘 **1.22** Listen to the recording to check your answers.

4 Work in pairs. Repeat the dialogues.

VOCABULARY: objects 1

1 🔘 **1.23** Listen and repeat the words.

> a desk   a computer   a chair   a pen   a coffee
> a piece of paper   a phone   a book

2 Find the things in the pictures.

3 🔘 **1.24** Listen to Alyssa and Margaret. Tick (✓) the words from exercise 1 you hear.

GRAMMAR:
verb *to be* – affirmative; possessive adjectives

> *I'm* new.
> They **are** Charles and Julian.
> She **isn't** Alison. She**'s** Alyssa.
>
> **Possessive adjectives**
> **Her** name is Margaret.
> What's **your** name?
> **Their** names are Baasim and Carla.

> ❯ SEE LANGUAGE REFERENCE PAGE 20

1 Complete the sentences with *is/are/am*.

1 Her name _____ not Alison.
2 Her name _____ Alyssa.
3 You _____ new.
4 I _____ the manager.
5 They _____ in the office.
6 He _____ in the hotel.
7 Baasim and Julian _____ not managers.
8 I _____ fine, thanks.

2 Say the sentences in exercise 1 with contractions.

3 <u>Underline</u> the correct word.

SPEAKING

1 Work in groups of three, A, B and C. Write a dialogue. Look at the diagram below and the dialogues 1 and 2 on page 12 to help you.

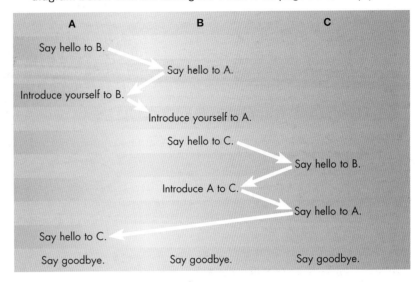

A	B	C
Say hello to B.		
	Say hello to A.	
Introduce yourself to B.		
	Introduce yourself to A.	
	Say hello to C.	
		Say hello to B.
	Introduce A to C.	
		Say hello to A.
Say hello to C.		
Say goodbye.	Say goodbye.	Say goodbye.

2 Change roles and repeat the dialogue.

1   This is *your / his* pen.

2   This isn't *my / your* sandwich!

3   *His / Her* name is George.

4   They're *her / their* earrings.

5   It's *my / our* computer.

6   *His / Her* name is Elizabeth.

1B | Personal application

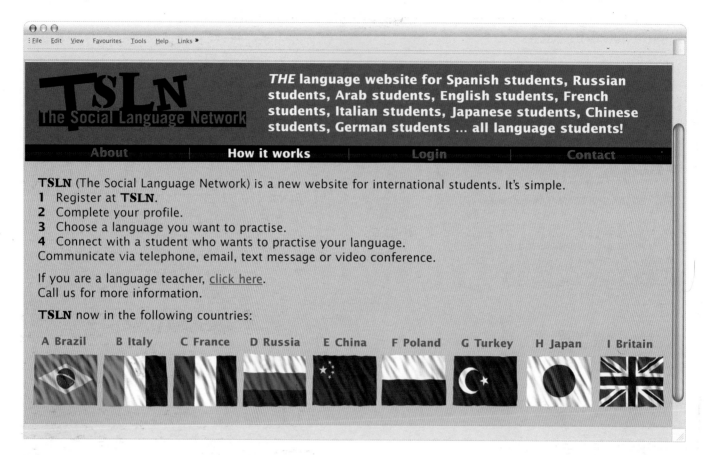

TSLN - The Social Language Network

THE **language website for Spanish students, Russian students, Arab students, English students, French students, Italian students, Japanese students, Chinese students, German students ... all language students!**

About | **How it works** | Login | Contact

TSLN (The Social Language Network) is a new website for international students. It's simple.
1 Register at **TSLN**.
2 Complete your profile.
3 Choose a language you want to practise.
4 Connect with a student who wants to practise your language.
Communicate via telephone, email, text message or video conference.

If you are a language teacher, click here.
Call us for more information.

TSLN now in the following countries:

A Brazil | B Italy | C France | D Russia | E China | F Poland | G Turkey | H Japan | I Britain

VOCABULARY: countries & nationalities

1 Match the sentences 1–3 to the correct flag or flags A–I.

1 The British and Russian flags are red, white and blue. ☐ ☐
2 The Chinese flag is red and yellow. ☐
3 The Italian flag is red, white and green. ☐

2 Write the nationalities for these countries in the correct column.

Brazil ~~Greece~~ Germany Poland Turkey France
Ireland ~~Japan~~ Italy ~~Britain~~ ~~Russia~~ China

-(i)an	-ish	-ese	other
Russian	*British*	*Japanese*	*Greek*

3 🔘 **1.25** Listen to the recording to check your answers. Listen and repeat.

4 Describe the other flags on the website. Use the words from exercise 1.

5 Work in pairs. Where are you from? What's your nationality? Tell your partner.

Where are you from? I'm from Poland. What's your nationality? I'm Polish.

LISTENING

1 Look at the web page. What is TSLN?

2 🔘 **1.26** Listen to a telephone call to TSLN. Underline the correct answer.

1 Mark is a *language teacher / language student*.
2 Mark is a(n) *German / English* student.
3 Mark's first language is *German / English*.
4 He is *26 / 25* years old.
5 He is *American / Australian*.
6 The woman is from *London / Sydney*.

3 **1.26** Listen again. Complete the form for Mark.

The Social Language Network – Personal Profile			
First name:	Mark	Sex:	male ☐ female ☐
Last name:		Age:	
Language student ☐		13–16 ☐	
Language teacher ☐		17–25 ☐	**upload photo**
Language of study:	German	26–35 ☐	
First language:	English	36–45 ☐	
Nationality:		46–55 ☐	
Email address:	Mark@mail.com	over 55 ☐	

GRAMMAR: verb *to be* – negative & questions

With the verb *to be*, change the position of the subject and the verb to make a question.

*You **are** a student.*

✗

***Are** you a student?*

In English, there are two kinds of questions:
Wh- questions = questions with a question word
  ***Where are** you from?*
Yes/no questions = questions with no question word
  ***Are** you a student?*

Yes/no questions have a short answer.
  Yes, *I **am**.*   **No**, *I'm **not**.*

> SEE LANGUAGE REFERENCE PAGE 20

1 Read about another TSLN member. Make questions and answers.

Ben Stark is a language student at university. He's 21 years old. He studies Chinese and Korean. Ben is from Los Angeles, in the US.

1 / Canadian?
  Is he Canadian? No, he isn't.
2 / American?
  Is he American? Yes, he is.
3 / his last name Stark?
4 / from New York?
5 / a language student?
6 / 43 years old?

2 Rearrange the words to make questions.

1 name   what's   your ?
2 last   what's   name   your ?
3 language   teacher   you   are   a ?
4 you   are   a   language   student ?
5 are   you   old   how ?
6 you   are   from   where ?

3 **1.27** Listen to the recording to check your answers. Repeat the questions.

SPEAKING

1 Work in pairs, A and B.

A: You want to be a member of TSLN.
B: You work at TSLN.

Read the dialogue.

B: Good afternoon, The Social Language Network.
A: Hello, I want to be a member.
B: Of course. What's your name?
A: …

2 Continue the dialogue. Use the questions in Grammar exercise 2 to help you.

DID YOU KNOW?

1 Work in pairs. Read about social networks and discuss the questions.

The world of social networks
Social networks are very popular on the internet now. Facebook is a big online network, but other countries have social networks too. Tuenti is a Spanish social network. Orkut is a social network popular with Brazilians and Indians. V Kontakte is a social network in Russia. Mixi is a Japanese online social network.

- Do you use an online social network? Which one?
- What are your favourite 'social' websites?
- Do you have a profile on a website?

1c | Personal possessions

VOCABULARY: objects 2

1 Look at the photos. How many things can you say in English? Make sentences with the words in the box.

| umbrella   mobile phone   glasses
| alarm clock   bottle of water   camera
| newspaper   diary   memory stick
| earphones   business cards   mirror   wallet

It's a …
It's an …
They're …
I don't know what this is.

2 🔘 **1.28** Listen to the recording to check your answers. Repeat the sentences.

LISTENING

1 🔘 **1.29** Listen and tick (✓) the objects you hear.

2 Check your answers in audioscript 1.29 on page 140.

3 Work in pairs. Read the dialogues on page 140.

GRAMMAR: *this, that, these, those*

this (pen)　　　*that* (pen)

these (pens)　　　*those* (pens)

> SEE LANGUAGE REFERENCE PAGE 20

1 Underline the correct word in the dialogues.

1 What's *those / this*?
It's my private book!

2 Wait a minute. Is *that / those* a camera?
Yes. Just one photo please!

3 I think *these / this* are your keys.
Yes, they are!

4 Is that the alarm clock?
No, *that / these* is my mobile phone.

5 Are *those / that* your glasses?
Yes, they are.

6 Are *this / these* my things?
This / These is your phone, but *those / that* are my earphones.

2 Complete with *this, that, these, those*.

1 Is _____ a taxi?
Yes, it is.

2 _____ are your keys.

3 Look. _____ are English buses.

4 Is _____ your ID card?

5 _____ is my business card. Please call me.

6 Hey! _____'s my wallet!

3 🔘 1.30 Listen to the recording to check your answers. Say the sentences.

SPEAKING

1 Work in groups of three. Play *What's This in English?* Each person puts three personal possessions from their bag on the table.

2 One person starts. Ask questions.

For things on the table, ask
What's this in English? What are these in English?
For things in the classroom, ask
What's that in English? What are those in English?

What's that/this in English?

It's a window.　　It's a door.　　I don't know.

That's right!　　Sorry, that's wrong.　　It's a window.

1D | In person

READING

1 Read the email. What is it about?

2 Read again and answer the questions.

1 What is Explore London Tours?
2 Who is Valerie?
3 Where is the welcome party?
4 When is the welcome party?

From: Valerie Hudson <v.hudson@explorelondon.org>
To: Mr and Mrs Curtis <herbcurtis@americainternet.com>
Subject: Welcome party
Date: Mon, 7 May 2012 09:15:53

Dear Mr Curtis,

My name is Valerie and I am your tour guide for the Explore London tour.

Explore London Tours would like to invite you to a welcome party at the Regent Hotel, London, on Sunday, 13 May at 7:30 pm. Come for a drink and meet the other people on your tour.

If you have any questions about your tour, please email me or phone our head office in London on 0207 954 6178.

We look forward to seeing you,

Valerie Hudson
Explore London Tours "London … In Style"

LISTENING

1 🔘 **1.31** Listen. Where are they? <u>Underline</u> the correct place in the hotel for each dialogue.

1 In the hotel *reception / restaurant*
2 In the hotel *reception / restaurant*
3 In the hotel *reception / restaurant*
4 In the hotel *reception / restaurant*

2 🔘 **1.31** Listen again. Is the <u>underlined</u> information correct? Tick (✓) or cross (✗) the sentences.

1 Their names are <u>Rob and Meg Sherman</u>.
2 They are in room <u>34</u>.
3 They are in the <u>bar</u>.
4 He has <u>tea</u> and she has a <u>Coke</u>®.
5 <u>Her</u> name is Sam Moore.
6 Valerie is the <u>tour guide</u>.
7 Herb and Hannah are from <u>America</u>.
8 Rob and Meg are from <u>England</u>.

VOCABULARY: drinks & snacks

1 Match the words in the box to the photos A–H.

> tea   coffee   orange juice   mineral water
> a sandwich   a cake   white wine   beer

2 🔘 1.32 Listen and repeat the words.

3 Work in pairs. Cover the words. Test your partner.

A: *What's this in English?*
B: *Coffee.*
A: *That's right.*

FUNCTIONAL LANGUAGE: offers & responses

1 Complete the words in the box to make phrases.

> **Offers**
> *Would you l___ a drink?*
>
> **Responses**
> *Yes, p_____.*
>
> *No, t_____ you. / No, t_____.*

> ❯ SEE LANGUAGE REFERENCE PAGE 20

2 🔘 1.33 Listen to the recording to check your answers.

3 🔘 1.34 Listen to the words and make offers.

> *a coffee   Would you like a coffee?*

4 Work in pairs, A and B.

A: Offer things to B.   B: Respond.

5 Work in groups of three. You are at the welcome party in the lounge of the Regent Hotel. One person is the tour guide, the other two people are on the tour. Prepare a dialogue. Use the menu and the useful language below to help you.

6 Present your dialogues to other groups in the class.

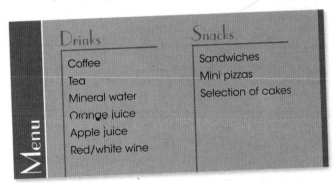

Menu

Drinks	Snacks
Coffee	Sandwiches
Tea	Mini pizzas
Mineral water	Selection of cakes
Orange juice	
Apple juice	
Red/white wine	

Useful language

Greetings	*Hello. Good afternoon …*
Introductions	*My name's … Nice to meet you.*
Personal information	*Where are you from? I'm from …*
Offers	*Would you like …?*
Responses	*Yes, please. No, thank you.*

Self-assessment (✓)

☐ I can introduce myself and another person.
☐ I can give basic personal information.
☐ I can spell my name.
☐ I can make and respond to offers.

GRAMMAR
Verb *to be*: present simple

Affirmative					
Full form			**Contraction**		
I	am		I'm		
He/She/It	is	from Canada.	He's/She's/It's		fine.
You/We/They	are		You're/We're/They're		

To make the verb *to be* negative, add *not* (or *n't*) to the verb.

Negative	
Full form	**Contraction**
I am not from Spain.	I'm not from Spain.
He/She/It is not a teacher.	He/She/It isn't a teacher.
You/We/They are not in class.	You/We/They aren't in class. or You're/We're/They're not in class.

To make questions with the verb *to be*, put the verb before the subject.

verb	**subject**	
Are	*you*	*married?*

Question		
Am	I	
Is	he/she/it	30 years old?
Are	you/we/they	
Short answer		
	I	am.
		'm not.
Yes, No,	he/she/it	is.
		isn't.
	you/we/they	are.
		aren't.

Possessive adjectives

I	my	*It's my book.*
you	your	*What's your name?*
he	his	*It's his mobile phone.*
she	her	*Is it her pen?*
it	its	*What's its name?*
we	our	*It's our class.*
they	their	*I am their teacher.*

Possessive adjectives go before a noun.

This, these, that, those

Use *this/these* to talk about things that are here.

Use *that/those* to talk about things that are there.

FUNCTIONAL LANGUAGE
Hello & goodbye

Hello
Hello.
Hi.
Good morning/afternoon/evening.

Goodbye
Goodbye.
Bye.
See you tomorrow/Monday/Tuesday.

Offers & responses

Would you like a ...?
Yes, please.
No, thank you.
No, thanks.

WORD LIST

Objects

alarm clock *n C* **	/əˈlɑː(r)m klɒk/
bottle of water *n C*	/ˈbɒt(ə)l əv wɔːtə(r)/
business card *n C*	/ˈbɪznəs kɑː(r)d/
camera *n C* ***	/ˈkæm(ə)rə/
chair *n C* ***	/tʃeə(r)/
computer *n C* ***	/kəmˈpjuːtə(r)/
desk *n C* ***	/desk/
diary **	/ˈdaɪəri/
earphones *n pl*	/ˈɪə(r)ˌfəʊnz/
glasses *n pl* *	/ˈglɑːsɪz/
memory stick *n C*	/ˈmem(ə)ri stɪk/
mirror *n C* ***	/ˈmɪrə(r)/
newspaper *n C/U* ***	/ˈnjuːzˌpeɪpə(r)/
paper *n C/U* ***	/ˈpeɪpə(r)/
phone *n C* ***	/fəʊn/
umbrella *n C* *	/ʌmˈbrelə/
wallet *n C*	/ˈwɒlɪt/

Countries & nationalities

Brazil *n*	/brəˈzɪl/
Brazilian *adj*	/brəˈzɪljən/
Britain *n*	/ˈbrɪt(ə)n/
British *adj*	/ˈbrɪtɪʃ/
China *n*	/ˈtʃaɪnə/
Chinese *adj*	/ˌtʃaɪˈniːz/
France *n*	/frɑːns/
French *adj*	/frentʃ/
Germany *n*	/ˈdʒɜː(r)məni/
German *adj*	/ˈdʒɜː(r)mən/
Greece *n*	/griːs/
Greek *adj*	/griːk/
Ireland *n*	/ˈaɪələnd/
Irish *adj*	/ˈaɪrɪʃ/
Italy *n*	/ˈɪtəli/
Italian *adj*	/ɪˈtæljən/
Japan *n*	/dʒəˈpæn/
Japanese *adj*	/ˌdʒæpəˈniːz/
Poland *n*	/ˈpɒlənd/
Polish *adj*	/ˈpɒlɪʃ/
Russia *n*	/ˈrʌʃə/
Russian *adj*	/ˈrʌʃ(ə)n/
Turkey *n*	/ˈtɜː(r)ki/
Turkish *adj*	/ˈtɜː(r)kɪʃ/

Drinks

beer *n C/U* ***	/bɪə(r)/
coffee *n C/U* ***	/ˈkɒfi/
(orange, apple) juice *n C/U* **	/dʒuːs/
tea *n C/U* ***	/tiː/
(mineral) water *n U* ***	/ˈwɔːtə(r)/
wine *n C/U* ***	/waɪn/

Other words & phrases

afternoon *n C/U* ***	/ˌɑːftə(r)ˈnuːn/
age *n C/U* ***	/eɪdʒ/
bar *n C* ***	/bɑː(r)/
cake *n C/U* ***	/keɪk/
country *n C/U* ***	/ˈkʌntri/
email *n C/U* ***	/ˈiːmeɪl/
evening *n C/U* ***	/ˈiːvnɪŋ/
glass *n C/U* ***	/glɑːs/
guide *n C* ***	/gaɪd/
invite *v* ***	/ɪnˈvaɪt/
language *n C/U* ***	/ˈlæŋgwɪdʒ/
meet *v* ***	/miːt/
morning *n C/U* ***	/ˈmɔː(r)nɪŋ/
nationality *n C/U* *	/ˌnæʃəˈnæləti/
new *adj* ***	/njuː/
online *adj* **	/ˈɒnlaɪn/
party *n C* ***	/ˈpɑː(r)ti/
practise *v* **	/ˈpræktɪs/
reception *n U/C* **	/rɪˈsepʃ(ə)n/
room *n C/U* ***	/ruːm/
sandwich *n C* **	/ˈsæn(d)wɪdʒ/; /ˈsæn(d)wɪtʃ/
social network *n C/U*	/ˈsəʊʃ(ə)l netˌwɜː(r)k/
telephone *n C/U* ***	/ˈtelɪˌfəʊn/
tour *n C* ***	/tʊə(r)/

2A | The expat files

VOCABULARY: common verbs 1

1 Complete the phrases with a verb from the box.

> live   eat   drink   have   speak   work   read   go

1 _____ in a house/in a flat
2 _____ tea/coffee
3 _____ to school/to work
4 _____ chocolate/bread
5 _____ a newspaper/a book
6 _____ English/French
7 _____ in an office/in a shop
8 _____ a cat/friends

2 Match these words to the correct verb in exercise 1.

> a dog   water   hamburgers
> in a hospital   Italian   in Britain

3 🔘 **1.35** Listen to someone talking about her life in Britain. <u>Underline</u> the words from exercises 1 and 2 that you hear.

READING

1 Read the article and answer the questions about the people.

1 Where are they from?
2 Where are they now?
3 Are they happy ☺?

These people are British, but they don't live in Britain anymore. They live in other countries. They are British expatriates, or expats. The Expat Files look at the lives of different British expats around the world.

The Expat Files

Name: Sandra
Job: Student
From: London
New home: US

How is your life different?

I go to an American university in Seattle. I have a very American life now. I have a big car and a big house. I live there with three friends. I eat a lot of Mexican-American fast food. I have friends from here and from South America.

How is your life similar?

I drink lots of tea. The Americans say I'm typically English in that way! I have my dog, Chelsea. That isn't very different because lots of people here have dogs.

YOUR OPINION: ☺☺ *I like it!*

Name: Carl and Anna Eder
Job: Retired
From: Liverpool
New home: Spain

How is your life different?

We don't work now, we're retired. We don't live in a house. We live in a flat in Malaga. We eat outside every day, that's different. We love Spanish food. We don't have our cats here.

How is your life similar?

Lots of English people live here. We have English shops and we read English newspapers. We watch the BBC on satellite television. We don't have an English garden, but we have plants on the balcony. We speak a little Spanish. We go to language classes every Thursday.

YOUR OPINION: ☺☺☺ *We love it!*

2 Read the article again. Complete the sentences with Sandra (S) or Carl and Anna (C/A).

1 _____ don't work.
2 _____ lives in a house.
3 _____ has friends from different countries.
4 _____ eat outside every day.
5 _____ has a dog.
6 _____ go to language classes.

3 Close your book. Choose Sandra or Carl and Anna. Make notes about them. Work in pairs. Compare your notes with your partner. Who remembers most?

LISTENING

1 🔘 **1.36** Listen to David. <u>Underline</u> the correct information.

Name: David *McKinnon / MacKinnon*
From: *Ireland / Scotland*
New home: *Istanbul / Edinburgh*
Job: *Teacher / Student*

OPINION: ☺☺ *I like it.* / ☹☹ *I don't like it.*

2 🔘 **1.36** Listen again and decide if the sentences are true (T) or false (F). Correct the false sentences.

1 He lives in a house.
2 He eats Scottish food.
3 He doesn't read the English newspapers.
4 He goes to football matches.
5 He speaks Turkish.
6 He works at the university.

3 Work in pairs. Ask and answer these questions.

• Do you know any expats?
• Where do they live?
• Would you like to live in a different country?

GRAMMAR: present simple affirmative & negative

Use the present simple to talk about things that are generally true.
*I **go** to an American university.*
*We **live** in a flat in Malaga.*

For *he, she, it* add *-s* to the verb.
*He **speaks** Turkish.*
*She **eats** fast food.*

Make negatives with *don't/doesn't* + infinitive.
*I **don't** live in England.*
*He **doesn't have** Scottish friends.*

> SEE LANGUAGE REFERENCE PAGE 30

1 Make sentences in the present simple.

1 She / work / in Germany.
2 We / live / in a big flat.
3 I / no speak English.
4 He / have / a dog.
5 They / no eat / a lot of pizza.
6 He / go / to an American school.

2 Complete the text. Put the verbs in brackets into the present simple.

Rosa (1) _is_ (*be*) an Italian expat. She (2) _is_ (*be*) from Rome and (3) _lives_ (*live*) in Brighton, a town in England. She (4) _is_ (*be*) a nurse, and (5) _works_ (*work*) in a hospital. She (6) _lives_ (*live*) with an English family. The family (7) _don't speak_ (*not speak*) Italian. Rosa (8) _drinks_ (*drink*) lots of tea now.

3 Complete the sentences with an affirmative or negative verb so that they are true for you.

1 I _____ in a house.
2 I _____ coffee.
3 I _____ in an office.
4 I _____ a dog.
5 I _____ a car.
6 I _____ Spanish.

4 Work in pairs. Compare your sentences. What's the same? What's different?

SPEAKING

1 Read about an American expat. Where is he?

I'm American. I live in a flat. I drink lots of tea and I eat lots of rice. I don't have a car. I read the newspaper *The South China Morning Post*. I work in a bank. I speak some Chinese. I like it.

2 Imagine you are an expat. Prepare a similar text about your new life. Don't say the country.

3 Work in pairs. Tell your partner about your new life. Guess your partner's country.

4 Introduce your partner to another student. Give information about your expat partner.

He's American. He lives in a flat …

2B Typical friends

Vocabulary: common verbs 2

1 Match the photos A–D to a phrase from the box.

> watch TV   go to the cinema   go dancing
> play sports   study   go shopping
> go to restaurants   listen to music   travel

2 Work in pairs. Ask and answer these questions.

- Which activities in exercise 1 do you do?
- Which activities do you usually do alone?
- Which activities do you usually do with friends?

I don't go to restaurants.
I play sports with friends.
I study alone.

He goes to the cinema alone.

Listening

1 Read the web page. What is it about?

THE WEEKLY PODCAST   *This week's topic …* **FRIENDS**

Are men and women the same? Do they like the same things? Men and women say friends are important. Men and women like the same things as their friends. But according to our psychologist, Simon Palmer, they are very different. Men friends play sports and do things together, women friends …

ⓘ Click here to listen to the full podcast.

2 🔘 1.37 Listen to the interview. Tick (✓) the words you hear.

> sports ✓   football   feelings ✓   personal ✓   tennis
> movies ✓   fashion   television ✓   politics ✓

3 🔘 **1.37** Listen again. Are the sentences about men (M), women (W), or both (MW)?

1 They like the same things.   *MW*
2 They play sports.   *M*
3 They talk about sports.   *MW*
4 They talk about personal things. *W*
5 They talk about their feelings.   *MW*
6 They listen more to their friends. *W*
7 They don't know a lot about their friends. *M*

4 What do you think? Put a tick (✓) if you agree and a cross (✗) if you disagree.

5 Work in pairs. Compare your answers.

> *Language note*
>
> *man* (singular) *men* (plural)
> *woman* (singular) *women* (plural)

GRAMMAR: present simple questions & short answers

> Make questions with *do/does* + subject + infinitive.
> **Do you have** *a lot of friends?*
> **Does he play** *sports with his friends?*
>
> Use the subject + *do/does/doesn't* in short answers.
> No, **they don't**.
> Yes, **he does**.

> ◗ SEE LANGUAGE REFERENCE PAGE 30

1 Make questions in the present simple.

Part 1

1 he / have a lot of friends?
   Does he have a lot of friends?
2 they / play sports?   *Do they play sports?*
3 they / talk about personal things?
4 he / have women friends?

Part 2

5 she / have a lot of friends?
6 they / talk about personal things?
7 they / do things together?
8 she / have men friends?

2 🔘 **1.38** Listen to a man and a woman talking about their friends. Mark the questions in exercise 1 yes (✓) or no (✗).

3 Work in pairs. Ask and answer the questions in exercise 1.

Does he have a lot of friends?
No, he doesn't.
Does she have a lot of friends?
Yes, she does.

4 Work in pairs. Ask and answer the questions.

you / have a lot of friends?
Do you have a lot of friends?

you / have more men friends or women friends?
you / know a lot about your friends?

PRONUNCIATION: word stress 1

1 🔘 **1.39** Listen to the words in the chart.

☐	☐ ◻	☐ ◻ ◻
sports	travel	personal
watch	shopping	politics
go	music	cinema
play	football	hospital
live	study	
	restaurant	

2 🔘 **1.40** Listen and put the words into the chart in exercise 1.

hamburger	have	English	newspaper	coffee	friend

3 Say the words in the chart. Pay attention to the word stress.

SPEAKING

1 Look at the words and phrases. What things do you do with your friends?

- Talk about personal things
- Watch TV
- Travel
- Speak English
- Eat at restaurants
- Go shopping
- Play sports
- Go to work

2 Work in pairs. Interview your partner about what they do with friends. Make questions with the words and phrases in exercise 1.

Do you talk about personal things?

3 Are you a 'typical' man friend or a 'typical' woman friend?

2c | Still at home

SPEAKING

1 Work in pairs. Discuss these questions about your country.

- How old are people when they leave the family home?
- How old are people when they get married?

READING

1 Read the article about the Castle family. What is the problem?

2 Read the sentences and <u>underline</u> the correct words.

1 Andy *is / isn't* 32 years old.
2 Andy *has / doesn't have* a car.
3 His mother *wants / doesn't want* Andy to live at home.
4 Emily *lives / doesn't live* with Andy.
5 Andy *is / isn't* married.
6 His father *loves / doesn't love* Andy.
7 Andy *likes / doesn't like* his house.

3 What's your opinion? Answer the questions in the article. Do you know a person in Andy's situation? Do you live at home?

> **Useful language**
>
> | It's not a problem. | It's a problem. |
> |---|---|
> | It's fine. | It's not right. |

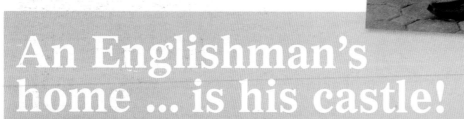

An Englishman's home ... is his castle!

The Castle family

Andy Castle lives in Brighton. He's not married. He has a nice car and a good job. Andy Castle lives with his parents, in his parents' house. He's thirty-seven years old.

His mother's opinion

I'm happy that Andy is at home. He is a very good boy. Andy doesn't have parties in the house.

Why does Andy live at home?

Because he likes it here. He helps me around the house. I have a daughter, Emily, but she's married. She doesn't live at home. Andy is my only son.

His father's opinion

It's not right. His mother says he's a good boy ... well, he's a man! And a thirty-seven-year-old man doesn't live with his mother and father. What about a family for Andy? I want to be a grandfather!

Why does Andy live at home?

I don't understand. He has money. He's a handsome young man. I love him, but it's better for Andy if he has his own house or flat.

Andy's opinion

It's fine. My father isn't very happy, but that's his problem. I don't have a girlfriend right now. When I meet the right girl, I'll get married and leave home.

Why do you live at home?

I have great parents, and I'm very happy to live with them. I like my house. A lot of my friends live at home.

What do YOU think of the situation?
Why does Andy live at home?
Send your answers to yourview@pointofview.co.uk

? YOUR VIEW

VOCABULARY: the family

1 Find all the family words in the article. What are they in your language?

parents, mother

2 Work in pairs, A and B. You are going to complete Emily's family tree.

A: Turn to page 134. B: Turn to page 136.

GRAMMAR: *Wh-* questions & possessive *'s*

> *What, where, when, who, why* and *how* are question words.
> Put them at the beginning of the question.
> **Where** *are you from?*   **Who** *does he live with?*
> **What** *is his name?*   **Why** *does he live at home?*
>
> Use *'s* to show possession.
> *Andy's mother   His parents' house.*

> **SEE LANGUAGE REFERENCE PAGE 30**

1 Complete the questions with a question word from the box.

who	why	what	how	where

1 _____ is he from?   Brighton, England.
2 _____ does he live with?   With his parents.
3 _____ does he live at home?   Because he likes it.
4 _____ old is he?   Thirty-seven.
5 _____ is his name?   Andy.

2 Rearrange the words to make questions.

1 live   do   where   you ?
2 with   who   live   you   do ?
3 their   what   names   are ?
4 old   they   how   are ?

3 Work in pairs. Ask and answer the questions in exercise 2.

4 Add *'s* or *'* to make possessives.

1 our sons__ names
2 John__ cousin
3 the teachers__ room
4 Andy__ books
5 his brother__ birthday
6 those families__ houses

5 Work in groups of three, A, B and C.

A: Close your eyes.
B and C: Put objects on the table.
A: Open your eyes and make sentences about the objects.

This is Ana's pen.   *This is Enzo's book.*

PRONUNCIATION: final *-s*

1 🔘 **1.41** Listen to the pronunciation of the final *-s* in these words. Sometimes the final *-s* is pronounced as an extra syllable.

no extra syllable	**extra syllable**
go goes	watch watches
computer computers	house houses
	class classes

2 🔘 **1.41** Listen again and repeat.

3 Say these words. Is there an extra syllable in the second word?

1 do does
2 listen listens
3 study studies
4 Charles Charles'
5 bus buses
6 sandwich sandwiches

4 🔘 **1.42** Listen to the recording to check your answers.

DID YOU KNOW?

1 Work in pairs. Read about the family in Britain and discuss the questions.

The family in Britain

Women now have an average of 1.96 children.
It is normal now for a British woman to have her first child when she is 29 years old.
40% (per cent) of the British population is married. 19% of children live with one parent, usually the mother.
On average, 45% of marriages end in divorce.

- How many children do women have in your country?
- Is divorce common in your country?
- How many people live in the family house or flat?
- Are the statistics for Britain similar in your country?

2D | Tour group

VOCABULARY: adjectives

1 Look at the pictures. Complete the sentences with words from the box.

> young   handsome   tall   fat
> beautiful   old   fair   dark   ugly
> thin   short

1   Height

He's _tall_. He's _____.

2   Age

She's _____. She's _____.

3   Weight

He's _____. He's _____.

4   Looks

He's _____. She's _____. They're _____.

5   Hair

She has _____ hair. He has _____ hair.

2 🔊 **1.43** Listen to the recording to check your answers. Say the sentences.

3 Are these adjectives for height, age or looks? Put them in the right category.

> middle-aged   medium height   average-looking   pretty

GRAMMAR: adjectives

> Adjectives go before the noun in English.
> *He's a **handsome** man.* He's a man handsome.
>
> Adjectives don't have a plural form.
> *They are **young** children.* They are youngs children.

> ❯ SEE LANGUAGE REFERENCE PAGE 30

1 Think of a famous person for each category. Write their names on a piece of paper.

A handsome film star   An ugly politician

A young film star   A fat man

A beautiful singer   A thin woman

A handsome film star   Robert Pattinson

2 Work in pairs, A and B.

A: Say a name.   A: *Robert Pattinson.*
B: Say the category.   B: *Is he a handsome film star?*
                         A: *Yes, he is.*

Change roles. Say the other names.

LISTENING

1 Look at the picture. Where is the man? Describe him.

2 🔘 **1.44** Listen to the dialogue. Answer the questions.

1 Where is Brian?
2 What does the woman talk to him about?

3 🔘 **1.44** Listen again. Match the people 1–3 to the pictures A–D. There is one extra picture.

1 Delilah Williams – from New Zealand
2 Patti Owen – from New Zealand
3 Dave Matthews – from Canada

FUNCTIONAL LANGUAGE: describing people

Asking about people

What	does … look like?
How	old is …? tall is …?
What colour	hair eyes	does … have?

Describing people

He's	tall/young/handsome.
She has	fair/dark/brown/black hair.
He has	blue/green/brown eyes.
She has	glasses.
She's (about)	thirty years old.

🔘 SEE LANGUAGE REFERENCE PAGE 31

1 🔘 **1.45** Listen to the words and make sentences with *She is* or *She has*.

1 glasses   *She has glasses.*
2 tall   *She's tall.*

2 Correct the questions and sentences.

1 What do they look?
2 Delilah is short pretty.
3 How old she?
4 Patti is around thirty years.
5 What he look like?
6 He has dark and glasses.
7 She blue eyes.

3 Work in pairs, A and B.

A: Choose a person in the class. Don't tell B.
B: Ask questions. Use the words below.
A: Answer the questions. Use the words below to help you.

What colour hair … have?
Fair/brown/dark/red.

What colour eyes … have?
Blue/brown/green.

Where is he/she from …?
He's from Brazil.

How old …?
He's young/old/about thirty/ about twenty-five.

How tall …?
She's about 1 metre 50/1 metre 73.

SPEAKING

1 Work in pairs, A and B.

A: Turn to page 132.
B: Turn to page 135.

Self-assessment (✓)

☐ I can describe a person.
☐ I can understand and use words relating to the family.
☐ I can ask simple questions using *where*, *what*, *who* and *why*.

Grammar
Present simple

Use the present simple to talk about things which are generally true.

> I **go** to an American university.
> We **live** in Malaga.

Affirmative		
I	speak	
He/She/It	speaks	English.
You/We/They	speak	

The form of the verb is the same except for *he/she/it*. For *he/she/it*, add *-s*.

Spelling: present simple verbs with *he/she/it*
For most verbs: add *-s*.

> work – work**s**   eat – eat**s**   like – like**s**   play – play**s**

For verbs ending in consonant + *y*: *y – ies*.

> study – stud**ies**

For verbs ending in *-ch, -sh, o*: add *-es*.

> do – do**es**   watch – watch**es**

Note: *have – has*

Make the negative with *don't* + infinitive or *doesn't* (for *he/she/it*) + infinitive.

subject	auxiliary + *not*	infinitive	
I	*don't*	*live*	*in Britain.*
She	*doesn't*	*have*	*a boyfriend.*

Negative			
I	don't		
He/She/It	doesn't	live	in a house.
You/We/They	don't		

For questions, put *do/does* before the subject, and the infinitive after the subject.

auxiliary	subject	infinitive	
Do	*you*	*speak*	*English?*
Does	*he*	*listen*	*to music?*

Answer these questions with short answers.

> *Do you speak English?* **Yes, I do.**
> *Does he have a big family?* **No, he doesn't.**

Question		
Do	I	
Does	he/she/it	work?
Do	you/we/they	
Short answer		
	I	do.
		don't.
Yes,	he/she/it	does.
No,		doesn't.
	you/we/they	do.
		don't.

Wh- questions

What, where, when, who, why and *how* are question words. Put them at the beginning of the question.

> **How** *are you?*
> **Where** *are you from?*
> **What** *is his name?*
> **Who** *does he live with?*
> **Why** *does he live at home?*

Possessive *'s*

Use *'s* to show possession.

> *John's cousin*
> *my son's bedroom*

If the word ends in an *-s*, add *'*.

> *His parents' house.*   *The babies' rooms.*

Not ~~the room of my son, the house of his parents~~.

Adjectives

Adjectives go before the noun.

> *a **black** cat*
> *the **big** house*

Adjectives also go after the verb *to be*.

> *Nancy is **tall**.*
> *Her hair is **long**.*

Adjectives do not have a plural form.

> *the old men*

Not ~~the olds men~~

Plurals

Plurals of words that end in -y

family = families
baby = babies

Irregular plurals

child = children
man = men
woman = women
person = people

FUNCTIONAL LANGUAGE

Asking about people

What	does …	look like?

How	old is …?
	tall is …?

What colour	hair	does … have?
	eyes	

Describing people

He's	tall/young/handsome.
She has	fair/dark/brown/black hair.
He has	blue/green/brown eyes.
She has	glasses.
She's (about)	thirty years old.

WORD LIST

Common verbs

drink *v* ***	/drɪŋk/
eat *v* ***	/iːt/
go *v* ***	/gəʊ/
have *v* ***	/hæv/
live *v* ***	/lɪv/
read *v* ***	/riːd/
speak *v* ***	/spiːk/
study *v* ***	/ˈstʌdi/
travel *v* ***	/ˈtræv(ə)l/
work *v* ***	/wɜː(r)k/

Free time activities

go dancing *v*	/gəʊ ˈdɑːnsɪŋ/
go shopping *v*	/gəʊ ˈʃɒpɪŋ/
go to restaurants *v*	/gəʊ tʊ ˈrest(ə)rɒnts/
go to the cinema *v*	/gəʊ tʊ ðə ˈsɪnəmə/
listen to music *v*	/ˈlɪs(ə)n tʊ ˈmjuːzɪk/
play sports *v*	/pleɪ spɔː(r)ts/
watch tv *v*	/wɒtʃ ˌtiː ˈviː/

Family

aunt *n C* ***	/ɑːnt/
brother *n C* ***	/ˈbrʌðə(r)/
child *n C* ***	/tʃaɪld/
cousin *n C* **	/ˈkʌz(ə)n/
daughter *n C* ***	/ˈdɔːtə(r)/
father *n C* ***	/ˈfɑːðə(r)/
grandchild *n C*	/ˈgræn(d)ˌtʃaɪld/
granddaughter *n C* *	/ˈgræn(d)ˌdɔːtə(r)/
grandfather *n C* **	/ˈgræn(d)ˌfɑːðə(r)/
grandmother *n C* **	/ˈgræn(d)ˌmʌðə(r)/
grandparent *n C* *	/ˈgræn(d)ˌpeərənt/
grandson *n C* *	/ˈgræn(d)ˌsʌn/
husband *n C* ***	/ˈhʌzbənd/
mother *n C* ***	/ˈmʌðə(r)/
parent *n C* ***	/ˈpeərənt/
sister *n C* ***	/ˈsɪstə(r)/
son *n C* ***	/sʌn/
uncle *n C* **	/ˈʌŋk(ə)l/

Descriptions

age *n C/U* ***	/eɪdʒ/
average-looking *adj*	/ˈæv(ə)rɪdʒ ˌlʊkɪŋ/
beautiful *adj* ***	/ˈbjuːtəf(ə)l/
dark *adj* ***	/dɑː(r)k/
fair *adj* ***	/feə(r)/
fat *adj* **	/fæt/
glasses *n pl* *	/ˈglɑːsɪz/
hair *n C/U* ***	/heə(r)/
handsome *adj* **	/ˈhæns(ə)m/
height *n C/U* ***	/haɪt/
medium height *adj*	/ˈmiːdiəm haɪt/
middle-aged *adj* *	/ˈmɪd(ə)l eɪdʒd/
old *adj* ***	/əʊld/
pretty *adj* ***	/ˈprɪti/
short *adj* ***	/ʃɔː(r)t/
tall *adj* ***	/tɔːl/
thin *adj* ***	/θɪn/
ugly *adj* **	/ˈʌgli/
weight *n C/U* ***	/weɪt/
young *adj* ***	/jʌŋ/

Other words & phrases

boy *n C* ***	/bɔɪ/
bread *n U* ***	/bred/
cat *n C* ***	/kæt/
chocolate *n C/U* **	/ˈtʃɒklət/
different *adj* ***	/ˈdɪfrənt/
divorce *n C/U* **	/dɪˈvɔː(r)s/
fashion *n C/U* ***	/ˈfæʃ(ə)n/
feelings *n pl* ***	/ˈfiːlɪŋz/
flat *n C* ***	/flæt/
friend *n C* ***	/frend/
get married *v*	/get ˈmærid/
girl *n C* ***	/gɜː(r)l/
home *n C/U* ***	/həʊm/
house *n C/U* ***	/haʊs/
leave *v* ***	/liːv/
life *n C/U* ***	/laɪf/
love *v* ***	/lʌv/
man *n C* ***	/mæn/
office *n C/U* ***	/ˈɒfɪs/
per cent *n* ***	/pə(r)ˈsent/
personal *adj* ***	/ˈpɜː(r)s(ə)nəl/
podcast *n C*	/ˈpɒdˌkɑːst/
point of view *n C* **	/pɔɪnt əv vjuː/
politics *n pl* ***	/ˈpɒlətɪks/
problem *n C* ***	/ˈprɒbləm/
same *adj* ***	/seɪm/
sports *n pl* ***	/spɔː(r)ts/
thing *n C* ***	/θɪŋ/
university *n C/U* ***	/ˌjuːnɪˈvɜː(r)səti/
woman *n C* ***	/ˈwʊmən/

3A | Houseswap

VOCABULARY: places to live

1 Match the adjectives in A to their opposites in B.

A	B
big	quiet
new	small
noisy	old
lovely	horrible

2 🔊 1.46 Listen to someone talking about where she lives. <u>Underline</u> the words that you hear.

> I live in a *small / big / old* flat on Herbert Street. It's in the centre of Dublin. It's a *lovely / dark / horrible* flat, but the street is *noisy / quiet / nice*. I *don't like / like* it.

3 Work in pairs. Tell your partner about where you live. Use the words in exercises 1 and 2 to help you.

> I live in a _____ on _____.
> It's in _____. It's a _____ _____.
> I like / don't like it.

READING

1 Read the introduction to the *Houseswap* web page. What does *swap* mean?

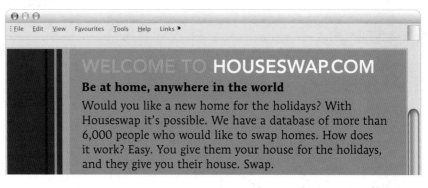

WELCOME TO HOUSESWAP.COM

Be at home, anywhere in the world

Would you like a new home for the holidays? With Houseswap it's possible. We have a database of more than 6,000 people who would like to swap homes. How does it work? Easy. You give them your house for the holidays, and they give you their house. Swap.

2 Read about some of the homes available on *Houseswap* below. Match the homes 1–5 to the photos A–F. There is one extra photo.

3 Read the texts again and decide if the sentences are true (T) or false (F). Correct the false sentences.

1 Hamed's house is in Luxor.
2 Hamed's house is very small.
3 Sean's house is in England.
4 Sean's house isn't in the mountains.
5 Michael and Catherine's house isn't very big.
6 Hugh's flat is in the city centre.
7 Hugh's flat isn't close to the shops or a market.
8 Gerard's flat is very quiet.

4 Work in pairs. Which of the five homes on *Houseswap* would you like for the holidays? Tell your partner.

1 This is my home. I live in a lovely white house. It's in Luxor, Egypt. It's next to the River Nile and near the mountains.
Email Hamed: hamed@houseswap.com

2 This is my home. It's a small house in Scotland. It's beautiful here and very quiet. The cottage is in the mountains. It's far from other people and noisy cities!
Email Sean: sean@houseswap.com

3 We have a lovely big family house on the beach. It's in Santa Monica, California. It is a very good area to see Hollywood stars. The famous Hollywood letters are near to our house!
Email Michael and Catherine: mikecathy@houseswap.com

4 I live with two friends in the centre of London. The flat is in Notting Hill. It's a little noisy. It's behind a market. It's close to a hospital and 30 minutes from Heathrow Airport.
Email Hugh: hugh@houseswap.com

5 My wife and I have a big flat at the end of the Champs-Élysées in Paris. It's a little noisy, but it's beautiful. We are opposite the Arc de Triomphe.
Email Gerard: gerard@houseswap.com

A

GRAMMAR: prepositions of place

 in on at

Other prepositions of place are:
close to/near to   *far from*
next to   *in front of*
behind   *opposite*

Prepositions of place go before a noun.
   in London   **close to** the school   **behind** the market

⊙ SEE LANGUAGE REFERENCE PAGE 40

1 Read the texts again and <u>underline</u> the prepositions of place and the nouns after them.

2 Complete the texts with prepositions.

> This is our home. It's (1) _____ New York. We are (2) _____ the centre of Manhattan. It's a flat (3) _____ Fifth Avenue.
>
> I have a very small house (4) _____ the beach. It's (5) _____ Vancouver, Canada. The house is (6) _____ front of a school and close (7) _____ the hospital and shops. Good for families. It's a little far (8) _____ the city centre, but it's quiet.

3 Choose a person in the class. Complete the sentences with information about that person.

1   I sit close to/far from the teacher.
2   I sit next to …
3   I sit in front of …
4   I sit behind …

4 Work in pairs. Read your sentences from exercise 3. Guess who the person is.

SPEAKING

1 Play *Class Houseswap*. On a piece of paper, write your name and a description of your home. Look at the web page to help you.

2 Walk around the class. Tell other students in the class about your home. Find someone who wants to swap homes with you. Swap papers.

3 Tell other students about your new home.

> *Useful language*
>
> *This is my home. It's …*
> *Would you like my house for the holidays?*
> *Yes, OK.*
> *No, thanks.*

3B | 1600 Pennsylvania Avenue

LISTENING

1 Look at the photos of the house at 1600 Pennsylvania Avenue. What do you know about this house? Answer the questions.

- [ ] How old is it?
- [✓] What is the name of the house?
- [ ] Who lives there?
- [ ] Are there public visits?
- [ ] How many rooms are there?
- [ ] Where is it?

2 ● 1.47 Listen to the beginning of a documentary about the house at 1600 Pennsylvania Avenue. Put the questions in exercise 1 in the order that you hear them.

3 ● 1.47 Listen again and complete the sentences with the numbers from the box.

| 4 | 10 | 32 | 7 | 200 |

1 There are __4__ names for the house at 1600 Pennsylvania Avenue.
2 It's more than __200__ years old.
3 There are 16 family bedrooms, 3 kitchens and __32__ bathrooms.
4 There are also 6 floors, __1__ staircases, 3 elevators, 147 windows and 412 doors.
5 Public visits are available for groups of __10__ people or more.

4 Work in pairs. Would you like to visit this famous house? Tell your partner.

VOCABULARY: parts of a house

1 ● 1.48 Listen and repeat the words in the box. Match the rooms to the numbers 1–7 on the plan of the flat.

| living room | hall | kitchen | balcony |
| bedroom | bathroom | dining room | |

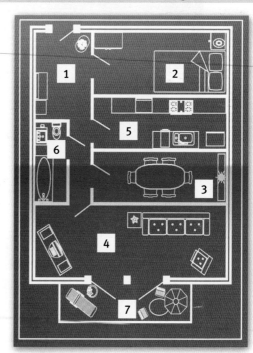

2 ● 1.49 Listen to the recording to check your answers.

3 Work in pairs. Ask and answer the questions.

In your house or flat …

1 where do you watch TV?
2 where do you eat?
3 where do you study?
4 where do you sleep?

GRAMMAR: *there is/there are & How many*

Affirmative
  There is *a tennis court.*
  There are *three kitchens.*

Negative
  There isn't *a restaurant.*
  There aren't *any public telephones.*

Question and short answer
  Is there *a bathroom? Yes,* **there is.** *No,* **there isn't.**
  Are there *any offices? Yes,* **there are.** *No,* **there aren't.**

Use *How many* to ask questions.
  How many *bedrooms are there?   There are 16 bedrooms.*

> SEE LANGUAGE REFERENCE PAGE 40

1 Make sentences about the White House. Use *There's …/There are …* for affirmative (+), and *There isn't …/There aren't any …* for negative (-).

1 a small cinema (+) *There's a small cinema.*
2 public bathrooms (-) *There aren't any public bathrooms.*
3 two swimming pools (+)
4 a restaurant (-)
5 three kitchens (+)
6 three elevators (+)
7 public telephones (-)

2 Make questions using the words in the table.

Is	there	a	bathroom dining room restaurant windows telephones	at your school? in your classroom? in your bedroom? in your house?
Are		any		

3 Work in pairs. Ask and answer the questions from exercise 2.

4 Make questions. Use *How many.*

1 bedrooms / your house
  How many bedrooms are there in your house?
2 students / class today
3 bathrooms / your house
4 teachers / your school
5 books / your bag today

5 Work in pairs. Ask and answer the questions in exercise 4.

SPEAKING

1 Draw a plan of your house or flat. Prepare a short presentation of your home. Use the words from the lesson and the useful language to help you.

Useful language

So, this is my home.
There are … rooms. This is the bedroom/living room/kitchen …
There's a bathroom/bedroom/study here.

DID YOU KNOW?

1 Work in pairs. Read about 10 Downing Street and discuss the questions.

Number 10 Downing Street,

also called Number 10, is the official residence of the Prime Minister of Britain. It is in the centre of London, in Westminster. It's a big house, and inside there are offices and a flat for the Prime Minister's family. There is one entrance through a black door on Downing Street. A police officer always stands outside the door. There aren't any public visits to Number 10, but thousands of tourists come every year to visit the street and look at the door.

• Does the president or prime minister of your country have a famous house? Where is it?
• Are there any other famous houses or flats in your country? Where are they?

3c | My first flat

VOCABULARY: furniture

1 Look at the pictures 1–4. What rooms are they?

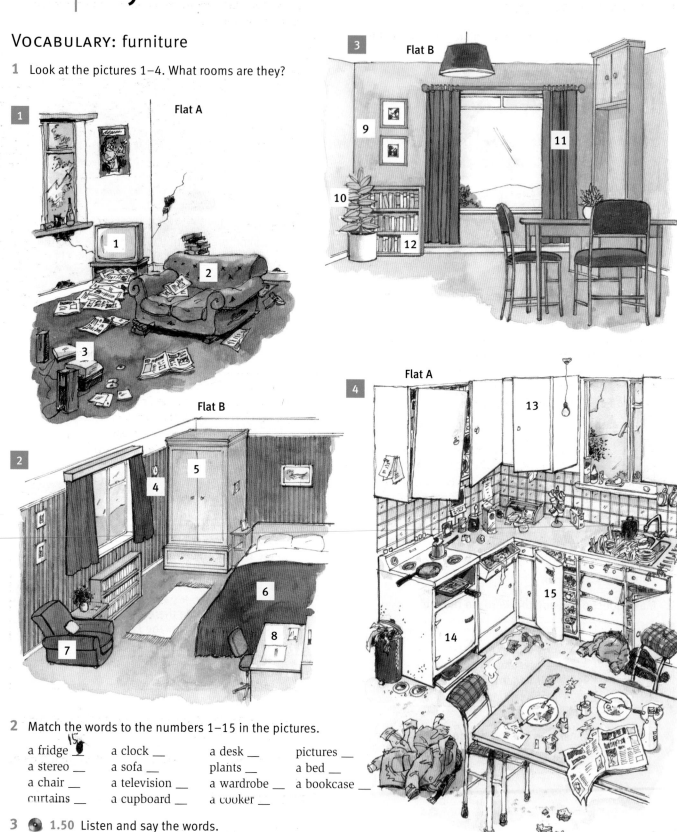

Flat A

Flat B

Flat B

Flat A

2 Match the words to the numbers 1–15 in the pictures.

a fridge 15   a clock __   a desk __   pictures __
a stereo __   a sofa __   plants __   a bed __
a chair __   a television __   a wardrobe __   a bookcase __
curtains __   a cupboard __   a cooker __

3 🔘 **1.50** Listen and say the words.

4 🔘 **1.51** Shelly and Claudia are students. They want to rent a flat. Listen. Which flat do they rent?

READING & LISTENING

1 🔘 1.52 Read and listen to the dialogue. Answer the questions.

1 Does Shelly like her flat?
2 Where is Claudia from?
3 Does Shelly want to see her parents?

Shelly: Hello?
Father: Hello, Shelly. It's your father here. How's your new flat? Do you like it?
Shelly: Yes, I do. It's ... perfect.
Father: Well, tell me about it. Is it big?
Shelly: Yes, it is.
Father: And what about furniture? Is there any furniture?
Shelly: Yes, I have a desk and a bed in my room.
Father: Would you like a lamp? We have an extra lamp at home.
Shelly: No, thanks, Dad. Claudia has a lamp for the living room.
Father: Who's Claudia?
Shelly: She's my flatmate. She's Italian. Don't worry, there aren't any boys here.
Father: Good. Your mother has some old curtains. Do you want them?
Shelly: No, that's fine. We have curtains.
Father: Really?
Shelly: Yes.
Father: Oh. So, when do we come and see the flat?
Shelly: This week isn't good. We don't have any chairs.
Father: No chairs? What does that mean, no chairs?
Shelly: I don't know. Sorry, that's the door. Talk to you later, OK, Dad? Bye.

2 Shelly doesn't tell the truth about her flat. Look at the pictures again. Read the text again and <u>underline</u> the false information.

3 Work in pairs and practise the dialogue.

GRAMMAR: *a, an, some & any*

Use *a/an* with single nouns.
*I have **a desk** in my room.*

Use *some* with plural nouns with affirmative verbs.
*There are **some lamps** here.*

Use *any* with plural nouns in questions.
*Do you have **any curtains**?*

Use *any* with plural nouns with negative verbs.
*There **aren't any boys** here.*

🔘 SEE LANGUAGE REFERENCE PAGE 40

1 Look at Shelly's bedroom. Complete the sentences with *some/any* or *a*.

1 She doesn't have _____ chairs in her room.
2 There's _____ bed.
3 There are _____ papers on the bed.
4 There's _____ pizza on the floor.
5 Does she have _____ CDs? Yes, she does.
6 There are _____ pictures on the wall.
7 Is there _____ wardrobe? No, there isn't.
8 There aren't _____ plants.

2 Make true sentences about your classroom. Use the words in the box.

There	are is aren't isn't	any some a	student(s) whiteboard(s) teacher(s) window(s) door(s) CD player(s) plant(s) cupboard(s) television(s) picture(s)	in the classroom.

3 Make five similar true sentences about one of these rooms in your house.

your bedroom   your living room   your dining room

SPEAKING

1 Work in pairs, A and B.

A: Turn to page 132.
B: Turn to page 136.

3D | Shopping mall

SPEAKING

1 Work in pairs. Look at the photos of the shopping malls. Ask and answer the questions.

- Do you like shopping?
- Are there any big shopping malls near your house?
- How often do you go to a shopping mall?

VOCABULARY: ordinal numbers

> ### Language note
> We use ordinal numbers to say the order or sequence of things.

1 Match the words to the ordinal numbers.

1st 2nd 3rd 4th 5th 6th 7th 8th 9th 10th

third	fifth	seventh	ninth	fourth	second	first
eighth	tenth	sixth				

2 🔘 **1.53** Listen and <u>underline</u> the word you hear. Practise saying the words.

1 *1 / 1st*   5 *10th / 10*
2 *3rd / 3*   6 *5th / 5*
3 *7 / 7th*   7 *2nd / 3rd*
4 *9th / 9*   8 *5th / 4th*

3 Work in pairs. Look at the diagram of a big shopping mall. Ask and answer questions about these places.

- car park
- cinema
- restaurants
- women's clothes shops
- supermarket

A: *What floor is the cinema on?*
B: *It's on the fifth floor.*

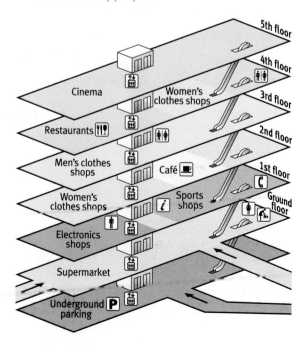

LISTENING

1 Match the words in the box to the symbols A–G.

public telephone	men's toilets	information	lift
women's toilets	baby changing room	café	

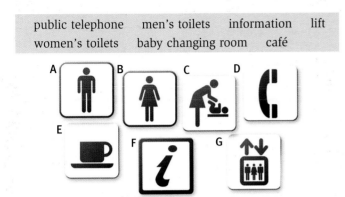

2 🔘 **1.54** Listen to the recording to check your answers. Say the words.

3 🔘 **1.55** Listen to four dialogues at the information desk in the shopping mall and tick (✓) the words from exercise 1 that you hear.

4 🔘 **1.55** Listen again and match the sentences to some of the places in exercise 1.

1 It doesn't accept coins. _____
2 You need a card. _____
3 Look, the brown doors. _____
4 It's next to the women's toilets. _____
5 It's behind you. _____
6 It's on the second floor. _____

FUNCTIONAL LANGUAGE: directions

1 Complete the directions with a word from the box.

left	up	down	right	along

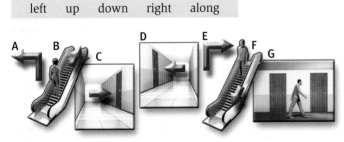

Giving directions
A *turn _____* B *go _____* C *on the _____* D *on the left*

E *turn right* F *go _____* G *go _____*

Asking for directions
Excuse me, where is the … ?
Is there a … near here?

▶ SEE LANGUAGE REFERENCE PAGE 40

2 🔘 **1.56** Listen and complete the sentences with a word or words.

1 Where _____ the café?
2 It's on the second floor. Go _____ the stairs and _____ right.
3 Where _____ the men's toilets?
4 They're over there. They're on the _____, next to the lift.
5 It's next to the stairs. It's on the _____.
6 Go _____ these stairs here. Then turn _____ and go _____ the hall.

3 Look at audioscript 1.56 on page 141 to check your answers.

4 Work in pairs. Practise the dialogues in the audioscript.

5 Work in pairs, A and B. Look at the plan of the Mini Mall.

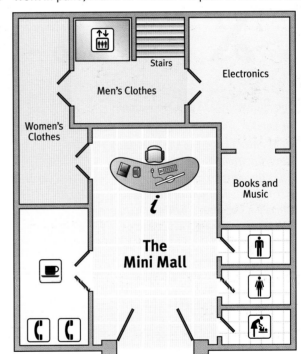

A: You work at the information desk. Listen to B's questions and give directions. Start each conversation with *Can I help you?*
B: You are a visitor to the Mini Mall. Choose a place on the floor plan and ask A for directions.

6 Swap roles and continue.

Self-assessment (✓)

- ☐ I can talk about where I live.
- ☐ I can use *there is* and *there are* to describe a building.
- ☐ I can understand the names of furniture in a room.
- ☐ I can ask for and give simple directions.
- ☐ I can understand and use ordinal numbers.

GRAMMAR
Prepositions of place

Other prepositions of place are:

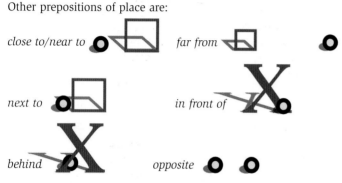

Prepositions of place go before a noun.

> **in** London   **close to** the school   **behind** the market

> I live **close to**/**near to** the city centre.
> I live **far from** the city centre.
> They live **next to** my house.
> Her house is **in front of** the school.
> There's a big garden **behind** the house.
> The flat is **opposite** the hospital.

> I work **at** home.
> Not I work **in** home.

There is/there are

Affirmative

There	is	a tennis court.
	are	three kitchens.

Negative

There	isn't	a restaurant.
	aren't	any public telephones.

Question & short answer

Is	there	a bathroom?	Yes,	there is.
			No,	there isn't.
Are		any offices?	Yes,	there are.
			No,	there aren't.

Use *How many* to ask questions:

> **How many** bedrooms are there?   There are 32 bedrooms.

A, an, some & any

a/an
Use *a/an* with single nouns.

> I have **a** desk in my room.

some
Use *some* with plural nouns and affirmative sentences.

> There are **some** lamps here.

any
Use *any* with plural nouns in questions and with plural nouns in negative sentences.

> Do you have **any** curtains?
> There aren't **any** boys here.

FUNCTIONAL LANGUAGE
Asking for directions

Excuse me, where is the ...?
Is there a ... near here?

Giving directions

Turn right/left.
Go right/left/straight on.
It's on the right/left.

WORD LIST

Places to live

city *n C* ***	/ˈsɪti/
city centre *n C*	/ˈsɪti ˈsentə(r)/
flat *n C* ***	/flæt/
house *n C/U* ***	/haʊs/
town *n C/U* ***	/taʊn/
village *n C* ***	/ˈvɪlɪdʒ/

Parts of a house

balcony *n C* *	/ˈbælkəni/
bathroom *n C* **	/ˈbɑːθˌruːm/
bedroom *n C* ***	/ˈbedruːm/
dining room *n C* *	/ˈdaɪnɪŋ ˌruːm/
door *n C* ***	/dɔː(r)/
hall *n C* ***	/hɔːl/
kitchen *n C* ***	/ˈkɪtʃən/
living room *n C* **	/ˈlɪvɪŋ ˌruːm/
staircase *n C* *	/ˈsteə(r)ˌkeɪs/
window *n C* ***	/ˈwɪndəʊ/

Furniture

bed *n C/U* ***	/bed/
bookcase *n C* *	/ˈbʊkˌkeɪs/
chair *n C* ***	/tʃeə(r)/
clock *n C* **	/klɒk/
cooker *n C* *	/ˈkʊkə(r)/
cupboard *n C* **	/ˈkʌbə(r)d/
curtain *n C* **	/ˈkɜː(r)t(ə)n/
desk *n C* ***	/desk/
fridge *n C* *	/frɪdʒ/
lamp *n C* **	/læmp/
picture *n C* ***	/ˈpɪktʃə(r)/
plant *n C* ***	/plɑːnt/
sofa *n C* *	/ˈsəʊfə/
stereo *n C* *	/ˈsteriəʊ/
television *n C* ***	/ˈtelɪˌvɪʒ(ə)n/
wardrobe *n C* *	/ˈwɔː(r)drəʊb/

Ordinal numbers

first ***	/fɜː(r)st/
second ***	/ˈsekənd/
third	/θɜː(r)d/
fourth	/fɔː(r)θ/
fifth	/fɪfθ/
sixth	/sɪksθ/
seventh	/ˈsev(ə)nθ/
eighth	/eɪtθ/
ninth	/naɪnθ/
tenth	/tenθ/

Other words & phrases

art *n C/U* ***	/ɑː(r)t/
baby *n C* ***	/ˈbeɪbi/
big *adj* ***	/bɪg/
café *n C* **	/ˈkæfeɪ/
dark *adj* ***	/dɑː(r)k/
easy *adj* ***	/ˈiːzi/
elevator *n C*	/ˈeləveɪtə(r)/
entrance *n C/U* ***	/ˈentrəns/
famous *adj* ***	/ˈfeɪməs/
film star *n C*	/fɪlm stɑː(r)/
floor *n C* ***	/flɔː(r)/
horrible *adj* **	/ˈhɒrəb(ə)l/
information *n U* ***	/ˌɪnfə(r)ˈmeɪʃ(ə)n/
lift *n C* ***	/lɪft/
lovely *adj* ***	/ˈlʌvli/
modern *adj* ***	/ˈmɒdə(r)n/
museum *n C* ***	/mjuːˈziːəm/
new *adj* ***	/njuː/
nice *adj* ***	/naɪs/
noisy *adj* *	/ˈnɔɪzi/
official *adj* ***	/əˈfɪʃ(ə)l/
old *adj* ***	/əʊld/
outside *adj* ***	/ˌaʊtˈsaɪd/
policeman *n C* **	/pəˈliːsmən/
quiet *adj* ***	/ˈkwaɪət/
residence *n C/U* **	/ˈrezɪd(ə)ns/
school *n C/U* ***	/skuːl/
shop *n C/U* ***	/ʃɒp/
stand *v* ***	/stænd/

4A MetroNaps

The EnergyPod

Will Cotton works in an office in New York. He goes to work at 7.30. He starts work at 8.15. He usually finishes work at 6.00, but has meetings after work. After his meetings, he goes to the gym or has a drink with friends in the café. He gets home at 9.00 and has dinner. He goes to bed at 12.15 am. It's a very busy day. How does he do it?

'Easy,' says Will, 'At 4.30 I go to MetroNaps.'

MetroNaps is a company in New York. At MetroNaps you get into a machine called the EnergyPod. You listen to quiet, relaxing music and then go to sleep. After twenty minutes, the pod moves with music and light and you wake up. MetroNaps also has a café, and there are sandwiches and drinks for you after your nap.

Will likes MetroNaps. 'I get my best ideas in bed, not at a desk,' says Will. 'When I go to work after having a nap, I'm relaxed. I'm not stressed in meetings after work. I do more with my day.'

The MetroNaps offices are in the Empire State Building in New York. It's open from 10.00 to 6.00. It's a very quiet place.

Glossary
nap *n* short sleep, usually during the day

M E T R O N A P S

READING

1 Look at the photo of an EnergyPod. Which activity do you think people do at MetroNaps?

1 go to sleep   2 have a shower   3 watch TV

2 Read the article to check your answer.

3 Read the article again. Answer the questions.

1 Where does Will Cotton work?
2 What time does he start work?
3 What time does he finish work?
4 What is a *nap*?
5 Where is MetroNaps?
6 Why does Will like MetroNaps?
7 What time does MetroNaps open and close?
8 How many hours is it open?

4 Put the events in the correct order for a typical MetroNap.

☐ You have a sandwich and a drink.
☐ You get into the EnergyPod.
☐ The EnergyPod pod moves.
☐ *1* You go to MetroNaps.
☐ You listen to quiet music.
☐ You wake up.
☐ You go to sleep.

5 Work in pairs. Do you have a nap during the day? Would you like a MetroNap? Tell your partner.

FUNCTIONAL LANGUAGE: telling the time

| He gets home at | nine thirty/half past nine. |
| He goes to bed at | twelve fifteen/a quarter past twelve. |

Asking the time	**Saying the time**
What time is it?	*It's four forty-five/a quarter to five.*
What's the time?	

> SEE LANGUAGE REFERENCE PAGE 50

1 Say the times for the clocks.

   1   2   3   4   5

2 🔊 **1.57** Listen to Will's dialogues and complete the clocks.

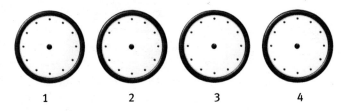

   1   2   3   4

3 Look at audioscript 1.57 on page 142 to check your answers. Practise the dialogues, but change the times.

VOCABULARY: collocations *have, go & get*

1 Find these words in the article on page 42 and put them in the correct boxes.

| to work/to the gym | meetings | a drink |
| dinner | to bed | to sleep | ideas | a nap |

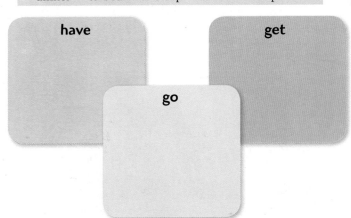

have

get

go

2 Put these words in the boxes.

| a shower | dressed | breakfast | classes |
| a break | lunch | | |

3 What is the difference between the <u>underlined</u> phrases? What are they in your language?

I <u>go home</u> at 6.00 and I <u>get home</u> at 6.15.
I <u>wake up</u> at 7.00 and I <u>get up</u> at 7.05.

PRONUNCIATION: vowels 1

1 🔊 **1.58** Listen and repeat the sounds and the words.

/æ/ **have**	/e/ **get**	/eɪ/ **wake**	/əʊ/ **go**

2 Put these words in the correct column in exercise 1.

| nap | break | home | bed | desk | make |
| seven | eight | any | day | flat | lamp | no |

3 🔊 **1.59** Listen to the recording to check your answers. Repeat the words.

SPEAKING

Language note

Use the present simple to talk about daily routines and habits.
  I wake up at 6.00.
To make questions, remember the word order.
Question word + auxiliary (*do/does*) + subject + verb
What time do you get up in the morning?

1 Work in pairs, A and B.

A: Turn to page 133.
B: Turn to page 136.

2 What do you do at these times? Tell your partner.

1 8.00   2 12.00   3 6.00   4 10.00

4B | A day off

A International Women's Day

B Teacher's Day

VOCABULARY: months

1 🔘 **1.60** Listen to the pronunciation of these months.

January	March	April	July	September
☐☐☐☐	☐	☐☐	☐☐	☐ ☐ ☐

2 Write the following months in the correct column in exercise 1.

> February   May   June   August
> October   November   December

3 🔘 **1.61** Listen to the recording to check your answers. Repeat the months.

4 Work in pairs. What is your favourite month? Why? Tell your partner.

LISTENING

C May Day

1 🔘 **1.62** Listen to people talking about special days that they like. Match the speakers 1–4 to the photos A–D.

2 🔘 **1.62** Listen again. What months are these special days in?

3 Work in pairs. Do you have these days in your country? Do people work on these days? What do they do? Tell your partner.

D New Year's Eve

FUNCTIONAL LANGUAGE: the date

We write the date:
1st May, 2012 or *1 May 2012* or *1/5/12* or *01/05/12*
We say the date:
the first of May two thousand and twelve or *May the first two thousand and twelve*

We ask the date:
What's the date today?   What date is it today?

⊙ SEE LANGUAGE REFERENCE PAGE 50

1 Say the dates.

1 13/10/2012   3 14/09/2000   5 21/03/2008   7 22/03/2011
2 03/07/1999   4 11/09/1991   6 30/10/2012   8 31/07/1990

2 Write five important dates for you on a piece of paper. Work in pairs. Ask your partner about his or her important dates.

Why is 5 March important for you?
Because it's my birthday!

READING

1 Read the interview with Christina East. Match the questions A–D to the answers 1–4.

A When is Nothing Day?
B What do people do on Nothing Day?
C Why Nothing Day?
D What is Nothing Day?

Christina East is a British mental health specialist. She thinks it's time for a new special holiday, called **Nothing Day**.

1 _____

The idea comes from Harold Coffin, an American journalist. It's a day for nothing. No parties, no gifts, no cards. It's a time to have a break, to sit and do nothing.

2 _____

It's on January 16. The first Nothing Day was in 1973.

3 _____

Because there are special days for everything. In March, we have Mother's Day, and in June, we have Father's Day. In October, there's United Nations Day and Halloween, and in April, there's Earth Day.

4 _____

Ideally, people do nothing. But that's very difficult. Here are some suggestions:
In the morning, wake up when you like. Have a relaxing breakfast. Do nothing.
In the afternoon, go for a walk. Sit in a park. Do nothing.
At night, telephone an old friend and talk. Read a book or go to bed. Do nothing.

2 ⊙ **1.63** Listen to the interview to check your answers.

3 ⊙ **1.63** Read and listen again to decide if the sentences are true (T) or false (F). Correct the false sentences.

1 The idea for Nothing Day comes from the United States.
2 Nothing Day is on 6 January.
3 United Nations Day is in April.
4 On Nothing Day, people do nothing.

GRAMMAR: prepositions of time *in, on, at*

Use the prepositions *in, on* and *at* to talk about time.
in + months, years, the morning/afternoon/evening
    in March, **in** the morning
on + days, dates
    on Monday, **on** 16 January
at + time of day, night
    at four o'clock, **at** night

⊙ SEE LANGUAGE REFERENCE PAGE 50

1 Complete the sentences with a preposition and a time word so that they are true for you.

1 I usually relax …
2 I watch television …
3 People in my country go on holiday …
4 My birthday is …
5 My English class is …
6 The next day off is …

2 Work in pairs. Read your sentences to your partner. Ask *What about you?*

SPEAKING

1 Work in groups. The government wants to create three new holidays. Decide on three reasons to celebrate and what dates they are on. What do people do on these days?

2 Present your ideas for new holidays to the class. Which are the most interesting?

Our idea for a new holiday is Student's Day. It's on 3 June. On this day, people …

4c | Do the housework!

VOCABULARY: verb collocations (housework)

1 Match the pictures A–F to the phrases in the box. There are four extra phrases.

> do the shopping   set the table   do the dishes   wash the clothes
> do the ironing   make the bed   clean the bathroom
> water the plants   take out the rubbish   make dinner

2 Work in pairs. Which activities in exercise 1 do you do at home? Which activities don't you do at home?

LISTENING

1 You are going to hear part of a radio show phone-in. Look at the newspaper headline. What is the number? Guess with a partner.

> ___ % of men don't do the housework, new survey says

2 🔘 1.64 Listen to the radio show and check your answer to exercise 1. Tick (✓) the phrases from Vocabulary exercise 1 you hear.

3 🔘 1.64 Who does it? Listen again and tick (✓) the correct column.

Name	Ralph	Ralph's mother	Tom	Tom's wife
does the shopping once a week				
is always on the phone				
always does all the housework				

GRAMMAR: frequency adverbs & phrases

> There are two ways to talk about how often we do things:
> Use frequency adverbs.
>   *How **often** do you do the housework?*
>   *I **often** do the dishes.*
>   *He's **always** on the phone.*
>
> | always | often | usually | sometimes | hardly ever/rarely | never |
> |---|---|---|---|---|---|
> | 100% | | | | | 0% |
>
> Use phrases like *every day/month/year*, *once a week/month/year*.
>   *I make the bed **every morning**.*
>   ***Once a year**, he washes the clothes.*

▶ SEE LANGUAGE REFERENCE PAGE 50

1 ● **1.65** Read and listen to the sentences, then use the words in brackets to answer.

1 You never do the dishes.
   That's not true. *I often do the dishes!*
   (often)
2 You don't clean the bathroom.
   That's not true. _____ (always)
3 You're always in front of the television.
   That's not true. _____ (hardly ever)
4 I always wash your clothes.
   That's not true. _____ (often)
5 This flat's always dirty.
   That's not true. _____ (rarely)
6 You're usually on the telephone.
   That's not true. _____ (sometimes)

2 Put an adverb of frequency in the sentence so that it's true for you. Then write two more similar sentences.

1 I am late for English class.
2 I work on Saturdays.
3 I watch English films.
4 I have coffee in the morning.
5 I go to bed before 10.00 pm.
6 I am tired in the morning.

3 Rewrite the sentences with one of the phrases.

> twice a week   once a year   every day
> three times a year   once a week

1 I read the newspaper on Mondays, Tuesdays, Wednesdays, Thursdays, Fridays, Saturdays and Sundays.
2 I go on holiday in August.
3 On Saturdays and Sundays, I have a nap in the afternoon.
4 I see my grandparents at Christmas, at Easter and on my birthday.
5 I do the shopping on Saturdays.

4 Choose two sentences from exercise 2 and two sentences from exercise 3. Make questions with *How often*.

How often do you watch English films?

5 Work in pairs. Ask and answer the questions.

PRONUNCIATION: vowels 2

1 ● **1.66** Listen and repeat the sounds and the words.

/aɪ/	/aʊ/	/uː/	/ʌ/
h**i**	**h**o**use**	r**oo**m	**u**p

2 Which word sounds different? Underline the different word.

1 time   hi   drink   wife
2 house   aunt   brown   now
3 son   bread   bus   some
4 blue   new   June   good

3 ● **1.67** Listen to the recording to check your answers. Say the words.

SPEAKING

1 Work in groups of three or four. Do the *Life and work at home* survey. Make questions with *How often …?* Ask and answer the questions. Make notes of the answers.

2 Compare your survey results with other groups in the class.

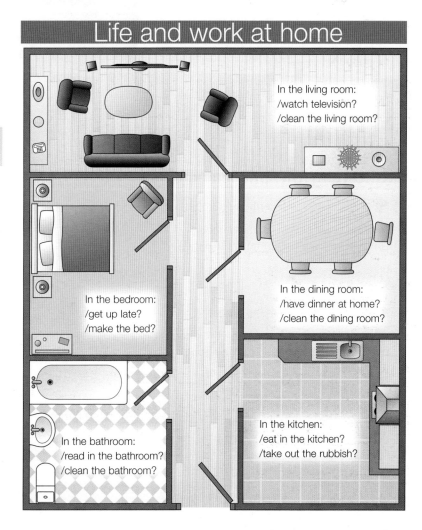

Life and work at home

In the living room:
/watch television?
/clean the living room?

In the bedroom:
/get up late?
/make the bed?

In the dining room:
/have dinner at home?
/clean the dining room?

In the bathroom:
/read in the bathroom?
/clean the bathroom?

In the kitchen:
/eat in the kitchen?
/take out the rubbish?

4D | I'm on the phone

SPEAKING

1 Work in pairs.
Do the phone survey.

PHONE SURVEY

| How many phones do you have in your house? Where are they?

| Do you have a mobile phone? What kind of mobile phone is it?

| How often do you use the phone?

| Do you use the phone in the car?

| How many phone calls do you make every day?

| How many phone calls do you get every day?

| Which of these things do you have on your phone?

☐ a calendar   ☐ internet access
☐ a camera   ☐ an mp3 player

| What other things do you have on your phone?

PRONUNCIATION: phone numbers

1 🔘 **1.68** Listen to two phone numbers.

- How do you say 0 in phone numbers?
- How do you say two numbers together?

0802 788 743
416 928 2212

2 🔘 **1.68** Listen again and repeat.

3 🔘 **1.69** Listen and <u>underline</u> the phone number you hear. Then say the phone numbers.

1   1 455 635 0403 / 1 455 635 0413
2   639 099 088 / 639 099 098
3   0802 788 743 / 0802 728 743
4   011 513 992 0732 / 011 516 992 0732

4 What's your phone number? Ask four other people in the class.

LISTENING

1 🔘 **1.70** Listen to three phone dialogues. <u>Underline</u> the correct word *makes* or *gets*.

1   The man *makes* / *gets* a phone call.
2   The man *makes* / *gets* a phone call.
3   The woman *makes* / *gets* a phone call.

2 🔘 **1.70** Listen to the dialogues again. Decide if the sentences are true (T) or false (F). Correct the false sentences.

Dialogue 1
1   The man is in class.
2   The woman doesn't want to talk.

Dialogue 2
3   The man calls the airport.
4   The man talks to Mr Green.

Dialogue 3
5   The man wants to call a restaurant.
6   The man calls the wrong number.

3 🔘 **1.71** Listen to two more dialogues. Complete the notes.

Message for Rob

Call Ms _____ Kerr.

Phone number: _____

Flight confirmation details for Mr and Mrs Curtis

Flight number _____

destination Dallas USA.

Terminal: 2

Date: Thursday, _____

Time: 8:45pm

FUNCTIONAL LANGUAGE: on the phone

1 There is one mistake in each of these phrases. Correct the mistake.

1 Just minute.
2 Can call you back?
3 I'd like to say to Mr Green.
4 Would you like to leave message?
5 Please tell him to call I.
6 Is Simon here, please?
7 Sorry, you have the number wrong.
8 Hi, I'm Rob.

2 Look at audioscripts 1.70 and 1.71 on page 142 to check your answers.

3 Read and complete these four phone dialogues with the correct sentence.

> No, he isn't. Can I take a message?
> Good morning, Acme Company.
> Is that 1823 556 0211?
> Hi, Sarah. How are you?

1
Hello.
Hello, it's Sarah.
(1) _____

2
(2) _____ Can I help you?
Good morning, can I speak to Mr James?
Yes. Just a minute.

3
Hello, is David there?
(3) _____
Please tell him to call me.
What's your phone number?
It's 662 4043.

4
Hello, is that Michelle?
I'm sorry, you have the wrong number.
(4) _____
No, it isn't.
Oh, sorry.

4 🔘 **1.72** Listen to the recording to check your answers.

5 Work in pairs. Roleplay the dialogues from exercise 3, but use information about you.

DID YOU KNOW?

1 Work in pairs. Read about phones and phone numbers in North America and discuss the question.

Phone facts: Canada and the US

The international code for Canada and the United States is 1.

All phone numbers have 10 digits. The first three digits are the area code.

The phone number for emergencies is 911.

The phone number for information is 411. This is free.

In American and Canadian films and television shows, all the phone numbers begin with 555.

Numbers which begin with 1-800, 1-888, 1-866 or 1-877 are free.

• What phone information is important for visitors to know in your country?

Self-assessment (✓)

☐ I can understand months and dates.
☐ I can talk about how often I do things.
☐ I can understand simple phone dialogues.
☐ I can ask for phone numbers and give my phone number.
☐ I can take a phone message.

GRAMMAR
Prepositions of time: *in, on, at*

Use the prepositions *in*, *on* and *at* to talk about time.

in + months, years, the morning/afternoon/evening

in *March,* **in** *the morning*

on + days, dates

on *Monday,* **on** *January 16th*

at + time of day; also *at night*

at *four o'clock*

We use *at* with *night, the weekend*:

at *night,* **at** *the weekend*

We use *at* with some special holidays:

at *Christmas,* **at** *Easter*

Frequency adverbs & phrases

Use frequency adverbs to say how often you do something.

How **often** *do you do the housework?*
I **never** *do the housework.*

always   often   usually   sometimes   hardly ever/rarely   never

100%	0%

Frequency adverbs go before the verb (except *to be*).

He **never** *makes the bed.*

Frequency adverbs go after the verb *to be*.

He's **always** *on the phone.*

You can also use phrases like:

every day/month/year
once a week/month/year

These phrases go at the beginning or end of a sentence.

I make the bed **every morning**.
Once a year, *he washes the clothes.*

FUNCTIONAL LANGUAGE
Telling the time

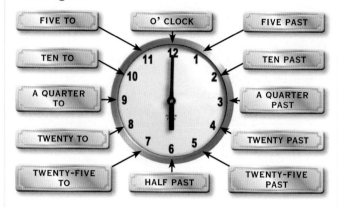

Use *It's* + time to say the time in English.

It's eight o'clock.
It's a quarter past five.
It's half past eleven.
It's ten to nine.

We can say the time in two ways:

It's twenty to six.
It's five forty.

We can also use *about* + time. We use *about* when we don't know the exact time.

It's about half past three.

We can ask the time in two ways:

What's the time?
What time is it?

The date

Write the date:

1st May, 2012 or *1 May 2012* or *1/5/12* or *01/05/12*

Say the date:

the first of May two thousand and twelve or
May the first two thousand and twelve

Ask the date:

What's the date today?
What date is it today?

We use ordinal numbers to say the date in English. For more on ordinal numbers, see lesson 3D.

Talking on the phone

Just a minute.
Can I call you back?
I'd like to speak to Mr Green.
Would you like to leave a message?
Please tell him to call me.
Is (Simon) there, please?
I'm sorry, you have the wrong number.
(Jerry) can't answer the phone right now.
Can I take a message?
Hi, it's (Rob).

WORD LIST

Phrases with *have, go & get*

have breakfast/dinner/lunch	/həv ˈbrekfəst, ˈdɪnə(r), lʌntʃ/
have a drink/a coffee/	/həv ə drɪŋk, ə ˈkɒfi,
a sandwich	ə ˈsæn(d)wɪdʒ/
have a break	/həv ə breɪk/
have a nap	/həv ə næp/
get dressed	/get ˈdrest/
get up	/get ʌp/
get home	/get həʊm/
go home	/gəʊ həʊm/
go to bed	/gəʊ tʊ bed/
go to sleep	/gəʊ tʊ sliːp/

Months

January *n C/U* ***	/ˈdʒænjuəri/
February *n C/U* ***	/ˈfebruəri/
March *n C/U* ***	/mɑː(r)tʃ/
April *n C/U* ***	/ˈeɪprəl/
May *n C/U* ***	/meɪ/
June *n C/U* ***	/dʒuːn/
July *n C/U* ***	/dʒʊˈlaɪ/
August *n C/U* ***	/ˈɔːgəst/
September *n C/U* ***	/sepˈtembə(r)/
October *n C/U* ***	/ɒkˈtəʊbə(r)/
November *n C/U* ***	/nəʊˈvembə(r)/
December *n C/U* ***	/dɪˈsembə(r)/

Housework

do the ironing	/duː ði ˈaɪə(r)nɪŋ/
do the shopping	/duː ðə ˈʃɒpɪŋ/
clean the bathroom	/kliːn ðə ˈbɑːθˌruːm/
make dinner	/meɪk ˈdɪnə(r)/
make the bed	/meɪk ðə ˈbed/
wash the clothes	/wɒʃ ðə ˈkləʊðz/
water the plants	/wɔːtə(r) ðə ˈplɑːnts/
do the dishes	/duː ðə ˈdɪʃɪs/
set the table	/set ðə ˈteɪb(ə)l/
take out the rubbish	/teɪk aʊt ðə ˈrʌbɪʃ/

Other words & phrases

breakfast *n C/U* ***	/ˈbrekfəst/
calendar *n C* **	/ˈkælɪndə(r)/
card *n C/U* ***	/kɑː(r)d/
class *n C/U* ***	/klɑːs/
closed *adj* **	/kləʊzd/
dinner *n C/U* ***	/ˈdɪnə(r)/
Earth *n C/U* ***	/ɜː(r)θ/
finish *v* ***	/ˈfɪnɪʃ/
gym *n C/U* *	/dʒɪm/
Halloween *n C/U*	/ˌhæləʊˈiːn/
idea *n C/U* ***	/aɪˈdɪə/
lunch *n C/U* ***	/lʌntʃ/
meeting *n C* ***	/ˈmiːtɪŋ/
nap *n C*	/næp/
nothing *prn* ***	/ˈnʌθɪŋ/
open *adj* ***	/ˈəʊpən/
shower *n C* **	/ˈʃaʊə(r)/
special *adj* ***	/ˈspeʃ(ə)l/
United Nations *n C*	/juːˈnaɪtɪd ˈneɪʃ(ə)nz/

5A | High-speed trains

SPEAKING

1 Work in pairs. Discuss these questions.

* What is more common in your country: to travel by train or travel by car?
* Do you travel by train? How often? Where do you go?
* What do you think of the trains in your country?

READING

1 Look at the photos of different popular trains. Check you understand the words in the box and <u>underline</u> the ones you think you will find in the article.

| fast | slow | comfortable | noisy |
| convenient | cheap | horrible | tall |

2 Read the article to check your answers.

3 Read the article again and answer the questions.

1 Why do many people like high-speed trains more than planes? Find three reasons.
2 Which train has a name that means bird?
3 Which train is called a bullet train?
4 Which train has a big network of cities?
5 Which train is the fastest?

4 Does your country have a high-speed train? Would you like to travel on one? Why or why not?

High-speed trains

The trains of the 21st century are here, and they are safe and comfortable. And they are fast. Super fast.

Today's high-speed trains can go up to three or four hundred km per hour. They can't fly, but in many ways they are more convenient than airplanes. Airports are usually outside city centres. With high-speed trains people can go from city centre to city centre. Many people like high-speed trains more than airplanes. Passengers on a high-speed train have more space than in an airplane. They can work on a computer and go for a walk. They can see the world go by – at 300 km per hour. In airplanes, you can't see anything.

These are some of the world's fastest trains:

The CRH (China)

China Rail High-Speed, the Chinese Rail system, uses many different trains. They have names like CRH1, CRH2, CRH3, etc. The CRH3 can travel at 350km per hour and travels between Beijing and Tianjin.

The TGV (France)

The TGV is French for *Train de Grande Vitesse*. It is France's famous high-speed train. The TGV has a big network. It can go to 150 different cities. The TGV's top speed is 320km per hour.

The AVE (Spain)

The AVE stands for *Alta Velocidad España*, but is also the Spanish word for *bird*. It is Spain's high-speed train. It can travel at 300 km per hour and has routes between the capital, Madrid, and other important cities in Spain.

Shinkansen (Japan)

The Shinkansen high-speed train network covers all of Japan. This Japanese train is called a *bullet train* and it can go up to 360 km per hour.

GRAMMAR: *can/can't*

> Use *can/can't* to talk about ability.
> It **can** travel very fast.
> It **can't** travel very fast.

> SEE LANGUAGE REFERENCE PAGE 60

1 Complete the English Language Ability Survey with *can/can't* so that it's true for you.

ENGLISH LANGUAGE ABILITY SURVEY –
Can you do it?

1 I ____ spell my first name and last name.
2 I ____ introduce myself and another person.
3 I ____ give my address and phone number.
4 I ____ understand the words in English songs.
5 I ____ talk about the people in my family.
6 I ____ describe someone in the class.
7 I ____ talk about where I live.
8 I ____ give simple directions.
9 I ____ answer a phone call and take a message in English.
10 I ____ speak on the telephone for a long time in English.

2 Work in pairs, A and B.

A: Turn to page 134.
B: Turn to page 136.

PRONUNCIATION: *can/can't*

1 🔘 **1.73** Listen how the words *can/can't* are pronounced in these sentences.

It can travel very fast.
It can't travel very fast.

In sentences and questions, *can* is pronounced /kən/.
In negatives, *can't* is pronounced /kɑːnt/.

2 🔘 **1.74** Listen and <u>underline</u> the word you hear. Then repeat the sentences.

1 We *can / can't* get there by plane.
2 We *can / can't* take the train.
3 You *can / can't* sit here.
4 They *can / can't* hear you.
5 It *can / can't* go very fast.

SPEAKING

1 🔘 **1.75** Listen to two dialogues. Match them to the pictures A and B.

2 Work in pairs. Look at audioscript 1.75 on page 142 to check your answers. Practise the dialogues with your partner.

3 Prepare a similar dialogue for the other picture.

Useful language

Excuse me, can you repeat that, please?
Can you write it for me on a piece of paper?
I'm sorry, I don't understand. Do you speak Spanish/French/Polish ...?
I only speak a little English.
Can you speak more slowly, please?

5B | Cross Canada trip

VOCABULARY: the weather

1 Look at the weather map of Canada. Complete the sentences with the names of the cities.

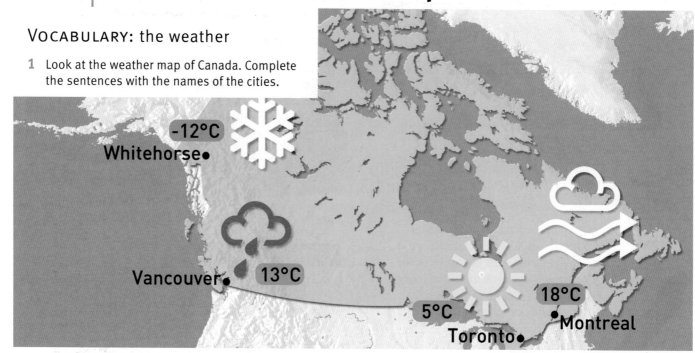

-12°C
Whitehorse●

Vancouver● 13°C

5°C
Toronto●

18°C
●Montreal

1 In _____ today, it's **cloudy** and **windy** but **warm**.
2 It's **cold** and **snowy** in _____, with temperatures of minus 12.
3 In _____, it's **sunny** and **cold**, 5 degrees.
4 You need your umbrellas in _____ today. It's **rainy** and **cool**.

> ### Language note
>
> Use the pronoun *it* to talk about the weather.
> *It's rainy and cold. It's sunny and warm.*
> To ask about the weather.
> *What's the weather like?*

2 🔘 1.76 Listen to the recording to check your answers. How do you say the words in **bold** in your language?

3 Work in pairs. Ask and answer these questions.

- What's the weather usually like on your birthday?
- What's your favourite weather?
- What weather don't you like?

LISTENING

1 🔘 1.77 Listen to two people talking about their holiday in Canada. Put the photos in the order you hear them. There is one extra photo.

☐ Montreal jazz

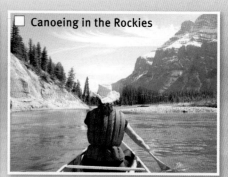
☐ Canoeing in the Rockies

☐ Toronto

☐ Train in Halifax

☐ Our hotel in Banff

2 🔊 **1.77** Listen again and <u>underline</u> the correct words.

1 The train journey was *ten / twelve* days.
2 The weather in Halifax was *good / bad*.
3 They were in Montreal for *two / four* days.
4 The shops were *open / closed* in Toronto.
5 Tom *can / can't* ski.
6 They were in Banff for *three / four* days.

3 Work in pairs. Imagine this was your Cross Canada trip. Talk about the photos on page 54. Use the sentences in exercise 2 to help you.

4 Would you like to visit these places? Why/Why not?

GRAMMAR: past simple *was/were*

> The past tense of the verb *be* is *was/were*.
> Our holiday **was** lovely.
> We **were** in Canada.
>
> The negative is *wasn't/weren't*.
> I **wasn't** very happy.
> The shops **weren't** open.

> ➤ SEE LANGUAGE REFERENCE PAGE 60

1 Read the sentences. Then make answers with the words in brackets.

1 We were in Dublin. (Glasgow) *No, we weren't. We were in Glasgow.*
2 The hotel was expensive. (cheap)
3 It was in a noisy part of town. (quiet)
4 It was sunny and warm. (rainy and cold)
5 Our tour guide was an Irish man. (Scottish man)
6 We were there for a week. (ten days)

2 Complete the dialogue with *was/wasn't*, *were/weren't* + the verb in brackets.

Lara: This is Toronto. You can see the CN Tower there. The shops (1) _____ (not open) that day. So we (2) _____ (be) in the park. I (3) _____ (not be) very happy.
Tom: No, you (4) _____ (not be). You (5) _____ (be) miserable.
Lara: It (6) _____ (be) cold!
Tom: How many days (7) _____ (be) we in Toronto?
Lara: We (8) _____ (be) there for two days.

3 Work in pairs. Practise the dialogue.

4 Work in pairs. Take turns making true sentences about one of the following times. Use *was* and *were*.

> last weekend   last night   a holiday

A: *Last weekend I was in the mountains.*
B: *Last weekend I was at home.*
A: *It was very cold.*
B: *It was nice and warm for me!*

DID YOU KNOW?

1 Work in pairs. Read about Canadian tourist destinations and discuss the questions.

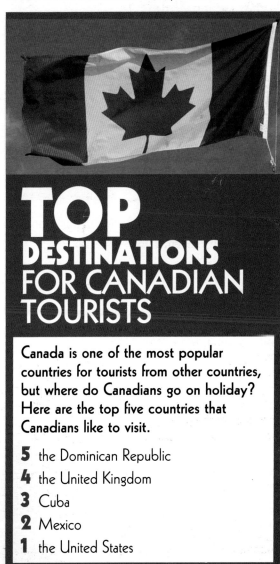

TOP DESTINATIONS FOR CANADIAN TOURISTS

Canada is one of the most popular countries for tourists from other countries, but where do Canadians go on holiday? Here are the top five countries that Canadians like to visit.

5 the Dominican Republic
4 the United Kingdom
3 Cuba
2 Mexico
1 the United States

- Do people in your country travel to other countries often?
- What are the popular destinations for tourists from your country?
- Would you like to visit any of the five countries on the list?

5c | Travel essentials

SPEAKING

1 Look at the picture. What can you see?
How many things can you say in English?

2 Work in pairs. Imagine you are going on a
last-minute holiday to a big city. It's time to
pack your bag. You can only take five things
from the picture. What do you take?

Useful language

I think the … is a good idea.
I agree. We can take the … and the …
I don't agree. I think the … is more
important.

READING & LISTENING

1 🔘 1.78 The Thompsons are going to the airport. Read and
listen to their dialogue. Who packed the bags – Walter or
Thelma Thompson?

Walter: Come on!
Thelma: I'm here. I'm here.
Walter: Did you turn off the lights?
Thelma: Yes, I did. I turned off the lights and your computer.
Walter: Good. Did you pack my digital camera?
Thelma: Yes, I did. It's in the black bag with your mobile
phone and book.
Walter: Which book?
Thelma: The book that was on the table next to your bed.
Walter: Oh. I didn't want a book. I wanted the
iPod.
Thelma: Well, I didn't know!
Walter: We don't have the iPod then.
Thelma: No, we don't.

Walter: Do you have the guidebook?
Thelma: Just a minute.
Walter: Oh no, you didn't remember
the guidebook.
Thelma: Yes, I did. Here it is!
Walter: Plane tickets?
Thelma: I remembered. They're here.
Walter: Good. Good. Well, darling,
we're on holiday.
Thelma: We can finally relax.

2 Read the dialogue again. Put a tick (✓) next to
the things they have in the car.

computer   digital camera   guidebook   iPod
mobile phone   book   torch   plane tickets

3 Work in pairs. Practise the dialogue.

4 🔘 1.79 Listen to Walter and Thelma at the
airport. What is the problem?

GRAMMAR: past simple regular verbs

> The past tense of regular verbs is verb + *ed*.
> I **wanted** the iPod.
> The past simple negative is *didn't* + verb.
> She **didn't remember** the iPod.
> The past simple question form is *did* + subject + verb.
> **Did you pack** my digital camera?

> ❯ SEE LANGUAGE REFERENCE PAGE 60

1 Complete the sentences. Put the verbs in brackets into the past simple.

1 They _____ (*remember*) the tickets but they _____ (*not remember*) the passports.

2 He _____ (*want*) a book but he _____ (*not want*) that book.

3 They _____ (*visit*) Washington but they _____ (*not visit*) the White House.

4 They _____ (*enjoy*) the city but they _____ (*not enjoy*) the weather.

5 They _____ (*like*) the hotel but they _____ (*not like*) the food.

2 Work in pairs, A and B. Look at the picture in Speaking exercise 1 on page 56. Write down the names of five things on a piece of paper. Don't show your partner.

A: Ask B questions to find out what B packed.
B: Answer.

Did you pack the iPod?
Yes, I did. / No, I didn't.

When you finish, swap roles.

3 Make questions about last night. Use the words in the box.

use	play	watch	study	cook	take out

1 you/television?
   Did you watch television?

2 you/the internet?

3 you/dinner?

4 you/English?

5 you/the rubbish?

6 you/football?

4 Work in pairs. Ask and answer the questions in exercise 3. Answer *Yes, I did* or *No, I didn't*.

PRONUNCIATION: past simple regular verbs

1 🔊 **1.80** Listen to the verbs and the past tense forms. What is different between group A and group B?

A		**B**	
pack	packed	want	wanted
open	opened	end	ended
watch	watched		

2 Choose the correct option to complete the rule about pronouncing past tense endings.

If the past simple verb ends in *-ted* or *-ded,* then
a) pronounce the *-ed* as an extra syllable /ɪd/.
b) don't pronounce the *-ed* as an extra syllable /ɪd/.

3 How do you pronounce the verbs in these sentences?

1 I **liked** it.
2 He **closed** the door.
3 They **remembered** it.
4 We **visited** her.
5 You **cooked** dinner.
6 English class **started** in September.

4 🔊 **1.81** Listen to the recording to check your answers.

SPEAKING

1 Make questions in the past simple.

Last year …

1 /travel by plane? Where?
2 /visit another country? Where?
3 /stay in a hotel? How was it?
4 /study English? In what school?
5 /play a sport? What sport?
6 /live in a different house or flat? Where?

2 Work in pairs, A and B.

A: Ask B questions from exercise 1.
B: Answer. Tell a lie about ONE thing that A asks.
A: Guess the lie.
You lied about question 2.
That's right.
That's wrong. That was the truth.

3 Swap roles and repeat the activity.

5D | Bed & breakfast

SPEAKING

1 Complete the sentences with information about you.

1 I often/sometimes/hardly ever/never stay in hotels.
2 The last time I stayed in a hotel was _____.
3 The hotel was in _____.
4 The hotel was very good/good/OK/not very good.
5 I was there for _____ nights.

2 Work in pairs. Compare your answers with your partner.

READING

1 Read the advertisements for two hotels. Which hotel do you like best?

2 Read the advertisements again and write *S* for the Shakespeare Inn, *CSC* for the Chicago Sky Central Hotel or *Both* if the sentence is true for both hotels.

1 It's an old house.   ____
2 It's good for business travellers.   ____
3 You can have breakfast in the hotel. ____
4 You can have dinner in the hotel.   ____
5 It is open every day.   ____
6 Children can play in the garden.   ____

3 Complete the definitions with a word from the advertisements.

1 Someone who is f_____ is nice and helpful to other people.
2 If something is w_____, it is hot in a comfortable, pleasant way.
3 An e_____ is a business or institution.
4 If something is c_____, then it's free.
5 A m_____ is a time when you eat, such as breakfast, lunch or dinner.
6 If something is a_____, then you can use, take or get it.

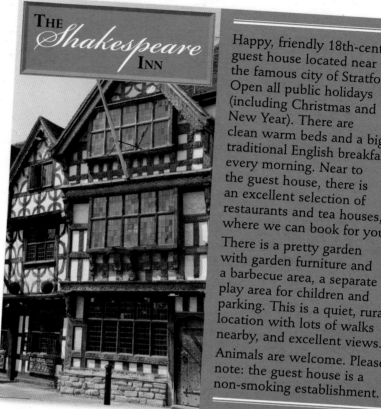

THE Shakespeare INN

Happy, friendly 18th-century guest house located near the famous city of Stratford. Open all public holidays (including Christmas and New Year). There are clean warm beds and a big traditional English breakfast every morning. Near to the guest house, there is an excellent selection of restaurants and tea houses, where we can book for you.

There is a pretty garden with garden furniture and a barbecue area, a separate play area for children and parking. This is a quiet, rural location with lots of walks nearby, and excellent views.

Animals are welcome. Please note: the guest house is a non-smoking establishment.

Chicago Sky Central Hotel

Our professional, modern hotel is in the centre of Chicago. We are open all year round and are only minutes away from shops, cinemas and discos. All our 81 rooms have a bathroom with shower, complimentary tea and coffee, internet access and modern furniture and design. Our hotel is perfect for business travellers and families.

Our famous Sky Central continental breakfast is included in the price of your room. You can eat in our breakfast lounge on the fifteenth floor. There is also a hotel restaurant for your evening meals: *The Sky Table.*

Children are welcome.

We have conference rooms available.

Free parking for hotel guests.

LISTENING

1 🔘 **1.82** Listen to some tourists visiting a hotel. Which hotel do they visit?

2 🔘 **1.83** Listen to four dialogues at the hotel. Match the dialogues 1–4 to the signs A–D.

A This phone is NOT for guests

B Beware of Dog!

C Sorry we do not take American Express

D Baggage Service £2.00

3 🔘 **1.83** Listen again and complete the dialogues with the correct word from the box.

public	credit card	fifteen	mobile phone
dangerous	private	take	bags	sorry	four

Cathy: I'm (1) _____. I was only looking. What's his name?
Owner: Rex.
Cathy: Can I touch him?
Owner: I'm afraid you can't. He's very (2) _____.

George: Hi. Excuse me, but could I use your phone? My (3) _____ doesn't work here.
Owner: I'm afraid we don't have a phone for the (4) _____.
George: What do you mean, no phone? What about that phone?
Owner: Sorry, it's (5) _____.

George: I'd like to pay the bill. Can I pay by (6) _____?
Owner: Of course. Visa? Mastercard?
George: American Express.
Owner: Oh no, I'm sorry but we don't (7) _____ American Express.

George: One more thing. Our bus leaves at a quarter past (8) _____. Is it OK to leave our bags here, please?
Owner: Certainly. It's £2 an hour.
George: But it's only for (9) _____ minutes!
Owner: I'm sorry, it's £2 minimum to keep (10) _____.

4 Look at audioscript 1.83 on page 143 to check your answers.

FUNCTIONAL LANGUAGE: asking for permission

Asking for permission		
Can I Could I May I	use your phone? wait here?	(please)
Is it OK if I/Is it OK to	(+ infinitive)	

Responding			
☺		☹	
(Yes)	Of course. Go ahead. Sure.	(No)	I'm sorry (but …) I'm afraid not.

❯ SEE LANGUAGE REFERENCE PAGE 61

Language note

It's very common to use *please* when we ask for permission.

1 Rearrange the words to make questions. Then ask the teacher the questions.

1 your   please   phone   I   may   use ?
2 to   the   go   toilet   please   can   I ?
3 alright   it   is   if   now   go   I ?
4 please   I   can   pen   your   use ?

2 Work in pairs. Take turns. Ask the questions in exercise 1. Respond to the questions ☺ or ☹.

3 Work in pairs, A and B.

A: You are a guest at the Chicago Sky Central Hotel. You are at reception. You want to do different things. Use the ideas on page 132 to help you. Ask permission at reception.

B: You are the receptionist at the Chicago Sky Central Hotel. Answer A's questions. Use the ideas on page 138 to help you.

4 Swap roles. Then change partners and repeat the roleplay.

Self-assessment (✓)

- ☐ I can use *can* and *can't* to talk about my abilities.
- ☐ I can understand expressions about the weather.
- ☐ I can use *was* and *were* to talk about the past.
- ☐ I can ask questions in the past simple.
- ☐ I can ask for permission and respond to a request.

5 | Language reference

GRAMMAR
Can/can't

Can is a modal auxiliary verb. This means:

- it goes with the infinitive without *to*.
- it has the same form for all subjects.
- the negative is with *not* (*n't*).
- to make a question, put *can* before the subject and the infinitive after the subject.

Affirmative

I You He/She/It We They	can	speak another language.

Negative

I You He/She/It We They	can't	speak another language.

I can speak French.
Not ~~I can to speak French~~.

I can't understand.
Not ~~I don't can understand~~.

Question & short answer

Can	I you he/she/it we they	do that, please?	
	Yes,	I you he/she/it we they	can.
	No,		can't.

Can you hear me?
Not ~~Do you can hear me?~~

Can has different uses.
Use *can* to talk about ability.

*I **can** speak English.*

Use *can* to ask for permission.

***Can** I use your phone?*

Past simple *was/were*

The past simple of *to be* is *was/were*.

*I **was** in Canada.*
*We **weren't** in a lovely hotel.*

Affirmative & negative

I He/She/It	was wasn't	
You We They	were weren't	on holiday.

Question

Was	I he/she/it	in Toronto?
Were	you/we/they	

Short answer

Yes, No,	I he/she/it	was. wasn't.
	you/we/they	were. weren't.

Past simple regular verbs

For most regular verbs, add *-ed* to the verb for the past simple.

*He **closed** the door.*
*He **walked** to work.*
*He **started** work at nine o'clock.*

Affirmative

I You He/She/It We They	packed	our bags.

For negatives, use the auxiliary *did* and *did not* (*didn't*) and the infinitive.

Negative			
I You He/She/It We They	didn't	visit	the museum.

For questions, use the auxiliary *did*. Put the auxiliary before the subject and the infinitive after the subject.

Question			
Did	I you he/she/it we they	remember	the passports?

FUNCTIONAL LANGUAGE

Asking for permission

Can I + infinitive?
Could I + infinitive?
May I + infinitive?

Is it OK if I + infinitive?
Is it OK to + infinitive?

Responses

Yes, of course.
Go ahead.
Sure.

No, I'm sorry but …
No, I'm afraid not.

WORD LIST

Things to take on holiday

alarm clock *n C* **	/ˈɑlɑː(r)m klɒk/
guidebook *n C* *	/ˈgaɪd ˌbʊk/
passport *n C* *	/ˈpɑːspɔː(r)t/
sunglasses *n pl*	/ˈsʌnˌglɑːsɪz/
ticket *n C* ***	/ˈtɪkɪt/

The weather

cloudy *adj*	/ˈklaʊdi/
cold *adj* ***	/kəʊld/
cool *adj* ***	/kuːl/
rainy *adj*	/ˈreɪni/
snowy *adj*	/ˈsnəʊi/
sunny *adj* *	/ˈsʌni/
warm *adj* ***	/wɔː(r)m/
windy *adj* *	/ˈwɪndi/

Other words & phrases

accessible *adj*	/əkˈsesəb(ə)l/
airport *n C* ***	/ˈeə(r)ˌpɔː(r)t/
animal *n C* ***	/ˈænɪm(ə)l/
available *adj* ***	/əˈveɪləb(ə)l/
barbecue *n C* *	/ˈbɑː(r)bɪˌkjuː/
bilingual *adj*	/baɪˈlɪŋwəl/
bird *n C* ***	/bɜː(r)d/
bullet *n C* **	/ˈbʊlɪt/
clean *adj* ***	/kliːn/
complimentary *adj*	/ˌkɒmplɪˈment(ə)ri/
convenient *adj* **	/kənˈviːniənt/
concert *n C* **	/ˈkɒnsə(r)t/
continental breakfast *n C/U*	/ˌkɒntɪˈnent(ə)l ˈbrekfəst//
cook *v* ***	/kʊk/
design *n C/U* ***	/dɪˈzaɪn/
destination *n C* **	/ˌdestɪˈneɪʃ(ə)n/
dictionary *n C* **	/ˈdɪkʃən(ə)ri/
draw *v* ***	/drɔː/
drive *v* ***	/draɪv/
electronic *adj* ***	/ˌelekˈtrɒnɪk/
establishment *n C/U* ***	/ɪˈstæblɪʃmənt/
exchange rate *n C* *	/ɪksˈtʃeɪndʒ reɪt/
friendly *adj* ***	/ˈfren(d)li/
go skiing *v*	/gəʊ ˈskiːɪŋ/
hear *v* ***	/hɪə(r)/
high-speed *adj*	/ˈhaɪˌspiːd/
iPod *n C*	/ˈaɪˌpɒd/
jazz *n U* *	/dʒæz/
machine *n C* ***	/məˈʃiːn/
meal *n C/U* ***	/miːl/
money *n U* ***	/ˈmʌni/
passenger *n C* ***	/ˈpæsɪndʒə(r)/
play chess/tennis *v*	/pleɪ tʃes, ˈtenɪs/
sing *v* ***	/sɪŋ/
swim *v* **	/swɪm/
torch *n C* *	/tɔː(r)tʃ/
translate *v* **	/trænsˈleɪt/
translation *n C/U* **	/trænsˈleɪʃ(ə)n/
type *v* *	/taɪp/
unnecessary *adj* **	/ʌnˈnesəs(ə)ri/
view *n C/U* ***	/vjuː/
warm *adj* ***	/wɔː(r)m/

6A | Celebrations

VOCABULARY & SPEAKING: celebrations

1 Put the life events in order. More than one answer is possible.

- **1** you are born
- **5** you get married
- **3** you graduate
- **2** you go to school
- **6** you have a baby
- **7** you retire
- **4** you get a job

2 Work in pairs. Discuss these questions.

- Do you celebrate the events in exercise 1?
- If you do, how do you celebrate them?

READING

1 Read the blogs. Match each blog to a life event from Speaking exercise 1.

2 Read the blogs again. Match the sentences 1–3 to the blogs A–C.

1 Anyway, we sat and talked for a long time.
2 This year, it was at my best friend's house.
3 He didn't know anything about it.

3 Read the sentences and decide if they are true (T) or false (F). Correct the false sentences.

1 Patrick got a watch at the party.
2 Richard was with the company in 1975.
3 Frank and Jessica didn't have a big wedding.
4 Frank and Jessica got married in an Indian restaurant.
5 The birthday party was outside.
6 People danced at the birthday party.

A | File Edit View Favourites Tools Help Links ➤

MEANY BLOG

Saturday 25th June
The Office Grind – Patrick Meany's life at an office
Richard's party was last night. It was at the Madison Hotel and around 60 people came. It was a big surprise for Richard.

_____ When he got to the hotel, we sang 'For he's a jolly good fellow'. We had a wonderful dinner and then we had the presentation. We gave him a gold watch. Nobody could believe Richard started with the company in 1975! I think he liked the party a lot, he looked happy anyway. Marjorie said some words about Richard, and we all congratulated him. I took some photos with my new camera. Here they are.
<u>Click here for photos of the party.</u>

B | File Edit View Favourites Tools Help Links ➤

MARISA'S BLOG

Thurs 6.45pm 16/05

Daily Shout – A blog for Marisa's family and friends
Can you believe it! My best friends Jessica and Frank finally got married last Saturday. I was so happy for them – ten years together! They didn't want a big wedding; it was a very quiet thing in the town hall. I didn't go to the ceremony, but I went to the party on Saturday night. It was in a big Indian restaurant. Guess what? Julian was there! It was great to see him again after all these years. _____ It was a great evening, I'm so happy for Jessica and Frank.

Wed 3.16pm 09/05

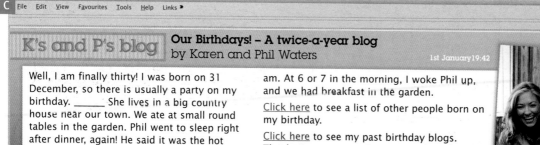

C | File Edit View Favourites Tools Help Links ➤

K's and P's blog | **Our Birthdays! – A twice-a-year blog**
by Karen and Phil Waters
1st January 19:42

Well, I am finally thirty! I was born on 31 December, so there is usually a party on my birthday. _____ She lives in a big country house near our town. We ate at small round tables in the garden. Phil went to sleep right after dinner, again! He said it was the hot weather. After dinner, people danced until 5

am. At 6 or 7 in the morning, I woke Phil up, and we had breakfast in the garden.

<u>Click here</u> to see a list of other people born on my birthday.

<u>Click here</u> to see my past birthday blogs. Thanks to everyone who came and made it a very good celebration.

GRAMMAR: past simple irregular verbs

There are two kinds of verbs in the past simple.
Regular verbs end in –ed in the affirmative form of the past simple.

Irregular verbs have a different form in the past simple affirmative.

eat – ate   go – went   make – made
see – saw   have – had

You can see a list of irregular past simple verbs on page 159.

The rules for questions and negatives are the same for regular and irregular past simple verbs.

Did you go to Richard's party? Yes, we did.
We didn't go to a disco.

▸ SEE LANGUAGE REFERENCE PAGE 70

1 Look at the blogs in Reading exercise 1. Underline eleven different irregular past tense affirmative verbs. Write the past form and the infinitive.

got – get

2 Complete the blog. Put the verbs in brackets into the past simple.

○○○

⋮ File Edit View Favourites Tools Help Links ➤

Scott's blog

**A magical journey –
Scott's travel blog**

On 31st December, my friend and I (1) _____ (be) on a train from Switzerland to Spain. We (2) _____ (have) a compartment for two people and some nice food for a picnic that we (3) _____ (buy) in Switzerland. We (4) _____ (want) to be on a train for December 31st. The train (5) _____ (not stop) at midnight, but it (6) _____ (stop) twenty minutes later. We (7) _____ (look) out the window and (8) _____ (eat) our picnic. We (9) _____ (not sleep) all night, we (10) _____ (sit) and (11) _____ (talk). We (12) _____ (get) home to Barcelona at 8am in the morning on January 1. It (13) _____ (be) a good New Year's Eve.

---

3 Make questions in the past with the words and with *you*.

1 where / go?
2 what / do?
3 who / go with?
4 what / eat?
5 what / drink?
6 what time / go to bed?

4 Work in pairs. Choose one of the following celebrations and interview your partner with the questions in exercise 3.

- A birthday party
- A wedding
- A New Year's Eve party
- Other (you choose)

SPEAKING

1 Work in pairs, A and B. You are going to tell a story of a celebration.

A: Begin. Complete sentence 1 with an idea of your own.
B: Continue the story with sentence 2.

1 Last night, we went to a _____ party.
2 It was in a _____.
3 It started at _____.
4 _____ and _____ were at the party.
5 We ate _____
6 and we drank _____
7 At the party, we met _____

2 Continue the story in turns. Choose phrases from the list below to give you ideas.

- called for a pizza
- had a coffee
- washed the dishes
- the music was loud and noisy
- danced in the street
- went out to the street
- the police arrived
- had a nap

3 Finish the story.

At _____, we went home. It was an interesting party!

6B | Actor! Author!

VOCABULARY & SPEAKING: films & books

1 Match the words in the box to the photos A–G.

> comedy horror love story/romance
> science fiction cartoon western
> thriller

2 Work in pairs. Think of a film or book you know for each category. Write their names.

3 Work with another pair. Read out the names of your films or books. Can the other pair say what the category is?

4 Work in pairs, A and B.

A: Turn to page 138.
B: Turn to page 135.

LISTENING

1 🔘 **2.1** Listen to the beginning of the TV programme *Actor! Author!* What are the rules?

2 🔘 **2.2** Listen to the extract. Can you guess the famous actor or author before Mike or Steph?

3 🔘 **2.2** Listen again. Underline the correct word(s).

Actor (1) _____
He was born in Kentucky, USA in *1963 / 1973*.
He *directed / acted* in many films by Tim Burton.
He made several films in his most famous role as a *pilot / pirate*.

Author: (2) _____
He is *Canadian / American*.
His books are translated into more than *14 / 40* languages.
He wrote a famous *thriller / love story*.
It's about symbols in the art of a famous *German / Italian* painter.

Author (3) _____
She was born in *England / Portugal*.
She taught *Spanish / English* in Portugal about twenty years ago.
She wrote a series of *seven / eleven* books.

Actress (4) _____
She was born in *1974 / 1964*.
She's from *Barcelona / Madrid*.
She got married to a famous *American / Spanish* actor.

GRAMMAR: past simple irregular verbs; past time expressions

> Past simple irregular verbs
> He **wrote** a thriller.
> She **taught** in Portugal.
>
> Past time expressions
> I saw Gladiator on DVD **last night**.
> I read that book **two years ago**.

> SEE LANGUAGE REFERENCE PAGE 70

1 Look at pages 64–65. Find the past simple of these verbs.

1 write _____   3 win _____   5 read _____
2 teach _____   4 see _____   6 make _____

2 Rearrange the words to make sentences.

1 weekend last a DVD I watched .
2 last didn't television I watch night .
3 bought ago two months I a book .
4 I didn't the Oscars® last year watch .
5 this read newspaper I the morning .
6 use didn't I the internet email or yesterday .

3 Change the sentences in exercise 2 so that they are true for you.

PRONUNCIATION: past simple irregular verbs

1 🔊 2.3 Listen to these verbs and their irregular past simple forms.

| think thought   understand   understood   say   said |
| speak   spoke   swim   swam   make   made |

2 🔊 2.3 Listen again and repeat.

3 Complete the table with an irregular past simple form from exercise 1.

/əʊ/	/ʊ/	/ɔː/	/e/	/eɪ/	/æ/
wrote woke	could took	taught bought	read went	ate gave	drank had

4 🔊 2.4 Listen to the recording to check your answers. Say the verbs.

SPEAKING

1 Work in groups of three. Write down the names of two famous actors and two famous authors. Don't show your names to your partners.

2 Prepare clues for your actors and authors.

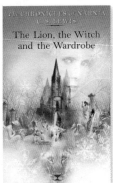

He/She was born in …
He/She won an Oscar®.
He/She wrote …
He/She acted in …

3 Play *Actor! Author!* One person gives clues, the others guess.

4 Swap roles.

DID YOU KNOW?

1 Work in pairs. Read about The Big Read and discuss the questions.

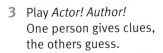

The Big Read

Some years ago, the BBC had a television show and competition to discover Britain's favourite books. More than 750,000 people voted for the book they liked the most. Here is the list of the top ten books in Britain.

1 **The Lord of the Rings**, J R R Tolkien
2 **Pride and Prejudice**, Jane Austen
3 **His Dark Materials**, Philip Pullman
4 **The Hitchhiker's Guide to the Galaxy**, Douglas Adams
5 **Harry Potter and the Goblet of Fire**, J K Rowling
6 **To Kill a Mockingbird**, Harper Lee
7 **Winnie the Pooh**, A A Milne
8 **Nineteen Eighty-Four**, George Orwell
9 **The Lion, the Witch and the Wardrobe**, C S Lewis
10 **Jane Eyre**, Charlotte Brontë

- Do you know any of these books?
- What are the titles in your language?
- What are the favourite books in your country, do you think?

6c | They cry easily

VOCABULARY: feelings

1 Match the sentences 1–5 to the pictures A–E.

1 He is bored. ☐
2 He is happy. ☐
3 He is sad. ☐
4 He is angry. ☐
5 He is nervous. ☐

2 💿 **2.5** Listen to the people at an important sports event. How do they feel? Number the sentences from exercise 1 in the correct order.

3 Work in pairs. Imagine you are in these situations. How do you feel? Tell your partner.

- You are in an exam.
- It's a beautiful sunny day and you have the day off.
- It's your birthday.
- It's Friday night and you finish work.
- You are at an important football match.
- You arc at the airport. Your plane is three hours late.
- You can't find an important piece of paper.

READING

1 Look at the photos. How do these people feel?

2 Read the article. Choose the best title.

1 # Men never cry

2 ## Crying – it's a man's thing

3 ### Crying – good for your health

4 # Men and sports

Men don't cry, or do they? British psychologists and researchers say that men cry easily, more easily than we think. One in three British men cry once a month, and in America, men cry on average
5 1.4 times a month.

Why do men cry more? In Britain and America it is more acceptable for men to cry today. Football star David Beckham cried when he took his children to school the first time. British Olympic athlete, Matthew Pinsent,
10 cried when he won a gold medal at the Olympics. Actors sometimes cry in front of millions of people when they win an Oscar®. Even two US presidents cried quietly on television.

In a survey on crying, men said that they often cry when
15 they are sad or when they feel bad. They said they don't cry when they are angry. But men cry a lot more than women when they are happy. For example, many British men cry when their favourite football team plays very well and wins a cup.
20 Doctors say that crying is good for your body. Most people say that they usually feel better after crying. So the next time you want to cry, go ahead. It's good for you!

3 Read the sentences and decide if they are true (T) or false (F). Correct the false sentences.

1 It's difficult for British men to cry.
2 American men cry more often than British men.
3 Matthew Pinsent cried because he lost a medal.
4 Actors always cry when they win an Oscar®.
5 Men cry when they are angry.
6 British men sometimes cry at sports, especially football.

4 Work in pairs. Discuss these questions.

- Is it common for people to cry in your country?
- Who cry more, men or women?
- Do you cry at sports events?
- Do you cry easily?
- When was the last time you cried?

GRAMMAR: adverbs of manner

> We use adverbs of manner to say how we do something.
> *The actor cried **quietly**.*
> *The football team played **well**.*

> SEE LANGUAGE REFERENCE PAGE 70

1 Find and <u>underline</u> the adverbs of manner in the article.

2 Complete the sentences with the correct form of the word in brackets.

1 He explained the rules very _____. (careful)
2 The winner at Wimbledon this year played tennis _____. (beautiful)
3 The manager of the football team answered the question _____. (angry)
4 Formula One cars go very _____. (fast)
5 She goes to the swimming pool every day, and she swims very _____. (good)

3 <u>Underline</u> the correct word.

1 He speaks very *quietly / quiet*. I can't hear him.
2 It's a very *sadly / sad* film.
3 My boyfriend cries very *easy / easily*.
4 It was a *well / good* party.
5 This is a very *hard / hardly* test.
6 He sat and ate his pizza *noisy / noisily*.

4 Work in pairs. Can you think of a famous sports person who …

- drives very fast?
- plays football very well?
- speaks English badly?

PRONUNCIATION: word stress 2, intonation 1

1 🔊 2.6 Listen and repeat the adverbs of manner. <u>Underline</u> the stressed syllable in these adverbs.

<u>an</u>grily	happily	nervously
slowly	carefully	quietly	noisily

2 🔊 2.7 Listen to four dialogues. Which adverb describes each dialogue?

SPEAKING

1 Play the *Dialogue Game*. Your teacher will explain the rules.

6D | I'm not crazy about it

SPEAKING

1 Work in pairs. Look at the different things to do in London. Imagine you have a free day/evening in the city. Choose three things that you would like to do.

2 Compare your answers with another pair in the class.

VOCABULARY: adjectives of opinion

1 🔘 **2.8** Listen and <u>underline</u> the word you hear. Say the sentences.

1 It was an *awful / excellent* film.
2 The shopping is *good / bad* here.
3 The boat ride was *great / terrible*.
4 The gardens are *nice / horrible*.
5 The football match was *good / terrible*.

2 Put the adjectives into the correct column.

> ~~good~~   ~~bad~~   nice   lovely   awful
> great   excellent   terrible   horrible

Positive adjectives	Negative adjectives
good	bad

3 Work in pairs. Give examples of ...

- excellent weather.
- terrible weather.
- a nice hotel.
- an awful hotel.
- a good film.
- an awful film.
- a great place to visit on holiday.
- a terrible place to visit on holiday.

Explore London recommends ...

- shopping in London's most famous shopping districts (Oxford Street, Knightsbridge)
- a trip on the Millennium Wheel
- a Chelsea or Arsenal football match
- a nightclub
- Kew Gardens
- a boat ride on the Thames
- St Paul's Cathedral
- the London Aquarium
- a tour round London on an open-top bus
- the Tower of London

London Aquarium

Kew Gardens

a boat ride on the Thames

LISTENING

1 🔊 2.9 Listen to three dialogues between tourists in London. Decide which activities from Speaking exercise 1 they are talking about.

2 🔊 2.9 Listen again and complete the phrases with words from the box.

| love | mind | crazy | stand | awful | really |

Dialogue 1
1 I _____ football. It's my favourite sport.
2 I'm not _____ about it.

Dialogue 2
3 It was _____. The actors were bad, the music was bad …
4 I don't _____ the actor.

Dialogue 3
5 I _____ liked it.
6 Usually I can't _____ boats.

FUNCTIONAL LANGUAGE: talking about likes & dislikes

1 Complete the table with words from Listening exercise 2 above.

☺☺
I really like football.
I (1) _____ rock music.
I think London is wonderful/great/excellent.

☺☺
I like the hotel.
I think the food is good.

☺
I don't mind sport.
It's OK.

☹
I don't like football.
I'm not (2) _____ about the hotel.

☹☹
I hate the food.
I can't (3) _____ the weather.
I think the book is/terrible/awful/horrible.

▶ SEE LANGUAGE REFERENCE PAGE 70

2 Rearrange the words to make questions.

1 you   of   think   do   what
   rock music ?
2 do   you   films   what   like ?
3 you   do   like   football ?
4 of   think   what   do   you
   your English class ?

3 Work in pairs. Discuss the questions in exercise 2.

SPEAKING

1 Write the names of real people or things that you like.

- An actor/actress from your country
- An American actor/actress
- A restaurant in your city
- A TV programme
- A film
- A singer/group

2 Work in small groups. Ask other people in your group about the things they wrote in exercise 1. Use different expressions from the functional language box to answer questions.

A: *What do you think of Avatar?*
B: *I think it's OK.*
A: *What about you? Do you like Avatar?*
B: *Yes, I do. I think it's great.*

3 Find two people or things that everybody in the group likes. Report back to the rest of the class.

We all like …

Self-assessment (✓)

☐ I can use past tense verbs to tell a simple story.
☐ I can ask and answer questions about celebrations.
☐ I can use adjectives to describe simple feelings.
☐ I can ask other people their opinions.
☐ I can give my opinion on simple things.

GRAMMAR
Past simple irregular verbs

Many common verbs are irregular in the past simple.

*eat – ate   go – went   make – made   see – saw
have – had*

There is a list of past simple irregular verbs on page 159.

Affirmative		
I You He/She/It We They	went	to the party.

The rules for the negative and question are the same as past simple regular verbs. See Language reference 5, page 60.

Past time expressions & *ago*

Use the following expressions with the past tense.
yesterday, last night/week/Saturday/month/year

These expressions go at the beginning or end of a sentence.

*I saw a film **last night**.*
***Yesterday** I had English class.*

We also use periods of time + *ago* with the past tense. It usually goes at the end of a sentence.

*I saw the film **two weeks ago**.*
*They booked their tickets **six months ago**.*

Adverbs of manner

Use adverbs of manner to say how we do something.

*The actor cried **quietly**.*
*The football team played **well**.*

Adverbs of manner usually go at the end of the sentence. To make an adverb of manner, you usually add *-ly* to the adjective.

quiet – quietly   slow – slowly   bad – badly

For adjectives that end in *-y*, change *y* to *-ily*.

easy – easily   noisy – noisily

There are some adverbs that do not change.

late – late   fast – fast   hard – hard   early – early

The adverb for *good* is *well*.

*They are **good** players. They play **well**.*

FUNCTIONAL LANGUAGE
Talking about likes & dislikes

☺ ☺
I really like …
I love …
I think … is wonderful/great/excellent.

☺
I like …
I think … is good.

☺
I don't mind …
It's OK.

☹
I don't like …
I'm not crazy about …

☹ ☹
I hate …
I can't stand …
I think … is/are terrible/awful/horrible.

WORD LIST

Celebrations

birthday *n C* **	/ˈbɜː(r)θdeɪ/
ceremony *n C/U* **	/ˈserəməni/
champagne *n U*	/ˌʃæmˈpeɪn/
congratulate *v* *	/kənˈgrætʃʊleɪt/
New Year's Eve *n C* **	/njuː jɪə(r)z iːv/
retirement *n C/U* *	/rɪˈtaɪə(r)mənt/
wedding *n C* ***	/ˈwedɪŋ/

Films & books

cartoon *n C* *	/kɑː(r)ˈtuːn/
comedy *n C/U* **	/ˈkɒmədi/
horror *n C/U* **	/ˈhɒrə(r)/
love story *n C*	/lʌv stɔːri/
romance *n C/U* *	/rəʊˈmæns/
science fiction *n U* *	/ˈsaɪəns fɪkʃ(ə)n//
thriller *n C* *	/ˈθrɪlə(r)/
western *n C* ***	/ˈwestə(r)n/

Feelings

angry *adj* ***	/ˈæŋgri/
bored *adj* **	/bɔː(r)d/
happy *adj* ***	/ˈhæpi/
nervous *adj* **	/ˈnɜː(r)vəs/
sad *adj* ***	/sæd/

Adjectives of opinion

awful *adj* **	/ˈɔːf(ə)l/
bad *adj* ***	/bæd/
excellent *adj* ***	/ˈeksələnt/
good *adj* ***	/gʊd/
great *adj* ***	/greɪt/
horrible *adj* **	/ˈhɒrəb(ə)l/
lovely *adj* ***	/ˈlʌvli/
nice *adj* ***	/naɪs/
terrible *adj* ***	/ˈterəb(ə)l/
wonderful *adj* ***	/ˈwʌndə(r)f(ə)l/

Other words & phrases

acceptable *adj* **	/əkˈseptəb(ə)l/
act *v* ***	/ækt/
actor *n C* ***	/ˈæktə(r)/
athlete *n C* *	/ˈæθliːt/
author *n C* ***	/ˈɔːθə(r)/
boat ride *n C*	/bəʊt raɪd/
buy *v* ***	/baɪ/
cry *v* ***	/kraɪ/
fall *v* ***	/fɔːl/
favourite *adj* **	/ˈfeɪv(ə)rət/
feel *v* ***	/fiːl/
health *n U* ***	/helθ/
horse *n C* ***	/hɔː(r)s/
medal *n C* **	/ˈmed(ə)l/
president *n C* ***	/ˈprezɪdənt/
psychologist *n C* **	/saɪˈkɒlədʒɪst/
stress *n C/U* ***	/stres/
symbol *n C* **	/ˈsɪmb(ə)l/
twice *adv* ***	/twaɪs/
was born *v*	/wəz bɔː(r)n/
weekend *n C* ***	/ˌwiːkˈend/
win *v* ***	/wɪn/

7A | Miracle diets?

VOCABULARY: food 1

1 Match the words in the box to the photos A–K.

> fish   chicken   potatoes   lettuce
> ice cream   bananas   bread
> apples   milk   eggs   cake

2 Complete the information for the *Nutrition Reference Guide* with words from exercise 1. Check you know the meaning of the other food words.

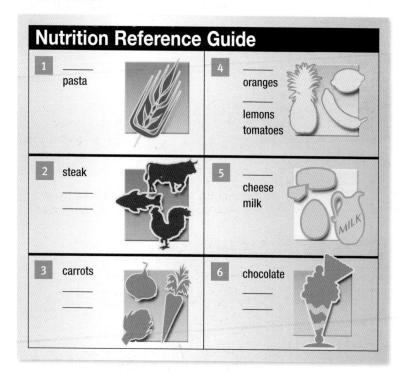

Nutrition Reference Guide

1 pasta ____	4 oranges ____ lemons tomatoes
2 steak ____	5 cheese milk ____
3 carrots ____	6 chocolate ____

3 🌐 2.10 Listen to the recording to check your answers. Say the words.

4 Work in pairs. Find out what food your partner likes. Ask questions.

> **A:** *Do you like pasta?*
> **B:** *Yes, I do.*
> **A:** *Do you like eggs?*
> **B:** *No, I don't.*

LISTENING

1 Read the extract from a TV magazine. What is the show about?

EXPOSED!

Film stars talk about them, doctors don't always believe them, and people pay a lot of money for them. Reporter Daniel Barber investigates the world of Miracle Diets. Do they work? Find out tonight at 9.15 pm on Channel 5.

2 🌐 2.11 Listen to part of the programme. What three diets does Daniel talk about? Underline the correct name.

Diet 1:   *The Two Fs diet / The Two Ss diet*
Diet 2:   *The High C diet / The Low C diet*
Diet 3:   *The Soup diet / The Fish diet*

3 🔊 **2.11** Listen again. <u>Underline</u> the correct word in Daniel Barber's notes.

<u>Diet 1</u>
- For breakfast, have some (1) fruit / milk.
- Don't eat any (2) meat / bread or drink any coffee.
- You can eat fish and (3) potatoes / tomatoes at lunch.
- Don't have any wine or beer, but fruit juice is OK.
- Lose (4) 2 or 3 / 5 or 6 kilos in a week.

<u>Diet 2</u>
Eat lots of fish, meat and (5) pasta / chicken.
Eggs are OK, too.
Don't eat any bread, pasta or (6) soup / fruit.
You can eat some lettuce, but don't eat any
(7) potatoes / cheese or carrots.
'Amazing results' – famous people use this diet?

<u>Diet 3</u>
Couldn't speak to a representative.
Website says you can eat all foods, but in soup form.
For example, fish soup, (8) pasta soup / chicken soup
and banana and (9) apple / chocolate soup?!?
Lose (10) 9 / 5 kilos in a week (?)

4 What do you think? Are these good diets? Do you know any miracle diets?

GRAMMAR: countable & uncountable nouns

Nouns can be countable or uncountable. Countable nouns have a plural form.
*You can eat **eggs** with this diet.*
Uncountable nouns do not have a plural form.
*Don't eat any **pasta**.*

Some/any
We use *some/any* with plural countable nouns and uncountable nouns. Use *some* in affirmative sentences and *any* in questions and negatives.

> SEE LANGUAGE REFERENCE PAGE 80

1 Mark the foods in the photos on page 72 countable (C) or uncountable (U).

2 <u>Underline</u> the correct word in the sentences.

1 I had some *coffee / coffees* for breakfast.
2 I don't have *any / some* beer at home.
3 I like *a French bread / French bread*.
4 I have *an / any* orange in my bag.
5 I ate some *pastas / pasta* yesterday.

3 🔊 **2.12** Listen to the recording to check your answers. Repeat if it's true for you.

4 Daniel Barber interviewed Susan Jeffreys about her experience with the *Two Fs* diet. Complete the dialogue with *some* or *any*.

Daniel: So, did the diet work for you?
Susan: No, it didn't. Every morning, I had three apples, two bananas and (1) _____ water for breakfast. I didn't eat (2) _____ bread or drink (3) _____ coffee or tea. I was tired all day!
Daniel: What else did you eat? Did you eat (4) _____ fish?
Susan: Yes, I did. On Monday, I ate (5) _____ fish. On Tuesday, I ate (6 _____ fish. On Wednesday, I ate (7) _____ tomato salad but I didn't eat (8) _____ fish. On Thursday, I ate (9) _____ fish again, with tomatoes.
Daniel: Did you eat (10) _____ meat, or vegetables?
Susan: No, I didn't. Only fish, fish, fish! At the end of the week, I was tired of it!
Daniel: What do you think of the *Two Fs* diet?
Susan: I didn't lose one kilogram! It's an awful diet!

5 Work in pairs. Read the dialogue.

SPEAKING

1 Work in pairs. Invent your own 'miracle diet'. Make a list of foods you can eat and a list of foods you can't eat. Give a name to your diet.

2 Work with another pair. Talk about your diet. Ask questions about the other diet.

Useful language

In the ... diet
You can eat ...   Eat lots of ...
You can eat some ...
You can't eat any ...
Don't eat any ...
The results are amazing/incredible. You can lose 10 kilos in a week.
Can I eat any ...?

7B | Rice

SPEAKING

1 Work in pairs. Discuss these questions.

- Do you like rice?
- Did you eat any rice last week?
- What do you eat rice with?

READING

1 Read the magazine article about rice. First, check you understand the words in **bold**, then decide if you think the sentences are true (T) or false (F).

1 Rice grows on **wet** land.
2 Rice grows on **dry** land.
3 **Almost** every country has rice in its diet.

2 Read the article again and check your answers. Then match the paragraphs 1–3 to the headings a–d below. There is one extra heading.

a Rice in danger   c Why I like rice
b Rice – an important food   d Why is rice so popular?

3 Read the article again and find the answers to the following questions.

1 How much rice do Europeans eat every year?
2 How much rice does a person in Myanmar eat every day?
3 How much rice does the world produce every year?
4 How many different types of rice are there?
5 What can you make with rice?

1 _____

Rice is life for millions of people around the world. It is the most important food for 50% of the world's population. Almost every country has rice in their diet. Europeans don't eat much rice, perhaps three kilograms per year. But in Myanmar, for example, each person eats half a kilogram of rice every day. Rice and fish is a popular combination in many Asian countries; rice and vegetables are important dishes in the Middle East and Southern Europe; and rice and beans is very popular in Latin America (in Colombia it is the national food).

2 _____

Every year, the world produces more than 500 million tonnes of rice. Rice is a popular food because it grows almost everywhere. You can grow rice on wet land and dry land, in rainforests and in deserts. Scientists think that there are more than 140,000 different types of rice in the world. Rice also has lots of uses. You can make paper, wine, bread, beer, sweets, cosmetics and even toothpaste with rice.

3 _____

Rice is in danger in many parts of the world, because of wars, environmental problems and pollution. Many of the poorest people in the world need rice. For these reasons, the United Nations declared 2004 the International Year of Rice and started many projects connected to rice. These programmes continue today.

Glossary
popular _adj_ liked by many people
cosmetics _n_ make-up

GRAMMAR: *how much/how many*

Use *How much* and *How many* to ask about quantities.
How much + uncountable nouns
   How much rice do people eat?
How many + countable nouns
   How many countries grow rice?

To talk about quantities, we use
a lot (of) / lots (of)
some
(not) much
(not) many

   Rice is in **a lot of** national dishes.
   People don't eat **much** rice in Europe.

> SEE LANGUAGE REFERENCE PAGE 80

1 Make questions using the words in the table.

	water coffee people rice hours eggs bread	do you buy every week? do you drink every day? are there in your English class? did you sleep last night? did you eat yesterday?
How much How many		

2 Work in pairs. Ask the questions from exercise 1. Answer *a lot, not much, not many* or *none*.

   How much coffee do you drink every day? A lot!

VOCABULARY: food 2

1 🔘 **2.13** Read and listen to descriptions of two rice dishes. Underline all the food and drink words. What are they in your language?

This is a dish I learnt in Mexico. It's called rice and beans. It's simple – it has rice, beans and corn. I like it for breakfast, with eggs and a large cup of coffee with lots of sugar. Delicious!

There are lots of different kinds of paella in Spain. For this paella, you need rice, different kinds of shellfish, Spanish sausages, an onion, some garlic, tomatoes, salt, pepper and a lemon. It's wonderful on a hot summer's day.

2 Which words are countable and which are uncountable? Write C or U. Say the words.

3 Work in pairs. Do you have a favourite rice dish? What is in it? Tell your partner.

PRONUNCIATION: word stress 3

1 🔘 **2.14** Listen and read the three shopping lists. How many syllables do the words have in each list?

Will's shopping list
* cheese
* bread
* milk

Jenny's shopping list
sugar
sausage
onion

Samantha's shopping list
banana
oranges
tomatoes

2 Who buys what? Put the words below into the correct shopping lists in exercise 1.

   rice   potatoes   ice cream   lettuce   cake   sausages

3 🔘 **2.15** Listen to the recording to check your answers. Add more words to each list.

4 Work in pairs. Read your lists to your partner.

SPEAKING

1 Work in pairs, A and B. Find six differences in the photos.
   A: Turn to page 133. B: Turn to page 134.

7c | Fussy eaters

SPEAKING & VOCABULARY: describing food

1 Work in pairs. What do you think of these dishes?

What do you think of sushi?
I like it. / I hate it. / I think it's … I don't know it.

brownies à la mode

chips

curry

spinach

sushi

2 🔊 **2.16** Listen and match the adjectives to the dishes in exercise 1. Say the words. What are these words in your language?

| salty | spicy | sweet | raw | cooked | hot | cold |

3 Work in groups. Find someone who …

- likes spicy food.
- doesn't like raw vegetables.
- likes sweet coffee.
- likes cold soups.
- always eats cooked vegetables.
- doesn't eat salty food.

Do you like spicy food?   *Yes, I do. No, I don't.*

LISTENING

1 Read the definition of a fussy eater. Do you know a fussy eater? Who is it? Why?

> A fussy eater is a person who eats only some types of food. They don't like trying new food.

My brother is a fussy eater. He doesn't eat vegetables or fruit.

2 🔊 **2.17** Listen to four dialogues. Put the food and drink words in the order you hear them. There are four extra words.

| burgers | rice | pasta | fish | wine |
| beer | cake | vegetable soup | | |

3 🔊 **2.17** Listen again and decide if the sentences are true (T) or false (F). Correct the false sentences.

1 The woman is a fussy eater.
2 The woman's brother is a fussy eater.
3 The man likes the wine.
4 The woman doesn't want the cake.
5 The boyfriend can only eat salty foods.

4 Work in pairs. Discuss these questions.

- What foods don't *you* like?
- Are you a fussy eater?

GRAMMAR: *too*

> *Too* + adjective means 'more than we want'
>   It's **too spicy**.
>
> *Too* + adjective and *very* + adjective are different.
>   The tea was **too hot**. I couldn't drink it.
>   The tea was **very hot**, but I could drink it.

> SEE LANGUAGE REFERENCE PAGE 80

1 Match the sentences in column A to the sentences in column B.

A	B
1 There's a lot of sugar in this coffee.	a You're too late.
2 I can't eat Mexican food.	b He's too short.
3 We can't move in this kitchen.	c It's too small.
4 Our baby needs to eat more.	d It's too spicy.
5 He can't reach the shelf.	e It's too sweet.
6 The film started ten minutes ago.	f He's too thin.

2 Rearrange the words to make sentences.

1 in   too   it's   here   hot .
2 tired   very   not   I'm .
3 easy   too   this   is   class .
4 very   food   is   expensive   in   country   my .
5 too   for   me   chocolate   is   sweet .
6 cloudy   it's   today   very .

3 🔘 2.18 Listen to the recording to check your answers. Repeat if it's true for you.

SPEAKING

1 🔘 2.19 Read and listen to the dialogue.

Man: Excuse me, waiter?
Waiter: Yes sir?
Man: I can't eat this soup. It's too cold.
Waiter: I'm sorry, sir.
Man: I hate cold soup!

2 Match the dialogue to one of the pictures A–C.

3 Work in pairs. Choose one of the other pictures. Write a similar dialogue.

4 Present your dialogue to another pair.

7D Eat out

Speaking & reading

1 Read the sentences below in the *Eating Out* survey. For each sentence, write a number 1 to 3 (1=usually; 2=sometimes; 3=hardly ever).

> **EATING OUT SURVEY**
>
> ☐ I have breakfast in a café or restaurant.
>
> ☐ I go to restaurants with my family.
>
> ☐ I go to restaurants with friends.
>
> ☐ I go to restaurants alone.
>
> ☐ I eat at a cafeteria at work or school.
>
> ☐ I go to fast food restaurants.

2 Work in pairs. Compare your results. Then calculate your points. Who has more points? Who eats out more?

Vocabulary: eating out

1 Match the words in column A to the words in column B to make sentences.

A		B	
1	We asked for a table	a	what we wanted to eat.
2	We looked	b	for two in the non-smoking section.
3	The waiter* asked us	c	for the waiter.
4	We had fish	d	for the main course.
5	We ate some chocolate cake	e	at the menu.
6	When we finished the meal	f	for dessert.
7	We left a tip	g	we asked for the bill.

* waiter = man   waitress = woman

2 🔘 **2.20** Listen to the recording to check your answers. Say the sentences.

Listening

1 🔘 **2.21** Listen to a couple at a restaurant. Tick (✓) the food and drink they order.

MENU for *Bella Pizza*

Salads
- Tomato and onion salad •
- Lettuce, tomatoes, onion and corn salad •

Pasta
- Spaghetti bolognese •
(with tomato sauce and meat)
- Four cheese pasta •
- Vegetarian lasagne •

Risottos
- Seafood risotto •
- Vegetable risotto •

Pizzas
- Margarita •
(tomato sauce and cheese)
- Special •
(tomato sauce, ham, mushrooms, green pepper, cheese)
- Vegetarian •
(tomato sauce, onion, green pepper, mushroom)
- Mexican spicy •
(tomato sauce, beef, corn, beans)

Drinks
- Cola, lemonade •
- Fruit juices •
- Mineral water •
(sparkling or still)
- Red wine, white wine •

2 🔊 **2.21** Listen again. Complete the dialogues with a word or words.

1 **Man:** Table for _____, please.
Waiter: This _____, please.

2 **Man:** Could we have the _____ too, please?
Waiter: Of course.

3 **Waiter:** Are you _____ to order?
Man: Yes, we are.

4 **Waiter:** Anything to _____?
Man: Yes, some red wine please.

5 **Man:** Do you have any salt?
Waiter: Here you are.
Man: _____ you.
Waiter: You're _____.

6 **Man:** No coffee for me, thank you. Just the _____.
Waiter: Of course. Here you are. That's 15 pounds, please.

FUNCTIONAL LANGUAGE: in a restaurant

Customer	
Can I have	fish/the menu/the bill, please?
Could I/we have	a table for two, please?
Can I pay	by credit card/by cheque?

Waiter/waitress	
Can I help you?	Are you ready to order?
Here you are.	That's X pounds, please.

▶ SEE LANGUAGE REFERENCE PAGE 80

1 Correct the mistakes in the sentences.

1 I can help you? *Can I help you?*
2 Here are you.
3 That are 15 pounds, please.
4 Could I has the fish, please?
5 Can I pay by the credit card?
6 Anything for drink?
7 Can we have a bill, please?

PRONUNCIATION: word linking 1

1 🔊 **2.22** Listen to six sentences. How many words do you hear in each sentence? (contractions=2 words)

2 Look at audioscript 2.22 on page 144 to check your answers.

3 🔊 **2.22** Listen to the sentences again and repeat.

SPEAKING

1 Work in pairs, A and B. Follow the directions below.

A: You are the waiter at Bella Pizza.
B: You are a customer at Bella Pizza.

2 Change roles and repeat.

A	B
Greet B.	Ask for a table.
Take B to table, give menu.	Read the menu.
Ask what B would like to drink.	Order a drink.
Bring B's drink, ask what B would like to eat.	Order food.
Bring B's food.	Thank A. Ask for the bill.
Bring the bill for B.	Pay the bill.

DID YOU KNOW?

1 Work in pairs. Read about eating out in the US and discuss the questions.

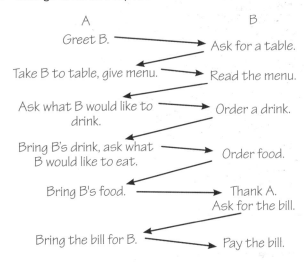

Restaurants by numbers – in the US

Eating out in the US is a big business. According to the National Restaurant Association, American restaurants sell $1.7 billion of food and drink every day.

88% of Americans say they enjoy going to restaurants.

71% of Americans say they try to eat more healthy food at restaurants now than in the past.

43% of Americans say that restaurants are an essential (very important) part of their life.

Restaurants in the US give jobs to 12.8 million people, more than any other industry in the private sector.

1 out of 4 Americans got their first work experience in a restaurant.

• Are these facts similar for your country?
• When do you eat out? Why?

Self-assessment (✓)
☐ I can talk about food I like and dislike.
☐ I can use *how much* and *how many* to ask about food.
☐ I can order food and drink in a restaurant.

GRAMMAR
Countable & uncountable nouns

Nouns can be countable or uncountable.

Countable nouns	Uncountable nouns

• have a plural form
  *This dish has five **eggs***.
	• do not have a plural form, they are always singular
	  *I love **fruit***.

• use *a/an* or *the* for the singular *Can I have **an orange**?*	• do not use *a/an*

• use *some* with plural nouns in affirmative sentences
  *I'd like **some carrots***.
	• use *some* with uncountable nouns in affirmative sentences
	  *She drank **some** water.*

• use *any* with plural nouns in negatives/questions
  *Does it have **any chocolate** in it?*
	• use *any* with uncountable nouns in negatives/questions
	  *Don't eat **any** bread.*

• in the dictionary, countable nouns are marked with a C
  pen (n/C)
	• in the dictionary, uncountable nouns are marked with a U
	  salt (n/U)

Some nouns can be countable or uncountable, but they mean different things.
juice (U) = the drink
a juice (C) = a glass or bottle of juice
Other nouns like this are *coffee, beer*.

How much/how many

Use *how much* and *how many* to ask about quantities.

How much + uncountable nouns
   ***How much** rice do people eat?*
How many + plural countable nouns
   ***How many** countries make rice?*

Use words like *lots, much, some* to talk about quantities.
These words go before the noun.

   a lot (of)/lots (of)

   some

   not much (with uncountable nouns)
   not many (with countable nouns)

*He has **lots of** friends.*
*They **don't** make **much** money.*

Too

Too + adjective means 'more than we want'.

   *It's **too** spicy.*

Too + adjective and *very* + adjective are different.

   *The tea was **too** hot. I couldn't drink it.*
   *The tea was **very** hot, but I could drink it.*

FUNCTIONAL LANGUAGE
In a restaurant

Can I have + noun, *please?*
Could I/we have + noun?
Can I pay by credit card/by cheque?

Can I help you?
Are you ready to order?
Here you are.
You're welcome.
That's X pounds, please.

WORD LIST

Food

apple *n C/U* **	/ˈæp(ə)l/
banana *n C/U* *	/bəˈnɑːnə/
bean *n C* **	/biːn/
bread *n U* ***	/bred/
butter *n U* **	/ˈbʌtə(r)/
cake *n C/U* ***	/keɪk/
carrot *n C/U* *	/ˈkærət/
cheese *n C/U* **	/tʃiːz/
chicken *n C* **	/ˈtʃɪkɪn/
chips *n pl* ***	/tʃɪps/
chocolate *n C/U* **	/ˈtʃɒklət/
corn *n U* **	/kɔː(r)n/
curry *n C/U*	/ˈkʌri/
diet *n C/U* ***	/ˈdaɪət/
egg *n C* ***	/eg/
fish *n C/U* ***	/fɪʃ/
fruit *n C/U* ***	/fruːt/
garlic *n U* *	/ˈgɑː(r)lɪk/
ice cream *n C/U* *	/aɪs kriːm/
lemon *n C/U* **	/ˈlemən/
lettuce *n C/U* *	/ˈletɪs/
milk *n U* ***	/mɪlk/
nutrition *n U* *	/njuːˈtrɪʃ(ə)n/
onion *n C* **	/ˈʌnjən/
orange *n C* **	/ˈɒrɪndʒ/
pasta *n C/U* *	/ˈpæstə/
pepper *n C/U* *	/ˈpepə(r)/
potato *n C/U* **	/pəˈteɪtəʊ/
rice *n U* **	/raɪs/
salt *n U* **	/sɔːlt/
sauce *n C/U* **	/sɔːs/
sausage *n C/U* *	/ˈsɒsɪdʒ/
shellfish *n C/U*	/ˈʃelˌfɪʃ/
soup *n C/U* **	/suːp/
spinach *n U*	/ˈspɪnɪdʒ/
steak *n C/U* *	/steɪk/
sugar *n U* ***	/ˈʃʊgə(r)/
tomato *n C* **	/təˈmɑːtəʊ/
vegetable *n C/U* ***	/ˈvedʒtəb(ə)l/
water *n U* ***	/ˈwɔːtə(r)/
wine *n C/U* ***	/waɪn/

Describing food

cold *adj* ***	/kəʊld/
cooked *adj*	/kʊkt/
delicious *adj* *	/dɪˈlɪʃəs/
healthy *adj* ***	/ˈhelθi/
hot *adj* ***	/hɒt/
raw *adj* **	/rɔː/
salty *adj*	/ˈsɔːlti/
spicy *adj*	/ˈspaɪsi/
sweet *adj* ***	/swiːt/

Eating out

bill *n C* ***	/bɪl/
dessert *n C/U* *	/dɪˈzɜː(r)t/
main course *n C*	/meɪn kɔː(r)s/
meal *n C* ***	/miːl/
menu *n C* **	/ˈmenjuː/
tip *n C* **	/tɪp/
waiter *n C* *	/ˈweɪtə(r)/
waitress *n C* *	/ˈweɪtrəs/

Other words & phrases

almost *adv* ***	/ˈɔːlməʊst/
dry *adj* ***	/draɪ/
wet *adj* ***	/wet/

8A | I hate flying

SPEAKING

1 Work in pairs. Ask and answer these questions about air travel.

- Did you travel to another country last year?
- Did you travel by plane?
- When did you travel?
- Where did you go?

READING

1 Read the magazine article and put the events in the correct order.

- ☐ The writer talked to a psychologist.
- ☐ The writer visited his brother in Hong Kong.
- ☐ The writer went on a course for people afraid of flying.
- ☐ The writer talked to a pilot.

2 Read the article again and answer the questions.

1 How many Americans hate flying?
2 Did the writer travel by plane before the course?
3 Why was the writer's phobia a problem?
4 Who taught the writer how to relax on a plane?
5 What did the people do when the flight started?
6 What did the writer do after his flight?

3 Work in pairs. What about you? What do you think of flying? Do you know someone who is afraid of going on a plane?

FEAR OF *FLYING*

PERSONAL STORY

If you don't like flying, you are not alone. Fear of flying is one of the most common phobias in the world. More than 10 million British adults are afraid of flying. In America, this number is more than 25 million. Many famous people
5 hate or hated flying: Ronald Reagan, Aretha Franklin, Mohammed Ali, Cher and Billy Bob Thornton are only some examples.

I hated flying. I knew that planes were very safe, that they were safer than cars (about 29 times safer), and
10 the chances of being in a plane accident were about 0.0000000004%. But every time I was at the airport, I felt terrible. I couldn't get on the plane. The only problem was that I loved travelling. And if you love travelling and hate flying, that is a problem.

15 After many years, I decided to do something. A friend told me about a special course for people like me. It was a one-day course at the airport. There were more than 100 people on this course. The first part of the course was a class with a pilot. He explained exactly how a plane
20 works, and showed us all the different parts. I liked that because it helped me a lot. Then we had a long talk with a psychologist. She gave us information about phobias and taught us a relaxation technique.

Then we had the most difficult part, a 45-minute flight.
25 We were all still very nervous. Some people held hands, and some people cried. But we all did it. At the end of the flight, I felt nervous and tired but very happy. I could get on a plane and survive. The next day, I booked a ticket to see my brother in Hong Kong. It was the first time I
30 visited him.

That was three years ago, and I don't mind flying now. But I don't like eating on planes, and no course can help me with that!

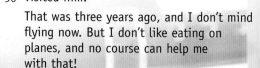

GRAMMAR: verb + -ing

> After the verbs *like, hate, love*, we use the verb + -*ing*.
> *Many famous people **hate flying**.*
> *I **don't like eating** on planes.*

> **SEE LANGUAGE REFERENCE PAGE 90**

1 Put the words in the correct order on the line.

> like   hate   don't like   love   don't mind

```
☺☺          ☺          ☺          ☹          ☹☹
```

2 Find examples of the verbs in exercise 1 in the article. Underline them and the verbs that go with them.

3 Here are some of the reasons why the writer doesn't like travelling on planes. Complete the sentences with a word from the box. Use the -*ing* form.

> wait   go   sit   talk   eat

1 I don't like _____ through security, it makes me nervous.
2 I hate _____ next to other people on planes. The seats are too small.
3 I don't like _____ to a stranger on a plane.
4 I don't like _____ for a long time at the airport.
5 I hate _____ airline food.

4 Work in pairs, A and B. Find out each other's likes and dislikes.

A: Turn to page 134.
B: Turn to page 136.

VOCABULARY: transport

1 Look at the words in the box. Put them into two groups.

> car   airport   car park   plane   boat
> motorbike   railway station   train   bicycle
> bus   underground   bus stop   port
> on foot

Group A: Places connected to transport
Group B: Kinds of transport

2 🔘 2.23 Listen to the recording to check your answers. Say the words.

Language note

> With the verb *go* and kinds of transport, use the preposition *by* + transport.
> *I went **by car**. They go to work **by train**.*

3 Work in pairs. Ask and answer the questions.

How do you get from your home to …	the city centre? English class? another city in your country? the sea? the US?

PRONUNCIATION: /ŋ/

1 🔘 2.24 Listen and repeat the words.

> waiting   young   flying   eating   think   English

2 🔘 2.25 Listen and complete the sentences.

1 I _____ flying.
2 I _____ speaking English.
3 I _____ watching horror films.
4 I _____ writing exams.

3 Complete the sentences with *like/don't like/hate* etc. so that they are true for you. Say the sentences.

SPEAKING

1 Do the *Travel* questionnaire below.

A: *Do you hate flying?*   **B:** *Yes, I do.*
A: *Why?*   **B:** *Because I'm afraid of planes.*

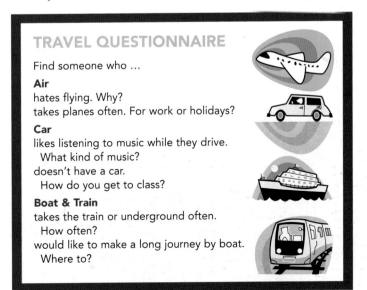

TRAVEL QUESTIONNAIRE

Find someone who …

Air
hates flying. Why?
takes planes often. For work or holidays?

Car
likes listening to music while they drive.
  What kind of music?
doesn't have a car.
  How do you get to class?

Boat & Train
takes the train or underground often.
  How often?
would like to make a long journey by boat.
  Where to?

2 Tell the class two things you found out about other students and travelling.

8B | Traffic jam

LISTENING

1 Work in pairs. Discuss these questions.

- How long is the journey from your house to class?
- How do you get to class? Do you walk, take public transport or drive?
- Is there a lot of traffic when you come to class?

2 🔘 **2.26** Listen to the traffic report. Match the pictures A–D to the stories 1–4.

3 🔘 **2.26** Listen again. What is the problem in each picture?

4 🔘 **2.26** Listen again and decide if the sentences are true (T) or false (F). Correct the false sentences.

1 There is a bus on fire in Regent Street.
2 Traffic isn't moving in Regent Street.
3 Some people are singing in Oxford Street.
4 These people are standing next to the cars.
5 The police are talking to the lion.
6 A car is on the wrong side of the road in East London.

5 Is traffic bad in your town?

GRAMMAR: present continuous

> Use the present continuous to talk about events happening now or around now.
>
> Form: *be* + verb + *-ing*
> *Traffic **is** not **moving**.*
> *Someone **is driving** on the wrong side of the road.*
> *What **are** they **doing**?*

> ▶ SEE LANGUAGE REFERENCE PAGE 90

1 Look at audioscript 2.26 on page 144. <u>Underline</u> examples of the present continuous.

2 Make questions and answers with the present continuous.

What / they / do?	They / move / a car to the side of the road.
What are they doing?	*They are moving a car to the side of the road.*
1 What / the people / do?	The people / stand / in the street.
2 Where / they / go?	They / go / to the city centre.
3 Who / the police / talk to?	They / talk to / the demonstrators.
4 What / the lion / do?	It / sit / in the road.
5 What / the car / do?	It / drive / on the wrong side of the road.
6 What / the woman / do?	She / talk / on her mobile phone.

3 Think of four people you know. What are they doing now? Make sentences about them. Use the verbs and phrases in the box to help you.

> watch TV   work   sleep   sit in traffic
> have breakfast/lunch/dinner   study
> talk on the phone   do the housework

4 Work in pairs. Write the names of the people in exercise 3 on a different piece of paper. Ask questions about the people on your partner's paper.

What's Michael doing?
He's working.

VOCABULARY: action verbs

1 Write the missing letters in the infinitive verbs.

1 s _ ng   3 dr _ ve   5 k _ ss
2 w _ lk   4 r _ n   6 sl _ _ p

2 Make sentences about what people are doing in the pictures. Use the verbs in exercise 1 in the present continuous.

SPEAKING

1 Work in pairs. Read the instructions for the *In Traffic Game*.

IN TRAFFIC GAME

- Work in groups of four or five. You are all in one car, in a traffic jam.
- Your teacher will give you a piece of paper with an action on it.
- Do the action. Don't say a word.
- The other students ask questions about the action,
- *Are you dancing?* Answer *Yes, we are* or *No, we aren't.*
- Take turns.

2 Play the game.

DID YOU KNOW?

1 Work in pairs. Read about traffic in London and discuss the questions.

London's CONGESTION CHARGE

London had the worst traffic in the UK and was one of the worst cities in Europe. Drivers spent 50% of their time in traffic jams, and the pollution was terrible. In 2003, the mayor of London made a new law to help reduce traffic. It now costs £10 (approximately €12) a day to drive in central London. More people use public transport and bicycles now in London because of this law. Traffic is bad, but not too bad now.

- What do you think of the congestion charge in London?
- Is it a good idea?
- Is there something similar in your country?

8c | Follow that car!

READING & LISTENING

1 Look at the advertisement. What does Tracy Dick do?

2 🔘 2.27 Tracy Dick is working for Mr Rogers, from the company Rogers and Lewis. Mr Rogers wants Tracy to follow his business partner, Mr Lewis. Read and listen to the story and put the pictures in the correct order. There is one extra picture.

Tracy: Mr Rogers, it's Tracy Dick here.
Mr Rogers: Yes?
Tracy: You asked me to call you. I'm outside your business partner's office now.
Mr Rogers: Oh, thank you. Jack doesn't leave work before 6 o'clock. And it's now only half past five.
Tracy: Well, Mr Rogers, Jack Lewis, your business partner, is leaving work now.

Mr Rogers: OK, Tracy. What is Jack doing now?
Tracy: He's taking a taxi.
Mr Rogers: A taxi! Jack hardly ever takes taxis. Interesting … is the company paying for this, I wonder?
Tracy: Do you want me to follow him?
Mr Rogers: Yes, yes! Follow that car!

Tracy: Mr Rogers? I'm in the centre of the city.
Mr Rogers: Where's Jack?
Tracy: Mr Lewis is paying the taxi driver … He's getting out of the taxi.
Mr Rogers: Where is he exactly?
Tracy: He's in front of a big office building. It says *Edwards and Horn* over the door.
Mr Rogers: Edwards and Horn! Our competition! I knew it. He's leaving our company!

Tracy: He's not going into the office. He's going into a café.
Mr Rogers: A secret meeting. It's a secret meeting. Tracy, I need to know what he says!
Tracy: I'm going to get closer.
Mr Rogers: Phone me back, please.

Mr Rogers: Hello?
Tracy: I'm just outside the café. Mr Lewis is sitting at a table.
Mr Rogers: What is he doing?
Tracy: He's meeting a middle-aged man. I think …
Mr Rogers: That's it! I'm going over there now! He's not going to give any of OUR secrets to Edwards and Horn!
Tracy: Wait! I think …

3 Read the story again. Choose the correct phrases to complete the sentences.

1 Mr Lewis usually leaves work …
   a) at 6 o'clock.
   b) at 5.30 pm.

2 He hardly ever …
   a) goes by bus.
   b) takes a taxi.

3 Tracy Dick follows …
   a) the taxi.
   b) the motorbike.

4 Mr Rogers …
   a) knows the big office building.
   b) doesn't know the big office building.

5 Mr Lewis …
   a) is meeting a man.
   b) is having lunch.

6 Mr Rogers …
   a) is going to the café.
   b) is leaving the café.

7 Tracy Dick …
   a) is talking to Mr Lewis.
   b) is watching Mr Lewis.

4 Work in pairs. What do you think is happening? Who is Mr Lewis meeting? Tell your partner.

5 🔘 **2.28** Listen to the end of the story. Were you correct?

VOCABULARY: collocations (transport)

1 Underline the correct word.

1 Can you *ride* / *drive* a motorbike?
2 Can you *ride* / *drive* a car?
3 How often do you *take* / *ride* a taxi?
4 Do you *take* / *drive* the train to work?

2 🔘 **2.29** Listen to the recording to check your answers.

3 Work in pairs. Ask and answer the questions in exercise 1.

GRAMMAR: present simple vs present continuous

Use the present simple to say what we usually do.
   *He **goes** to work by bus **every day**.*

Use the present continuous to say what we are doing now.
   *He's **taking** a taxi **now**.*

❯ SEE LANGUAGE REFERENCE PAGE 90

1 Decide if these sentences are present simple (PS) or present continuous (PC). Write *PS* or *PC* in the space.

1 Jack Lewis is leaving work now. ____
2 What is he doing? ____
3 He's taking a taxi. ____
4 He hardly ever takes taxis. ____
5 He's not going into the office. ____

2 Complete the conversation. Put the verbs in brackets into the present simple or the present continuous.

Jack: So, what (1) _____ you (2) _____? (do)
Tracy: I'm a private detective.
Jack: That's interesting. (3) _____ you (4) _____ (work) now?
Tracy: Yes, I am. At the moment I (5) _____ (follow) a man.
Jack: How exciting! Is he in this café?
Tracy: Yes, he is. Right now he (6) _____ (talk) with a woman.
Jack: So … who asked you to follow this man?
Tracy: I can't tell you. He (7) _____ (wait) for me to call him now.
Jack: Well, my brother and I are (8) _____ (have) a coffee. Would you like to join us?
Tracy: No, thank you. I'm (9) _____ (leave).

3 🔘 **2.28** Listen to the recording to check your answers. Work in pairs. Read the dialogue with your partner.

SPEAKING

1 Work in pairs, A and B.

A: Turn to page 137.
B: Turn to page 133.

8D | Let's take the bus

SPEAKING

1 Look at the photo.
Describe what is happening.

LISTENING

1 🔘 **2.30** Listen to the dialogue. Where are the man and woman going? How many different forms of transport do they take?

2 🔘 **2.30** Listen again. Complete the sentences with words from the box.

> a man   by bus   a taxi   the wrong train
> an umbrella   the directions

Dialogue 1
1 The woman asks _____ for help.
2 They don't understand _____.

Dialogue 2
3 They went on _____.
4 The man wants to go _____.

Dialogue 3
5 The woman didn't take _____.
6 The woman calls _____.

FUNCTIONAL LANGUAGE: suggestions

Suggestions	
Why don't we/you	*take a taxi?*
Let's	
We/You can/could	*take the underground.*

Responses
That's a good idea.
OK.
No.
I don't think that's a good idea.

> ⟩ SEE LANGUAGE REFERENCE PAGE 90

1 Rearrange the words to make suggestions.

1 go   the   concert   to   we   could .
2 the   underground   we   can   take .
3 the   man   ask   over   let's   there .
4 a   traditional   taxi   see   London   could   we .
5 now   take   we   that   taxi   don't   why ?
6 the   street   go   up   let's .

PRONUNCIATION: intonation 2

1 🔘 **2.31** Listen to these two suggestions said in different ways. Which way is friendlier? <u>Underline</u> 1 or 2.

1 We can take the underground. *1 / 2*
2 Let's take a bus. *1 / 2*

2 🔘 **2.31** Listen again and repeat.

3 🔘 **2.32** Listen to these suggestions. Put a tick (✓) if they are friendly and a cross (✗) if they are not.

1 Why don't we wait for the bus?
2 We can go on foot.
3 We could take a taxi.
4 Let's go by train.

4 Work in pairs. You want to get to the other side of your town quickly. Use the pictures to make suggestions. Respond to the suggestions.

VOCABULARY: *take*

1 We can use the verb *take* in different ways in English. Look at the examples in the box.

1 *take* + transport: *We can take a bus.*
2 *take* + things: *I didn't take an umbrella.*
3 *It* + *take* + time: *It takes 15 minutes (to get to the Waterfront Hall).*

take a photo

2 Look at audioscript 2.30 on pages 144–145 and <u>underline</u> all the examples of *take* + noun(s).

3 Complete the man's email about the concert with words from the box.

> a photograph   a sandwich   twenty minutes
> a taxi   the camera

In the end, we took (1) _____. Margaret was happy and of course, she took (2) _____ of us in the car. It took us (3) _____ to get to the Waterfront Hall, and I was right, it cost a lot of money. When we got there, I wanted to take (4) _____ into the hall. The man at the door said I couldn't. No eating in the concert, he said. And he said Margaret couldn't take (5) _____ in. The concert was wonderful, though. We loved it!

4 Work in pairs. Think of the last long journey you took. Ask and answer these questions and describe your journey.

- What form of transport did you take?
- Did you take a lot of things with you?
- How long did it take for you to get there?
- Did you take any photos?
- What did you take photos of?

SPEAKING

1 Work in two groups, Group A and Group B. Imagine there is no English class next week. What would you like to do?

A: Think of a suggestion for something to do. Use the ideas below to help you. When you are ready, make your suggestions to the students in Group B.

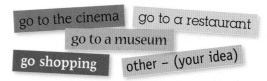

go to the cinema   go to a restaurant
go to a museum
go shopping   other – (your idea)

B: When a student from Group A makes a suggestion, ask him/her questions. Use the questions below to help you.

Is it expensive?
Where is it?
How do we get there?

Self-assessment (✓)

☐ I can talk about events and actions happening now.
☐ I can describe a journey.
☐ I can make and respond to suggestions.

GRAMMAR

Verb + -ing

After the verbs *love, like, hate, don't mind,* we use the verb + *-ing.*

☺ ☺   *I love*
☺   *I like*
☺   *I don't mind*   +   *flying.*
☹   *I don't like*
☹ ☹   *I hate*

Spelling

The *-ing* form can sometimes change the spelling of the verb.

Most infinitives = + *-ing*

   fly – flying   *talk – talking*   *go – going*

Infinitives that end in 'e' = ~~e~~ + *-ing*

   arrive – arriving   *hate – hating*

Infinitives that end in vowel + consonant = double consonant + *-ing*

   sit – sitting   *run – running*

Present continuous

Use the present continuous to talk about events happening now or around now.

To form the present continuous, we use the auxiliary verb *be* in the present with the *-ing* form of the main verb.

Affirmative			
Full form		Contraction	
I am		I'm	
You are		You're	
He/She/It is	working.	He's/She's/It's	working.
We are		We're	
They are		They're	

Negative				
Full form			Contraction	
I am			I'm not	
You are			You aren't	
He/She/It is	not	working.	He/She/It isn't	working.
We are			We aren't	
They are			They aren't	

Question	
Am I	
Are you	
Is he/she/it	working?
Are we	
Are they	

Present simple vs present continuous

Use the present simple to say what we usually do.

   *He **leaves** work at six o'clock.*

With these expressions we usually use the present simple:

   every day/month/year/afternoon …
   once a week/month/year …
   always/sometimes/hardly ever/often …

Use the present continuous to say what we are doing now.

   *He**'s leaving** work at 5.30 today.*

With these expressions we usually use the present continuous:

   at the moment
   now
   right now
   today

Remember: with questions and negatives in the present simple, use the auxiliary verb *do/does.* See page 30.

FUNCTIONAL LANGUAGE

Suggestions

Why don't we/you + verb?
Let's + verb.
We/You can/could + verb.

Responses

That's a good idea.
OK.
No.
I don't think that's a good idea.

WORD LIST

Transport

airport *n C* ***	/ˈeə(r)ˌpɔː(r)t/
bicycle *n C* **	/ˈbaɪsɪk(ə)l/
boat *n C* ***	/bəʊt/
bus *n C* ***	/bʌs/
bus stop *n C*	/ˈbʌs stɒp/
car *n C* ***	/kɑː(r)/
car park *n C*	/ˈkɑː(r) pɑː(r)k/
drive *v* ***	/draɪv/
motorbike *n C* *	/ˈməʊtə(r)ˌbaɪk/
on foot	/ɒn ˈfʊt/
plane *n C* ***	/pleɪn/
port *n C* ***	/pɔː(r)t/
ride *v* ***	/raɪd/
station *n C* ***	/ˈsteɪʃ(ə)n/
train *n C* ***	/treɪn/
underground *n U*	/ˈʌndə(r)ˌgraʊnd/

Action verbs

kiss *v* ***	/kɪs/
run *v* ***	/rʌn/
sing *v* ***	/sɪŋ/
sleep *v* ***	/sliːp/
smoke *v* **	/sməʊk/
walk *v* ***	/wɔːk/

Other words & phrases

accident *n C/U* ***	/ˈæksɪd(ə)nt/
adult *n C* ***	/ˈædʌlt/
alone *adj* ***	/əˈləʊn/
business partner *n C*	/ˈbɪznəs pɑː(r)tnə(r)/
company *n C* ***	/ˈkʌmp(ə)ni/
common *adj* ***	/ˈkɒmən/
course *n C* ***	/kɔː(r)s/
exactly *adv* ***	/ɪgˈzæk(t)li/
fear *n C/U* ***	/fɪə(r)/
flight *n C/U* ***	/flaɪt/
follow *v* ***	/ˈfɒləʊ/
hand *n C* ***	/hænd/
law *n C/U* ***	/lɔː/
phobia *n C*	/ˈfəʊbiə/
photograph *n C* ***	/ˈfəʊtəˌgrɑːf/
pilot *n C* ***	/ˈpaɪlət/
police station *n C* *	/pəˈliːs steɪʃ(ə)n/
safe *adj* ***	/seɪf/
secret *n C* ***	/ˈsiːkrət/
security *n C* ***	/sɪˈkjʊərəti/
stranger *n C* **	/ˈstreɪndʒə(r)/
survive *v* ***	/sə(r)ˈvaɪv/
take *v* ***	/teɪk/

9A | A good impression

SPEAKING

1 What do you notice about a person when you meet them for the first time? Put the following in order from 1 to 5 (1=very important ➝ 5=not important).

eyes ☐   face ☐   clothes ☐   voice ☐   body ☐

2 Work in pairs. Compare your lists. Do you notice the same things when you meet someone for the first time?

VOCABULARY: clothes

1 Match the pictures A–M with the words in the box.

shoes	trainers	jacket	dress	jeans
jumper	shirt	skirt	tie	trousers
T-shirt	boots	sock		

2 🔊 **2.33** Listen to the recording to check your answers. Say the words.

3 Complete the sentences so that they are true for you.

1 I never wear …
2 I only wear … at home.
3 I sometimes wear …
4 Right now I am wearing …
5 … is wearing …

READING

1 Read the web page. What is it about?

2 Read the web page again and answer the questions.

1 What are the three Vs?
2 Which Vs are more important?
3 Who writes about body language?
4 Who writes about clothes?
5 Who writes about men and women?

3 Work in pairs. Put a tick (✓) next to the sentences in the web page you agree with.

PRONUNCIATION: final -e

1 💿 **2.34** Listen to the pronunciation of these words and read the rule.

/eɪ/ make	/aɪ/ rice	/eɪ/ ate	/əʊ/ phone

In English, we don't pronounce the letter -e at the end of words.

2 How do you pronounce the underlined letters in these words?

sm<u>i</u>le	cl<u>o</u>thes	f<u>a</u>ce	t<u>i</u>me	t<u>a</u>ke	f<u>i</u>ne
phr<u>a</u>se	arr<u>i</u>ve	w<u>i</u>ne	c<u>a</u>ke	n<u>i</u>ce	

3 💿 **2.35** Listen to the recording to check your answers. Say the words.

GRAMMAR: *should/shouldn't*

We use *should/shouldn't* + verb to give advice about something.

*You **should wear** clean and neat clothes.*
*You **shouldn't wear** a short skirt for a meeting or an interview.*

▶ SEE LANGUAGE REFERENCE PAGE 100

1 Make new sentences using the information in brackets.

1 You should wear formal clothes. (not)
You shouldn't wear formal clothes.
2 You shouldn't talk loudly. (they)
3 I should listen to the other person. (?)
4 They should do something. (he; ?)
5 I should wear smart clothes. (she; not)
6 I should ask the teacher. (you; not)
7 We shouldn't talk in English. (you; should)

www.agoodimpression.com

Every personal or business relationship starts with a first impression. Psychologists say that when you meet someone for the first time, they make an impression on you in less than thirty seconds.

We evaluate another person using three Vs: visual (how you look, your clothes), vocal (your voice) and verbal (what you say). When you meet someone for the first time, your body language and your clothes make 93% of the first impression. Only 7% are the words you say.

There is an expression in English: You never get a second chance to make a first impression. But what makes a good impression on you? Send us your emails.

✱ For me, eye contact. You should look at the other person when you meet them. I don't trust a person if he or she doesn't make eye contact.
David Hill, USA

✱ You should wear clean and neat clothes. A dirty shirt makes a very bad impression, and so do dirty shoes.
Bahiya Wasti, Pakistan

✱ Your physical appearance and body language say a lot about you. Sit up straight. Your body should say "I am a friendly and confident person".
Gill Launders, Australia

✱ In Canada, you should shake a person's hand, man or woman. You shouldn't kiss them for the first meeting. It's also a good idea to use the other person's first name quickly. It's more friendly.
Michael Dobbs, Canada

✱ I think you shouldn't wear a very short skirt for a first meeting, or an interview. It can give the wrong first impression. For a man, I think a shirt and tie make a good impression at an interview.
Marta Wójcik, Poland

✱ You should smile when you meet someone for the first time. A smile is the best introduction. It's friendly. A smile is universal.
John Wong, Singapore

2 Cristiano is from Brazil. He is on a study trip to England and is meeting his host family for dinner. He asks an English friend for advice. Match Cristiano's questions 1–5 to the friend's answers a–e.

1 What should I wear?
2 What time should I arrive?
3 Should I buy a gift?
4 What should I talk about with them?
5 Should I tell them I don't eat meat?

a You should be there at the time they said. Don't be more than ten minutes late.
b A shirt and trousers is fine. No trainers.
c Don't worry! They're nice people. But you shouldn't talk about politics or religion.
d Yes, a lot of people cook meat for guests.
e It's not necessary, but a plant is always a good idea.

SPEAKING

1 Imagine someone wants to make a good impression on your parents. What are your answers to the questions in Grammar exercise 2? Is there anything else he/she should know?

2 Work in pairs. Tell your partner how to make a good impression.

If you want to make a good impression on my parents, you should …

9B | Body moving

SPEAKING & READING

1 Work in pairs. Ask and answer the questions.

> ### HEALTH — ARE YOU SITTING COMFORTABLY?
>
> - Are you sitting comfortably?
> - Do you spend a lot of your day sitting down?
> - Do you work in an office?
> - Do you work in front of a computer?
> - Do you play computer games?
> - Are you in a classroom for many hours a day?
> - Do you travel on long plane journeys frequently?
> - Do you spend a long time in a car, or on a bus every day?
>
> If you answered 'yes' to more than two of these questions, then read on …

2 The text in exercise 1 comes from a magazine article. What do you think the rest of the article is about?

1 Working in an office and going on holiday
2 A history of chairs
3 Problems and advice for people who sit for a long time

3 Read the rest of the article below to check.

4 Read the article again and match the headings 1–4 to the paragraphs A–D.

1 Take breaks often   3 Move your body
2 Drink water   4 Sit correctly

5 Which of the things in exercise 4 do you do when you are sitting for a long time?

It is not normal for the human body to sit for a long time. Sitting for a long time is new in human history. Now, sitting
5 for many hours every day is common. It is also dangerous for your health.

You can hurt your back, your arms, your neck and your wrists
10 if you sit for a long time every day. People who work in offices often have health problems because they sit too long in front of a computer. People who travel
15 many hours on planes often say they feel bad at the end of a long trip. Experts say you should do the following if you don't want problems:

A ____
20 Keep your back straight and your feet on the floor. You should have a good, comfortable chair.

B ____
Don't sit for more than thirty
25 minutes. Stand up and walk around. Several studies showed that people who take frequent 'microbreaks' do more work in the day.

C ____
30 Water cleans your body and keeps you healthy. It's good for you and gives you energy. Don't drink lots of coffee or tea.

D ____
Stretching is a simple and quick
35 way of doing some exercise while you are sitting down. Stretch your arms, your hands and your shoulders. Don't stretch a lot if it hurts.

VOCABULARY: body

1 Find and <u>underline</u> seven words in the article on page 94 related to the body.

2 Match the parts of the body A–O with the words in the box.

leg	foot/feet	knee	chest	back	hand
arm	wrist	shoulder	elbow	neck	
head	stomach	eyes	fingers		

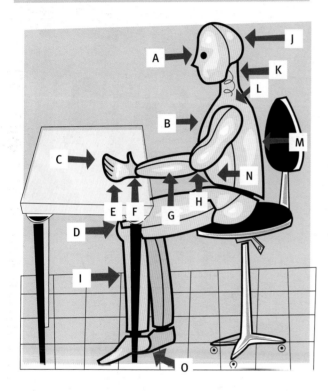

3 🔘 **2.36** Listen and tick (✓) the words you hear. Say the parts of the body.

4 Play *Simon Says*. Your teacher will explain the rules.

GRAMMAR: imperatives

We use the imperative to give orders. The imperative form of the verb is the same as the infinitive.
> ***Drink*** *water.*
> ***Sit*** *straight.*

We use *don't* + verb to make negative imperatives.
> ***Don't sit*** *for a long time.*
> ***Don't move.***

> ⟩ SEE LANGUAGE REFERENCE PAGE 100

1 <u>Underline</u> all the examples of verbs in the imperative in the article on page 94.

2 Make a sentence for each picture. Use the verbs and phrases in the box in the imperative.

take photos	smoke	speak	walk
turn right	drive slowly		

LISTENING & SPEAKING

1 🔘 **2.37** Look at the picture and listen to the instructions for a 'microbreak' exercise. Point to the parts of the body on the picture that the person says.

2 🔘 **2.37** Listen again and follow the instructions.

3 Work in pairs, A and B.
A: Look at page 133.   B: Look at page 135.

9c | Never forget a face

SPEAKING

1 Work in pairs. Read the sentences. Are they true for you?

1 I can remember what we learnt in our last English class.
2 I can remember the teacher's first name and last name.
3 I can remember the names of all the people in the class.
4 I never forget a face.

2 Change the sentences in exercise 1 so that they are true for you.

VOCABULARY: face

1 Match the parts of the picture A–H to the words in the box.

| nose   chin   eye   ear   hair |
| mouth   cheek   tooth/teeth |

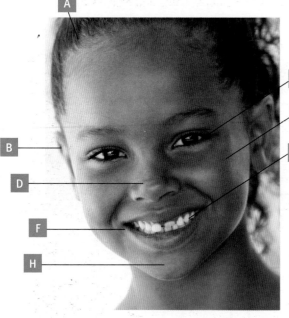

2 🔊 2.38 Listen and touch the parts of the face you hear. Say the words.

LISTENING

1 Work in pairs. Look at pictures A and B. Describe the pictures with your partner. Do you see anything strange?

2 🔊 2.39 Listen to the interview from a television interview about memory and the human face. What is wrong with the pictures in exercise 1?

3 🔊 2.39 Listen again and answer the questions.

1 Who doesn't have a very good memory: the woman or the man?
2 Which is the more important for memory: the top of the face or the bottom of the face?
3 What is strange about picture A?
4 Whose face is in picture B?
5 Whose hair is in picture B?
6 What do famous people do?

4 Look at audioscript 2.39 on page 145 to check your answers.

PRONUNCIATION: /h/

1 🔘 2.40 Listen to the words in the box. Tick (✓) the words that begin with a /h/ sound.

> house   hot   hospital   what   whose   hair
> happy   have   his   has   hamburgers   who
> her   hour

2 Complete the sentences with words from exercise 1.

1 Helen and Harry work in a _____.
2 They _____ lunch together every day.
3 He has _____ and she has _____ soup.
4 Helen's _____ with Harry.
5 But Helen _____ a problem.
6 She hardly ever remembers _____ name.

3 🔘 2.41 Listen to the recording to check your answers.

4 🔘 2.41 Listen again and repeat.

GRAMMAR: *whose* & possessive pronouns

> We use *whose* to ask about possession.
> **Whose** *face is that? It's* <u>George Washington's face</u>.
>
> We can replace the underlined words with a possessive pronoun.
> *Whose face is that? It's* **his**.
> *My memory isn't very good. How is* <u>your memory</u>?
> *My memory isn't very good. How is* **yours**?
>
> ⊙ SEE LANGUAGE REFERENCE PAGE 100

1 Rewrite the sentences using possessive pronouns.

1 It's his face. *It's his.*
2 They're her children.
3 It's my money.
4 Here's your coffee.
5 Is this our room?
6 It isn't their flat.
7 Where's your book?
8 That's his cat.

2 <u>Underline</u> the correct word.

1 Whose face is that? It's *her's / hers*. It's the Mona Lisa's.
2 I can remember his name but I can't remember *their / theirs*.
3 She always forgets *her / hers* glasses.
4 *Who's / Whose* in the picture?
5 *Who's / Whose* face is in the picture?
6 I brought my old photos today. Where are *yours / your*?

SPEAKING

1 Work in pairs. You are going to test your memory. Look at the pictures for one minute. Turn to page 134.

DID YOU KNOW?

1 Work in pairs. Read about coins and discuss the questions.

FACES ON COINS

The design of coins and money can say a lot about that country's culture and history. Countries often put an animal, a symbol or a person's head on their money. Many English-speaking countries have the Queen of England's head on their coins (Australia, Belize, Bermuda, Canada, Fiji, Great Britain and New Zealand are some examples). The United States has pictures of different presidents' heads on their coins.

• Whose face is on the money of your country?
• Do you have other symbols or animals on your money?

9D Not feeling well

VOCABULARY: health problems

1 Match the sentences 1–4 to the photos A–D.

1 My back hurts.   3 I've got a cold.
2 I've got a headache.   4 I'm ill.

2 Complete the sentences with the words in the box.

| tired   stomach   sick   toothache |
| head   arm   a stomach ache |

I'm I feel	ill. (1) _____ . (2) _____ .	
My	back (3) _____ (4) _____ (5) _____	hurts.
I've got I have	a headache. a cold. (6) _____ . (7) _____ .	

How do you say these in your language?

3 Work in pairs. Discuss these questions.

- Are you often ill?
- When was the last time you had a cold?
- How often do you go to the doctor?
- When was the last time you went to the doctor?

LISTENING

1 Read the text message. What was the problem?

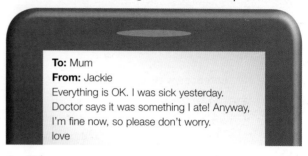

To: Mum
From: Jackie
Everything is OK. I was sick yesterday.
Doctor says it was something I ate! Anyway,
I'm fine now, so please don't worry.
love

2 🔘 **2.42** Listen to the dialogues to find out what happened to Jackie at work yesterday. Tick (✓) the phrases you hear.

1 Are you alright?   6 Take off that jacket.
2 I don't feel well.   7 Is there a doctor here?
3 It was lovely.   8 I've got a toothache.
4 Put on my jacket.   9 How's your stomach?
5 I'm fine, really.   10 She's got a cold.

3 🔘 **2.42** Listen to the dialogues again and put the events in the correct order.

☐ The woman calls a doctor.
☐ The doctor gives Jackie some aspirin.
☐ Jackie takes off the jacket.
☐ Jackie feels sick.
☐ Jackie goes to the toilet.
☐ Jackie sits down and puts on the man's jacket.

4 Match the words in column A to the words in column B to make phrases and questions.

A		**B**
1	Was it something	a too much wine?
2	Take off	b a minute.
3	Did she drink	c two aspirin.
4	Take	d you ate last night?
5	Wait	e that jacket.

FUNCTIONAL LANGUAGE: asking/saying how you feel

> **Asking how you feel**
> *How are you?*
>
> *Are you*   *alright?*
>   *OK?*
>
> *What's*   *the matter?*
>   *wrong?*
>
> **Saying how you feel**
> *I'm fine, thanks.*
> *I'm very well, thanks.*
>
> *I don't feel (very) well.*
> *I feel sick/ill/tired.*
> *I've got a …*

> ❯ SEE LANGUAGE REFERENCE PAGE 101

1 Look at audioscript 2.42 on page 145. Find examples of the phrases in the box.

2 Work in pairs. Ask and answer how you feel. Use the pictures.

How are you?   *I don't feel well.*

3 Complete the dialogues using the words in the box.

Dialogue 1

> well   got   are   matter

A: Hi, how (1) _____ you?
B: Oh, I don't feel very (2) _____.
A: What's the (3) _____?
B: I've (4) _____ a headache.
A: You should lie down.

Dialogue 2

> fine   wrong   home   I'm

A: Are you alright? What's (1) _____?
B: I'm (2) _____, thanks. I'm a little tired.
A: Do you want to go (3) _____?
B: No, (4) _____ fine. Really.

Dialogue 3

> fine   cold   head

A: Can I go out now?
B: No, you can't. You've got a (1) _____.
A: I feel (2) _____. My (3) _____ doesn't hurt now.
B: You should stay in bed.

4 🔘 2.43 Listen to the recording to check your answers. Practise the dialogues.

5 Work in pairs, A and B.

A: You feel ill. You have got a headache and you feel very sick. You are very tired. You don't think you can go to work. Phone your work and explain.

B: You are A's boss. When A phones you, listen to what he/she says and respond.

A: You are B's father/mother. You think B is ill and shouldn't go out tonight. Listen to B and respond.

B: You are A's son/daughter. You are often tired because you go out a lot! You want to go out tonight, but you don't feel well. Ask permission to go out.

> ## Self-assessment (✓)
> ☐ I can name parts of the body and parts of the face.
> ☐ I can talk about my clothes.
> ☐ I can give instructions using the imperative.
> ☐ I can talk to someone about their health.

GRAMMAR
should/shouldn't

Should is a modal auxiliary verb. This means:

- it goes with the infinitive without *to*.
- it has the same form for all subjects.
- the negative is with *not* (*n't*).
- to make a question, put *should* before the subject, and the infinitive after the subject.

We use *should* to give advice.

> You **should** say hello when you meet someone for the first time.

Affirmative	I/You/He/She/It/We/They	should	wear a tie.
Negative	I/You/He/She/It/We/They	shouldn't	wear a tie.
Question	Should	I/you/he/she/it/we/they	wear a tie?
Short answer	Yes,	I/you/he/she/it/we/they	should.
	No,	I/you/he/she/it/we/they	shouldn't.

Do not use *to* after *should*.

> You should arrive early.   Not ~~You should to arrive early.~~

Imperative

The imperative form of the verb is the same as the infinitive without *to*.
Use the imperative to give orders and instructions.

> **Drink** water.   **Sit** straight.

Use *don't* + verb to make negative imperatives.

> **Don't sit** for a long time.   **Don't move.**

You can also use imperatives to give directions (see Unit 3D page 39).

Whose & possessives

Use the question word *whose* to ask about possession. We can use *whose* with or without a noun.

Whose money is that?   **Whose** is that money?

Use possessive pronouns to avoid repeating the noun.

Possessive adjective	Possessive pronoun
It's my book.	It's mine.
It's your book.	It's yours.
It's his book.	It's his.
It's her book.	It's hers.
It's our book.	It's ours.
It's their book.	It's theirs.

Do not use possessive pronouns with a noun.

> It's mine.   Not ~~It's mine book.~~

have got

Have got means the same as *have*. It is common in spoken British English.

Use *have got*:

- to talk about possession.

  I've got a car.
- to talk about relationships.

  I've got two brothers and sisters.
- to talk about states.

Affirmative

I/You/We/They	have got 've got	a headache.
He/She/It	has got 's got	

Negative

I/You/We/They	haven't got	a headache.
He/She/It	hasn't got	

Question

Have	you/I/we/they	got	a headache?
Has	he/she/it		

Short answer

Yes,	you/I/we/they	have.
	he/she/it	has.
No,	you/I/we/they	haven't.
	he/she/it	hasn't.

The past of *have got* is *had*.

FUNCTIONAL LANGUAGE
Asking how you feel

How are you?   Are you alright?   Are you OK?

What's the matter?   What's wrong?

Saying how you feel

I'm fine, thanks.   I'm very well, thanks.

I don't feel (very) well.

I feel + adj

I've got a + noun

WORD LIST

Clothes

boot *n C* ***	/buːt/
dress *n C* ***	/dres/
jacket *n C* ***	/ˈdʒækɪt/
jeans *n C* *	/dʒiːnz/
jumper *n C* *	/ˈdʒʌmpə(r)/
shirt *n C* ***	/ʃɜː(r)t/
shoe *n C* ***	/ʃuː/
skirt *n C* **	/skɜː(r)t/
tie *n C* **	/taɪ/
trainers *n C* *	/ˈtreɪnə(r)z/
trousers *n C* **	/ˈtraʊzə(r)z/
T-shirt *n C* *	/ˈtiːʃɜː(r)t/

Body

arm *n C* ***	/ɑː(r)m/
back *n C* ***	/bæk/
chest *n C* ***	/tʃest/
elbow *n C* **	/ˈelbəʊ/
finger *n C* ***	/ˈfɪŋɡə(r)/
foot (plural feet) *n C* ***	/fʊt, fiːt/
hand *n C* ***	/hænd/
head *n C* ***	/hed/
knee *n C* ***	/niː/
leg *n C* ***	/leɡ/
neck *n C* ***	/nek/
shoulder *n C* ***	/ˈʃəʊldə(r)/
stomach *n C* **	/ˈstʌmək/
wrist *n C* **	/rɪst/

Face

cheek *n C* **	/tʃiːk/
chin *n C* **	/tʃɪn/
ear *n C* ***	/ɪə(r)/
eye *n C* ***	/aɪ/
hair *n U* ***	/heə(r)/
mouth *n C* ***	/maʊθ/
nose *n C* ***	/nəʊz/
tooth (plural teeth) *n C* ***	/tuːθ, tiːθ/

Health problems

cold *n C* **	/kəʊld/
headache *n C* *	/ˈhedeɪk/
hurt *v* ***	/hɜː(r)t/
ill *adj* ***	/ɪl/
stomach ache *n C/U*	/ˈstʌmək eɪk/
tired *adj* ***	/ˈtaɪə(r)d/
toothache *n U*	/ˈtuːθeɪk/

10A | It's illegal

VOCABULARY: places in a city

1 Complete the sentences with a word from the box.

shop	library	bank	town hall
stadium	cinema	supermarket	
chemist	pool		

1 A _____ is the building that has all the offices of the town government.
2 A _____ is a place where you can keep money or change money.
3 A _____ is a large place where you can buy things to eat and drink and things for the home.
4 A _____ is a place where there are sports events, like football matches.
5 A _____ is a place where you can look at books, CDs and films.
6 A _____ is a place where you buy things.
7 A _____ is a place where you can go swimming.
8 A _____ is a place that sells medicine.
9 A _____ is a place where you can see films.

2 Make similar sentences for these places.

school	hotel	hospital	disco

A school is a place where …

3 Look at these signs. In which places in exercise 1 or exercise 2 do you see these signs?

READING

1 Read a magazine article about different laws and choose the best title for the article.

1 Important laws for visitors to American cities
2 School laws in American cities
3 Strange laws in American cities

Several years ago, two American students started a collection of interesting American laws and put them on the internet. It was part of a high school project. They now have several hundred different bizarre* laws from different parts of the United States on their web page.

Here are some examples:

* If you want to go swimming in Destin, Florida, you must get dressed in your hotel room and not in your car.

* You must not look into car windows on the street in Milford, Massachusetts.

* You mustn't ride a bicycle in a swimming pool in the town of Baldwin Park, California.

* In Cathedral City, California, it's illegal to take a dog to school.

* In the state of Virginia, you must wear shoes while you are driving.

* A law in Walnut, California, says that a man must not wear women's clothes.

* In Toledo, Ohio, it's against the law to throw a snake at another person.

* You must not shout or sing in public at night in the town of Topeka, Kansas.

* In the majority of American cities, you needn't have a permit to buy or carry a gun.

Glossary
bizarre *adj* strange

2 Read the article again. Which cities or states have:

- a law about swimming?
- a law about transport?
- a law about clothes?
- a law about animals?

3 Work in pairs. Discuss these questions.

- Which law do you think is the most interesting?
- Do you have any strange laws in your town or country?

GRAMMAR: *must/mustn't/needn't*

Use *must/mustn't* to talk about obligation.
In affirmative sentences, *must* means 'this is necessary'.
   You **must** wear shoes while you are driving.
In negative sentences, *mustn't* means 'don't do this'.
   You **mustn't** take a pig to the beach.
In negative sentences, *needn't* means 'this isn't necessary'.
   You **needn't** have a permit to buy a gun.

⊙ SEE LANGUAGE REFERENCE PAGE 110

1 Write different sentences using the words in brackets.

1 They must drive slowly. (you).
   You must drive slowly.
2 You needn't wear a tie. (must)
3 You must have a permit to buy a dog. (needn't)
4 You must go now. (he; not)
5 I mustn't call the police. (you; must)
6 The teacher must prepare the lesson. (students; needn't)

2 Complete the sentences with *must* or *mustn't* and a verb.

A library

have	~~speak~~	bring

1 You *mustn't speak* loudly.
2 You _____ a library card to take out books.
3 You _____ the books back to the library.

A bus

buy	pay	smoke

4 You _____ for a ticket.
5 You _____ the ticket from the driver.
6 You _____ in the bus.

SPEAKING

1 Work in pairs. You are going to make some classroom laws. Look at the phrases in the box. Are they for the teacher, the students or the teacher *and* the students?

- come to class late
- explain again if the students don't understand
- do the homework every day
- speak in English all the time
- speak quickly
- turn off mobile phones in class
- correct the homework
- use the book in every lesson

2 Now make sentences with the phrases. Use *must*, *mustn't* or *needn't*. Add at least one more sentence of your own.

3 Work with another pair. Read your classroom laws. Do you agree? Decide on the five most important classroom laws.

DID YOU KNOW?

1 Work in pairs. Read about smoking and discuss the questions.

Many countries now have strong anti-smoking laws. The biggest English-speaking country in the world, India, passed a law in 2008 against smoking in all public places. You mustn't smoke now in any offices, banks, restaurants or pubs in India.

If you want to smoke a cigarette, you must go outside. Many people said the law was very important, as India had up to 250 million smokers. Today, there are still many smokers but more and more people now know about the dangers of tobacco.

- Are there anti-smoking laws where you live?
- Where mustn't you smoke in your city or town?
- Do you think these laws are a good idea?

10B | Life in the capital

SPEAKING

1 Work in pairs. Answer the questions.

Were you born in the capital of your country?

Yes   No

Do you live there now?   Where were you born?

Do you live in the same place?

Yes   No

Do you like living there?
Why or why not?   Would you like to live in the capital?
                Why or why not?

VOCABULARY: adjectives

1 Read the questionnaire. Check the meaning of any words you don't understand in a dictionary.

Seven questions about: Rome

		Yes	No
1	Are the people friendly?		
2	Is it an expensive place?		
3	Is it dangerous to walk on the streets at night?		
4	Can you visit interesting things in your city?		
5	Is it very noisy?		
6	Are there any beautiful or historical buildings?		
7	Is the air polluted?		

2 🔘 **2.44** Listen to Giovanni talk about life in Rome. Tick (✓) his answers in exercise 1.

3 Match the words in the box to their opposites in exercise 1.

> safe   boring   quiet   ugly   clean
> unfriendly   cheap   modern

4 🔘 **2.45** Listen to the recording to check your answers. Say the words.

5 Work in pairs. Choose a city, town or village that you know well. Interview your partner about his/her city.

LISTENING

1 Look at the photos of different capital cities. How many can you recognize?

A

B

C

D

E

F

2 2.46 Listen to Nick and Sofia talking about life in different capital cities around the world. What capital cities do they talk about?

3 2.46 Listen again and decide if the sentences are true (T) or false (F). Correct the false sentences.

1 Sofia lives in the capital.
2 Sofia lives with her family.
3 You can see bigger families in Alicante.
4 Life in Madrid is not expensive.
5 Nick lives in the capital.
6 Nick's city is very clean and quiet.
7 Nick's city has big stadiums.
8 Nick thinks that people have the wrong opinion about the capital.

GRAMMAR: comparatives

Use comparatives to compare people and things with other people and things.

Alicante **is smaller than** Madrid.
Life in small cities **is more romantic**, and **calmer, than** life in the capital.
Mexico City **is more modern than** other cities in Mexico.

> SEE LANGUAGE REFERENCE PAGE 110

1 Make the comparative form of the adjective.

cold	bad	small	interesting
big	cosmopolitan	friendly	good
happy	dangerous	safe	polluted

2 Complete the text with the adjectives in brackets in the comparative form.

Many people think that Toronto is the capital of Canada. Actually, Ottawa is the capital. Ottawa is (1) _____ (small) than Toronto. It's also (2) _____ (cold) in winter. Lots of people say that Toronto is (3) _____ (interesting), because it's (4) _____ (big) and (5) _____ (cosmopolitan). I think that Ottawa has more historical buildings than Toronto. Canadians also say that people from other cities are (6) _____ (friendly) than Torontonians. Traffic in Toronto is (7) _____ (bad) than traffic in Ottawa. There are too many cars. Toronto and Ottawa are both safe cities. They are (8) _____ (safe) than many other North American cities.

3 Look at the statistics for two cities in the state of New York. Make sentences and put the adjectives in brackets into the comparative form.

NEW YORK

		New York, NY	White Plains, NY
1	Became a city in	1626	1683
2	Population	8,008,278	52,105
3	Cost of living	$193.4	$172.7
4	Air quality (100=excellent)	15	21
5	Violent crimes/year	1,063.1	380
6	Distance to Washington DC	373.1 km	406.8 km

1 (old) *New York City is older than White Plains.*
2 (big)
3 (cheap)
4 (polluted)
5 (safe)
6 (close to the capital)

PRONUNCIATION: word stress 4

1 2.47 Listen to these words and count the syllables.

	1	2
1 f r i e n d l y	frien /	dly

2 c o l d
3 p o l l u t e d
4 e x p e n s i v e
5 n o i s y
6 c l e a n
7 b e a u t i f u l

2 Mark the stress in each word and say the words.

☐
frien / dly

3 2.47 Listen again to check your answers.

SPEAKING

1 Work in groups of three, A, B and C.

A: Turn to page 133.
B: Turn to page 138.
C: Turn to page 135.

2 Is life better in the capital or outside the capital in your country? Why?

10c | Best of the best

SPEAKING

1 Work in pairs. Imagine some friends are coming to visit your town or city. They only have time to see three things. What three things should they see? Make a list.

2 Compare your list with another pair. Who has the more interesting list?

READING

1 Work in pairs. What do you know about the city of Cape Town? Make some notes.

2 Read the extract from a guide book for Cape Town. Match the photos A–C to the correct paragraphs 1–6.

BEST OF THE BEST CAPE TOWN

Cape Town is one of South Africa's most beautiful cities. Cape Town is famous for its beaches, mountains and wine. There are lots of things to do and see during your visit. We have collected here a small sample of the best Cape Town has to offer.

1 The most exciting thing to do

5 Cape Town sits next to the beautiful Table Mountain. Table Mountain is 1,086 metres high and is the most famous mountain in South Africa. If you visit Cape Town, you must take a cable car up to the top of the mountain.
10 (1) _____.You can also go walking around the top of the mountain, which is 3km long.

2 The most frightening activity

The ocean near Cape Town is famous for sharks.
15 On special adventure tours you can go diving with a great white shark. (2) _____.This is an experience that you will never forget!

3 The best shopping

For many reasons the Victoria and Albert
20 Waterfront is the best and most popular shopping centre in the city. You can find cheap jewellery, good books and quality clothes at the shopping centre. If you want African paintings and souvenirs, go shopping at the Green
25 Point Market on Sundays.
(3) _____. There are hundreds of little shops at the market, and some have better prices than others.

30 **4 The most expensive place to stay**

The Cape Grace is a five-star hotel next to the sea in Cape Town. At Cape Grace you can go swimming in
35 the pool, relax in the spa or read in the library. (4) _____.
There is even a luxury boat for hotel guests to go on!

5 The most historical place

40 If you want to go sightseeing, you must go to Robben Island. Robben Island was one of South Africa's worst prisons during apartheid. (5) _____. Nelson
45 Mandela, former president of South Africa, spent 27 years in prison on Robben Island.

6 The wildest night out

Cape Town is home to the
50 biggest nightclub in South Africa, the Dockside. (6) _____. The giant building has a dancefloor for 5,000 people.

3 Match the sentences a–f with the gaps 1–6 in the article.

a A special cage protects you from the most dangerous animal in the world.

b The 360° views are incredible.

c It is now a national memorial and museum.

d This is the best place to go dancing and have a good time.

e The 122 rooms have beautiful furniture, flat-screen high-definition televisions, X-Box 360 consoles, complimentary tea and coffee and beautiful bathrooms.

f Some advice: you should always compare prices before you buy.

4 Work in pairs. Imagine you have a free trip to Cape Town but you can only see three things. Which three places in the brochure would you like to visit most?

VOCABULARY: *go* + verb + *-ing*

1 Match column A to column B to make sentences about things you can do in Cape Town. All the expressions are in the brochure.

A
1 You can **go walking**
2 You can **go sightseeing**
3 You can **go diving**
4 You can **go dancing**
5 You can **go shopping** for souvenirs
6 You can **go swimming**

B
a at the Dockside nightclub.
b on Robben Island.
c at the Green Point Market on Sundays.
d with sharks in Gansbaai, Cape Town.
e at some of the beaches around Cape Town.
f on the top of Table Mountain.

2 Work in pairs. Discuss these questions.

- Which of the activities in **bold** can you do in your city?
- Where can you do them?

GRAMMAR: superlatives

We use superlatives to compare people and things with *all the other* people and things in that group.

*Table Mountain is **the most famous** landmark in South Africa.*
*The V&A Waterfront is **the most popular** shopping centre.*

> SEE LANGUAGE REFERENCE PAGE 110

1 Look at the guide book extract on page 106. <u>Underline</u> all the superlatives.

2 🔘 2.48 Listen and make the superlative.

A safe city. *The safest city.*

3 Simona and Nicky are visiting Cape Town. Complete the sentences and put the adjectives in brackets into the superlative form. Where are they in each conversation?

1 What about this souvenir for my brother? I don't know. It's _____ souvenir in the shop! (expensive)

2 Look at this place! I think it's the _____ club in town. It's also very expensive, and I don't like dancing. Let's go to a different place. (big)

3 Why don't you want to go? Because it's _____ thing in the guidebook! It's also _____. (crazy, dangerous)

4 The guidebook says this is _____ part of Cape Town. Wow. You can see everything from up here. (high)

5 Who is Nelson Mandela? He's _____ person in modern South African history! (important)

SPEAKING

1 Make questions with the phrases below. Use the superlative. Make two more questions of your own.

1 good place to go shopping for clothes? *What's the best place to go shopping for clothes?*
2 interesting monument?
3 dangerous part of the city?
4 nice park?
5 bad time of year to visit the city?
6 important festivals in the city?

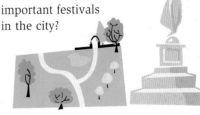

2 Work in pairs, A and B.

A: Choose a city that you know.
B: Ask the questions in exercise 1 about A's city. Swap roles.

3 Work with a different partner. Repeat the same activity.

10D | City souvenirs

SPEAKING

1 Work in pairs. Discuss these questions.

• Do you have any souvenirs from other cities/ countries? What are they? Where are they from?
• When you visit another city/country, do you buy souvenirs? Who do you buy them for? What do you buy?
• What do people buy as souvenirs from your city/country?

VOCABULARY: size & colours

1 Look at the photos of the souvenirs. Complete the descriptions of the souvenirs with a word from the box.

> brown   blue (x2)   red   white
> silver (x2)   black (x2)

1 It's a light _____ T-shirt.
2 It's a big _____ keyring.
3 It's a small _____ and _____ taxi.
4 It's a large _____ and _____ football shirt.
5 It's a big _____, _____ and _____ teddy bear.

Language note

Remember: colour words are adjectives – they come BEFORE the noun.
Not ~~A taxi black.~~ A black taxi.

2 Use the words in the box to describe things in the gift shop.

	SIZE		COLOUR	NOUN
It's a They're	small big		black white silver gold	T-shirt. towels. pen.
		(light) (dark)	yellow red blue green brown	teddy bear. taxi. football shirt. mug.

LISTENING

1 🔘 2.49 Listen to two people in the gift shop. What do they buy? How much does it cost?

2 🔘 2.49 Listen again and answer the questions.

1 What section of the gift shop does the man look at?
2 How many mugs does the woman take?
3 How much are the pens?
4 Does the man like the keyrings?
5 What is the book about?
6 How many bags does the woman want?

FUNCTIONAL LANGUAGE: in a shop

1 Complete the dialogues with the phrases in the box.

Dialogue 1

> You're welcome.   I can't see a price.
> can I help you?

Shop assistant: Hello, (1) _____
Customer: Yes, please. How much is this book?
                (2) _____
Shop assistant: Just a minute. It's £7.95.
Customer: Thank you.
Shop assistant: (3) _____

Dialogue 2

> No, I'm sorry we don't.   OK, thanks.
> Do you have any keyrings?

Customer: (4) _____
Shop assistant: Yes, we do. There are silver ones and
                these black ones.
Customer: Do you have any with the cathedral on
                it?
Shop assistant: (5) _____
Customer: (6) _____

Dialogue 3

> How much are they?
> The book and these postcards then, please.
> Anything else?

Shop assistant: (7) _____
Customer: Yes, I'd like some postcards please.
Shop assistant: They're over here.
Customer: (8) _____
Shop assistant: They're four for a pound.
Customer: Fine. (9) _____

Dialogue 4

> Would you like a bag for that?   Bye.   Here you are.

Shop assistant: That's £8.95.
Customer: (10) _____ Ten pounds.
Shop assistant: Here's your change. (11) _____
Customer: No, thanks, that's alright. Goodbye.
Shop assistant: (12) _____

2 🔘 **2.50** Listen and check your answers. Choose
one dialogue and practise it in pairs.

PRONUNCIATION: word linking 2

1 🔘 **2.51** Listen to these sentences. Notice how some
of the words are joined together.

Can‿I help you?   They're‿over there.
How much‿is it?   Would‿you like‿a bag?
Just‿a minute.   Here you‿are.
Anything‿else?

2 Practise saying the sentences in exercise 1 quickly.

SPEAKING

1 Work in groups of three, A, B and C. Choose a city.

A and B: You are tourists. You would like to buy
souvenirs from the city (decide what souvenirs you
want). Buy some souvenirs.

C: You are the shop assistant. Help the tourists.

> ### Useful language
>
> Can I help you?   How much is/are ...?
> I'm sorry, we don't have any. Here you are.
> Yes, I'd like ... / Do you have ...? Anything else?

> ### Self-assessment (✓)
>
> ☐ I can compare two or more places.
> ☐ I can describe the size and colour of things.
> ☐ I can ask for things in a shop.

GRAMMAR
Must/mustn't/needn't

Must is a modal auxiliary verb. This means:
- it goes with the infinitive without *to*.
- it has the same form for all subjects.
- the negative is with *not* (*n't*).
- to make a question, put *must* before the subject, and the infinitive after the subject.

Must, mustn't, needn't		
I You	must	
He/She/It We They	mustn't must not needn't	wear shoes in this place.

We use *must* to talk about obligations.

Must has two possible negatives.

Mustn't (*must not*) means *don't do this*.
Needn't (*need not*) means *this isn't necessary*.

We can also say *don't/doesn't need to = needn't*.

You can make questions with *must*, but this is not very common.

Must *I bring a pen to the exam?*

Comparatives

Use the comparative form of the adjective to compare two people or things.

*The capital is **more expensive than** my town.*

Use *than*, not *that*, to connect the two things we are comparing.

The city is bigger than the town.
Not ~~The city is bigger that the town.~~

For most short adjectives (one syllable), add *-er*.

old   older
small   smaller

If the adjective ends in consonant + vowel + consonant, double the consonant + *-er*.

big   bigger

Longer adjectives (more than one syllable), use *more* + adjective.

expensive   more expensive
dangerous   more dangerous

Adjectives that end in *-y*, drop the *-y* and add *-ier*.

noisy   noisier

Good and *bad* have irregular comparative forms.

good   better
bad   worse

Superlatives

Use the superlative form of the adjective to compare more than two people and things.

*It's **the most dangerous** part of the city.* (more dangerous than all the others)
*It's **the highest** mountain.*

With superlatives, use the article *the*.

He is the best player.
Not ~~He is best player.~~

For most short adjectives (one syllable), add *-est*.

short   the shortest
cheap   the cheapest
nice   the nicest

If the adjective ends in consonant + vowel + consonant, double the consonant and add *-est*.

big   the biggest
hot   the hottest

Longer adjectives (more than one syllable), use *the most* + adjective.

expensive   the most expensive
popular   the most popular

Adjectives that end in *-y*, drop the *-y* and add *-iest*.

happy   the happiest
funny   the funniest

Good and *bad* have irregular superlative forms.

good   the best
bad   the worst

FUNCTIONAL LANGUAGE
In a shop

Can I help you?
That's + price
Would you like a bag for that?

Here you are.
How much is/are ...?
Do you have any + noun?
I'd like + noun

WORD LIST

Places in a city

bank *n C* ***	/bæŋk/
chemist *n C* **	/'kemɪst/
cinema *n C* **	/'sɪnəmə/
disco *n C* *	/'dɪskəʊ/
hospital *n C* ***	/'hɒspɪt(ə)l/
hotel *n C* ***	/həʊ'tel/
library *n C* ***	/'laɪbrəri/
nightclub *n C*	/'naɪtˌklʌb/
pool *n C* ***	/puːl/
school *n C/U* ***	/skuːl/
shop *n C* ***	/ʃɒp/
shopping centre *n C*	/'ʃɒpɪŋ sentə(r)/
stadium *n C* *	/'steɪdiəm/
supermarket *n C* **	/'suːpə(r)ˌmɑː(r)kɪt/
town hall *n C*	/taʊn 'hɔːl/

Describing a town/city

beautiful *adj* ***	/'bjuːtəf(ə)l/
boring *adj* **	/'bɔːrɪŋ/
cheap *adj* ***	/tʃiːp/
cosmopolitan *adj*	/ˌkɒzmə'pɒlɪt(ə)n/
dangerous *adj* ***	/'deɪndʒərəs/
expensive *adj* ***	/ɪk'spensɪv/
friendly *adj* ***	/'fren(d)li/
historical *adj* ***	/hɪ'stɒrɪk(ə)l/
interesting *adj* ***	/'ɪntrəstɪŋ/
modern *adj* ***	/'mɒdə(r)n/
noisy *adj* *	/'nɔɪzi/
polluted *adj* *	/pə'luːtɪd/
quiet *adj* ***	/'kwaɪət/
safe *adj* ***	/seɪf/
ugly *adj* **	/'ʌgli/
unfriendly *adj* *	/ʌn'fren(d)li/

go + *-ing*

go dancing	/gəʊ 'dɑːnsɪŋ/
go diving	/gəʊ 'daɪvɪŋ/
go sightseeing	/gəʊ 'saɪtˌsiːɪŋ/
go shopping	/gəʊ 'ʃɒpɪŋ/
go swimming	/gəʊ 'swɪmɪŋ/
go walking	/gəʊ 'wɔːkɪŋ/

Size & colours

big *adj* ***	/bɪg/
dark *adj* ***	/dɑː(r)k/
gold *adj* ***	/gəʊld/
large *adj* ***	/lɑː(r)dʒ/
light *adj* ***	/laɪt/
silver *adj* **	/'sɪlvə(r)/
small *adj* ***	/smɔːl/
tiny *adj* ***	/'taɪni/

Other words & phrases

apartheid *n U*	/ə'pɑː(r)tˌheɪt/
at least	/æt 'liːst/
bizarre *adj* *	/bɪ'zɑː(r)/
carry *v* ***	/'kæri/
dance floor *n C*	/dɑːns flɔː(r)/
get dressed *v*	/get drest/
gun *n C* ***	/gʌn/
illegal *adj* **	/ɪ'liːg(ə)l/
jewellery *n U* **	/'dʒuːəlri/
keyring *n C*	/'kiː rɪŋ/
lose *v* ***	/luːz/
mug *n C* *	/mʌg/
offer *v* ***	/'ɒfə(r)/
permit *n C*	/'pɜː(r)mɪt/
pig *n C* **	/pɪg/
quality *n C/U* ***	/'kwɒləti/
shark *n C* *	/ʃɑː(r)k/
shout *v* ***	/ʃaʊt/
skill *n C/U* ***	/skɪl/
snake *n C* *	/sneɪk/
spa *n C*	/spɑː/
strange *adj* ***	/streɪndʒ/
teddy bear *n C*	/'tedi beə(r)/
throw *v* ***	/θrəʊ/
towel *n C* **	/'taʊəl/

11A Working behind the scenes

VOCABULARY & SPEAKING: jobs

1 Complete the sentences with words from the box.

> a doctor   a security guard
> an accountant   an actor
> a secretary   a waiter

What do you do?

1 I'm _____.

2 I'm _____.

3 I'm _____.

4 I'm _____.

5 I'm _____.

6 I'm _____.

2 🔊 **2.52** Listen to the recording to check your answers.

3 🔊 **2.53** Listen and underline the correct words.

1 I work *for / to* a big company.
2 I'm in charge *for / of* other people.
3 I work *in / to* a restaurant.
4 I work *in / at* home.
5 I work *with / to* the public.
6 I often work *on / in* a computer.

4 Work in pairs. Discuss these questions.

• What do you do?
• Do you like your work?
• Do you know people who do the jobs in exercise 1?
• Which job would you like to do?

PRONUNCIATION: /w/, /v/ & /b/

1 🔊 **2.54** Listen and say the words.

/w/	/v/	/b/
waiter	vet	builder
Will	Victoria	Bob
Washington	Vincent	Barbara
Wendy	vegetables	Brighton
working	vocabulary	bread
weekends	Vienna	beer

2 🔊 **2.55** Listen and read the text.

Will is a waiter. He lives in Washington. He likes working and weekends.

3 Make similar texts with other words from the box in exercise 1.

_____ is a _____. He/She lives in _____.

He/She likes _____ and _____.

LISTENING

1 Read the description of the TV documentary programme *Behind the Scenes*.

Behind the scenes

Every week, *Behind the Scenes* visits a big organization and talks to the people who do the invisible jobs, the work behind the scenes. This week, we visit a _____ in England and talk to a _____ and an _____.

2 🔘 2.56 Listen to the programme and complete the description in exercise 1.

3 🔘 2.56 Listen again and decide if the sentences are true (T) or false (F). Correct the false sentences.

1 Janet works with two men.
2 Janet got the job two years ago.
3 Janet's father likes her job.
4 Michael works with two people in the accounts department.
5 Michael got his job last year.
6 Michael thinks his job is boring.

4 Work in pairs. Think of two or three people you know. Discuss the questions.

• What are their jobs?
• Do they work behind the scenes?

GRAMMAR: question review

Why, when, where, who, what and *how* are all question words.
We can combine *how* and *what* with other words to begin questions.
How + many/much/often/old ...
What + time

Remember the word order with questions: (auxiliary) + subject + verb.

▶ SEE LANGUAGE REFERENCE PAGE 120

1 Look at the interviewer's questions from *Behind the Scenes*. Decide which questions are correct and which questions are incorrect. Correct the incorrect questions.

1 What do you do?
2 When did start you here?
3 What do other people thinks of your job?
4 You like your job?
5 Where do you work in the hospital?
6 Why do you do like your job?

2 Look at audioscript 2.56 on page 145 to check your answers.

3 Complete the questions about work with a question word from the box.

what	what	when	who	how many	why	where

1 _____ are you from?
2 _____ did you study at school?
3 _____ do you work with?
4 _____ did you start work today?
5 _____ did you do today at work?
6 _____ do you like your job?
7 _____ days do you work every week?

4 Work in pairs. Ask and answer the questions in exercise 3.

SPEAKING

1 Play *Guess The Job*. Work in pairs, A and B.

A: Choose a job.
B: Ask questions and guess the job. Use the questions from grammar exercise 3 to help you.

2 Swap roles and repeat the activity.

DID YOU KNOW?

1 Work in pairs. Read about the National Health Service and discuss the questions.

The NHS (National Health Service) is a public health care service in Britain. It's free for all British people. In Britain, there are men and women nurses, but there are more women nurses than men nurses. There are many nurses from other countries in the NHS. In a 2009 report, around 75% of NHS workers said that it was difficult work, but they liked their jobs.

• Are hospitals in your country public or private?
• Are nurses usually women in your country?
• Do you know someone who works in another country? What do they do?

11B The future of work

SPEAKING

1 Read the sentences and circle *I agree/ I disagree / I don't know*.

1 It is normal to change jobs many times.
I agree.   *I disagree.*   *I don't know.*

2 It is easy to get a job in my country.
I agree.   *I disagree.*   *I don't know.*

3 Many people work at home in my country.
I agree.   *I disagree.*   *I don't know.*

4 You must know how to use a computer to get a job.
I agree.   *I disagree.*   *I don't know.*

2 Work in pairs. Compare your answers. Explain why you agree or disagree.

READING

1 Read the article. What is *Futurework*?

1 A book about the future of work in Britain.
2 A webpage about the best jobs in the future in Britain.
3 A magazine article about work and life in Britain.

2 Read the article again and decide if the sentences are true (T) or false (F). Correct the false sentences.

1 *Futurework* is about the future of work around the world.
2 Lancaster wrote *Futurework* quickly.
3 Lancaster thinks that people will change jobs often.
4 Mobile phones will create more stress in the future.
5 Lancaster thinks that working at home is a good thing.
6 There are more old people in Britain now than in the past.
7 It will be important to know other languages to get a good job.

3 Work in pairs. Look at the predictions about work. Do you think these are true for your country? Discuss with your partner.

THE FUTURE WON'T WAIT ... will you?

In *Futurework*, author Lee Lancaster describes the world of work for the rest of the 21st century. Lancaster makes these predictions several years after investigation into jobs in Britain and around the world. Chapters include:

How many jobs?
You won't have a permanent job for life in the future. People will change jobs many times during their lives. Part-time jobs will be more common than full-time jobs.

Work/life balance?
With mobile phones, laptop computers, email and the internet, it will be difficult to separate your job and your personal life. People will be more stressed.

Office in the living room?
Working from home will be more popular in the future. That is good news and bad news. If your job is at home, where will you go for a day off?

A life of service?
Britain's population is getting older, and the economy is changing. This means that more people will be employed in the service sector: shops, hospitals, centres for old people, hotels and restaurants.

Languages and jobs?
How many languages do you speak? Yes, English will be a very important language in the future of work, but it won't be the only language. Many people in Britain only speak English at the moment. People who speak two or more languages will have better opportunities.

Other important skills for future jobs?
Computers, the internet and communication skills. You need to know these important things if you want a good, well-paid job in the future.

'If you want to know what the future is, you must read Lancaster's work!'
Daily Sun Times

'Lancaster explains clearly and completely what the dangers of future work will be, and how we can prepare for them.'
Publisher's Circle

VOCABULARY: describing work

1 Find the opposites of these words in the text.

> part-time badly-paid temporary
> unemployed

2 Complete the sentences with a word from exercise 1.

1 There is a _____ job at the school. They are looking for a person to work from February to July.
2 She has a _____ job in the bank. She only works Tuesdays and Thursdays.
3 He hates his job. It's dirty, dangerous and _____. He never has any extra money.
4 I'm _____ at the moment. I can't find a job.

3 Work in pairs. Discuss these questions.

- What jobs are well-paid in your country? What jobs are badly-paid?
- What are some problems with work in your country, for example, unemployment, overwork, low pay, temporary work?
- Do students have part-time jobs? What kind of jobs do they do?

GRAMMAR: predictions (*will*)

> Use *will* to talk about predictions in the future.
> Use *will* when we are certain something will happen in the future.
> The negative of *will* is *will not* (*won't*).
> *Part-time jobs* **will** *be more common than full-time jobs.*
> *You* **won't** *have a permanent job for life in the future.*
> *Where* **will** *you go for a day off?*

> ❯ SEE LANGUAGE REFERENCE PAGE 120

1 Complete the sentences with *will/will not* + the verb in brackets. Use contractions.

1 Public transport, like buses, _____ (*not use*) petrol. They _____ (*work*) on electricity.
2 A computer _____ (*control*) everything in your house: lights, fridge, television ...
3 Every car _____ (*have*) a computer with satellite technology.
4 There _____ (*be*) more problems with bad meat and people _____ (*be*) ill.
5 People _____ (*not cook*), they _____ (*buy*) prepared food.
6 People _____ (*not live*) in tall buildings, they _____ (*live*) underground.

2 Match the sentences in exercise 1 to the other books about life in the future in the box below.

> Futurelive Futuredrive Futureeat

3 🔘 2.57 What is your future? Listen to the words and make sentences with *I'll* or *I won't*.

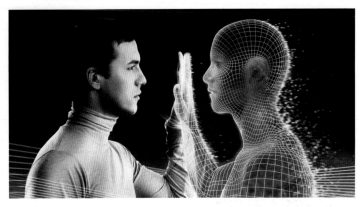

1 be rich *I'll be rich.* or *I won't be rich.*

4 🔘 2.57 Work in pairs. Listen to the recording again. Now make questions and answers.

1 be rich *Will you be rich? Yes, I will. / No, I won't.*

SPEAKING

1 Do the *My Future Working Life* quiz.

MY FUTURE WORKING LIFE

In 10 years ...

1 I'll have (a) a good job (b) an OK job (c) no job.
2 I'll work (a) many hours (b) part-time (c) not many hours.
3 Work will be (a) the most important part (b) very important (c) not important in my life.
4 I'll work (a) close to home (b) far from home (c) at home.
5 (a) Some people (b) Lots of people (c) Nobody will work for me.
6 I'll be (a) happy (b) satisfied (c) unhappy with my job.
7 In my work, (a) I'll travel to other countries (b) I'll travel inside my country (c) I won't travel.
8 I'll go to work (a) in the company limousine (b) in my own car (c) by bus.

2 Work in pairs. Tell your partner about your future working life. Who will have a better future?

11c | 16 before 60

SPEAKING & READING

1 Work in pairs. Complete the sentences.

1 If you want to be happy at work, you should …

2 If you want to live a long time, you shouldn't …

3 If you want to be happy when you're 60 years old, you should …

2 Compare with another pair in the class.

3 Read the magazine article *16 things to do before you're 60*. Match the photos A–D to the correct paragraphs in the article.

16 things to do before you're 60

Are you living your life as best as you can? Are you working to live, or living for your work? We have collected a list of 16 things that usually make people happier and healthier. It's time to take a look at your life critically. Which of these things do you do? Which are you going to do?

1 Take a break
Take a break from work to do something different: go back to school, try a different job or travel to a different country. Make plans now.

2 Say 'no'
It's difficult to say 'no' when someone asks you to do a job. If you say 'yes' to things that are impossible for you, then you will be unhappy and more stressed.

3 Exercise
If you do more exercise, you feel better and look better.

4 Learn from your mistakes
When you make a mistake, see this as a chance to learn something new. Don't make the same mistake again and again.

5 Make things simple
People often have too many things. If you don't use it, or love it, then you don't need it!

6 Do some volunteer work
Help others and it helps you. Research shows that helping other people who need you makes you happier and live longer.

7 See the positive side
One American study showed that optimists live 7.5 years longer than pessimists. Happy people make friends more easily too.

8 Make a difference in society
If you can vote, then you should.

9 Sleep well
We sleep more than 30% of our lives. Experts say you should have a good bed and sleep between seven and eight hours every night.

10 Save money
It's never too late to save money, and it needn't be a lot. Start now!

11 Eat well
A healthy diet, with lots of fruit and vegetables, protects you from health problems.

12 Quit
If you smoke, today is the best day to stop. Your body notices the difference in 24 hours.

13 Check your teeth
Many people hate the dentist, but if you don't go, you will regret it later. Make an appointment with the dentist twice a year for a healthy smile.

14 Laugh more
According to an American doctor, if you laugh more, you will be healthier. A good laugh is good exercise.

15 Drink water
Water makes you healthier, more beautiful and more relaxed.

16 Don't worry!
Don't feel bad about all the things you can't do – enjoy what you can do!

4 Read the article again. Which paragraphs talk about …

1	food and drink. ___ ___	6	money. ___
2	exercise. ___	7	your teeth. ___
3	feelings. ___ ___	8	sleep. ___
4	cigarettes. ___	9	politics. ___
5	school. ___	10	work. ___ ___ ___

5 Match the highlighted words and phrases in the article to the definitions 1–6.

1 _____ work for no money
2 _____ to stop and relax for a short time
3 _____ to feel bad about something you did
4 _____ to stop doing something
5 _____ opportunity
6 _____ to put money in the bank for the future

6 Read the article again. Put a tick (✓) next to the things that you already do, or did in the past.

7 Work in pairs. Compare your lists. Which are the same?

VOCABULARY: collocations *make* & *do*

1 Find all the examples of *make* and *do* used as a main verb in the text. Underline them and the words that come after them.

2 Make sentences that are true for you using the words in the box.

I never I always I sometimes I usually	do make	my homework every night. friends easily. a good job when I'm motivated. mistakes in English. coffee in the morning. plans for the future.

LISTENING

1 🔘 2.58 Listen to five people talk about *16 things to do before you're 60*. Put a tick (✓) next to points in the article you hear.

2 🔘 2.58 Listen again and match the sentences to the people – David (D), Sandra (S), Will (W), Ali (A) and Jarvis (J).

1 He's a student.
2 She's going to go to a gym next year.
3 Her husband is a pessimist.
4 He's going to live in France.
5 He plays football.
6 He is 64 years old.
7 She's going to talk to her husband about things on the list.
8 He isn't going to live in another country.

GRAMMAR: *going to*

> We use *be* + *going to* + infinitive to talk about plans in the future.
> Affirmative   She**'s going to go** to a gym next year.
> Negative   I**'m not going to stop** smoking.
> Question   What **are you going to do**?

> ❯ SEE LANGUAGE REFERENCE PAGE 120

1 Rearrange the words to make sentences.

1 to   a   is   going   buy   David   good   bed .
2 going   water   drink   she   is   to   more .
3 in   live   country   Will   is   not   another   going   to .
4 stop   smoking   going   to   I'm .

2 Complete the reporter's questions to Jarvis about the trip he is going to make.

1 Where / go? *Where are you going to go?*
  To China.
2 Who / go with? _____
  My best friend, Charlie.
3 When / make this trip? _____
  In two years, when I finish my studies.
4 How / get there? _____
  By plane.
5 What / do? _____
  We're going to ride around the country on motorbikes.

3 Think of a trip you are going to make in the future. Make notes about the trip.

4 Work in pairs. Interview your partner about his/her trip. Use the questions in exercise 2.

PRONUNCIATION: /tə/

1 🔘 2.59 Listen to the pronunciation of the word *to* in these sentences.

1 I'm going to drink more water.
2 I'm going to stop smoking.
3 What are you going to do?
4 Who are you going to go with?

2 Practise saying the sentences.

SPEAKING

1 Look at the list of *16 things to do before you're 60*. Make sentences about things you are going to do in the future and things you aren't going to do in the future.

2 Work in pairs. Compare your lists. Are there other things you are going to do?

11D | In the workplace

READING

1 Read the signs from a workplace. Match the signs A–F to the places where you can see them 1–4.

1 on the computer
2 in the kitchen
3 next to the lights
4 next to the rubbish bin

A Please clean up your coffee cups when you finish with them.

B PLEASE CLEAN UP WHEN YOU FINISH YOUR BREAK.

C TURN OFF ALL LIGHTS AT THE END OF THE DAY. *DON'T FORGET!*

D *Log on with your username and password.*

E When you finish, please shut down the computer.

F Do **not** throw away paper. Please recycle.

VOCABULARY: phrasal verbs

> ### Language note
> A phrasal verb is a combination of two or three words that you use like a verb. *Go out*, *take off* and *get up* are phrasal verbs.

1 Find and <u>underline</u> the phrasal verbs in the signs.

2 Complete the phrases with phrasal verbs from exercise 1.

1 _____ the kitchen   the room   the mess
2 _____ to the computer   with your username   to the system
3 _____ the lights   the computer   the television
4 _____ paper   rubbish   things you don't need
5 _____ the computer   the business   the system

3 <u>Underline</u> the correct preposition in the phrasal verbs.

1 Take *off / on* your jacket if you feel hot.
2 Will Cotton gets *out / up* at 6 o'clock every morning.
3 You look tired. Maybe you should sit *down / up*.
4 OK, everybody please stand *up / out* to do this exercise.
5 Did you take *off / out* the rubbish last night?
6 Can you turn *along / on* the radio please?

4 🔘 2.60 Listen and check your answers. Say the sentences.

LISTENING

1 🔘 2.61 Listen to three dialogues at a workplace. Match the dialogues 1–3 to the situations A–C.

A An interview

B   A retirement party

C   A tea break

2 🔊 **2.61** Listen again and decide if the sentences are true (T) or false (F). Correct the false sentences.

Dialogue 1
1   The man is going to drive to the party.
2   The woman is going to meet the man at 5:30 tomorrow.

Dialogue 2
3   It's almost eleven o'clock.
4   The women are going to stop work now.

Dialogue 3
5   The woman does not have the letter.
6   The woman does not have an interview today.

FUNCTIONAL LANGUAGE: invitations

Invitations

	go to the theatre	
Would you like to	*have dinner*	*(with me/us)?*
	come	

Responses

Yes,	*I'd love to.*
	that would be nice.
	I'm working/going shopping.
No,	*thanks.*
	sorry. I can't. I'm busy.

▸ SEE LANGUAGE REFERENCE PAGE 121

1 Correct the mistakes in the sentences.

1   Would you like go?
2   I'm sorry, I can't. I busy.
3   Would you like to have a cup of tea me?
4   Yes, I love to.
5   Do you like to come with me?

2 Look at audioscript 2.61 on page 146 to check your answers.

SPEAKING

1 💿 **2.62** Read and listen to the dialogue.

A: Hello.
B: Hi. How are you?
A: Fine, thanks. What are you doing?
B: Oh, nothing much.
A: Would you like to have a cup of tea with me?
B: Oh, yes. That would be nice.
A: I know a very good café near here.
B: Good. Let's go.

2 Work in pairs. Practise the dialogue.

3 Work in pairs. Choose one of the roles in the box. Prepare a similar dialogue.

- The President of the United States and the president of your country
- Two students after class
- Two famous film stars (you decide who)
- Other (you decide the roles)

Self-assessment (✓)

☐ I can ask someone about their job.
☐ I can make simple predictions about the future.
☐ I can talk about my plans for the future.
☐ I can make and respond to invitations.

GRAMMAR
Question review

When, where, what, how, who and *why* are all question words. We use them to begin a question.

Remember these rules about questions in English.

We make questions with the verb *be* by putting the verb in front of the subject.

	verb	subject	
	Are	*you*	*a doctor?*
Where	*were*	*you*	*yesterday?*

We make questions in the present simple and past simple with an auxiliary verb (*do/does/ did*) and the infinitive. We put the auxiliary verb before the subject and we put the infinitive after the subject.

	auxiliary	subject	infinitive	
	Do	*you*	*work*	*at night?*
When	*did*	*you*	*finish*	*today?*

Other verb forms (present continuous, *can*, *should*) already have an auxiliary verb and a main verb. We put the auxiliary verb before the subject and we put the infinitive after the subject.

	auxiliary	subject	infinitive	
	Is	*he*	*working*	*today?*
	Can	*you*	*speak*	*English?*
What	*should*	*he*	*do?*	

Will/won't

We use *will* to talk about predictions in the future.

Will is a modal auxiliary verb. This means:

* it goes with the infinitive without *to*.
* it has the same form for all subjects.
* the negative is with *not* (*n't*).
* to make a question, put *will* before the subject, and the infinitive after the subject.

Affirmative & negative

I	will	
You	'll	
He/She/It	won't	have a job in ten years.
We		
They		

Question & short answer

Will	I you he she it we they	have a job in ten years?	Yes, No,	I you he she it we they	will. won't.

Going to future

Use *be* + *going to* + verb to talk about plans for the future.

*She's **going to** go to the gym next year.*

Affirmative

Full form				Contraction		
I am You are He/She/It is We are They are	going to	vote in the next election.		I'm You're He's/She's/It's We're They're	going to	do exercise.

Negative

Full form					Contraction			
I am You are He/She/It is We are They are	not	going to	learn another language.		I'm not You aren't He/She/It isn't We aren't They aren't	going to	learn another language.

Question & short answer

Am I Are you Is he/she/it Are we Are they	going to	visit England?	Yes, I am. No, I'm not. Yes, he/she/it is. No, he/she/it isn't. Yes, you/they/we are. No, you/they/we aren't.

FUNCTIONAL LANGUAGE

Invitations

Would you like to + verb (*with me/us*)?

Responses

Yes, I'd love to.
That would be nice.
No, thanks.
Sorry, I can't.
Sorry/Thanks, but I'm busy.

WORD LIST

Jobs

accountant *n C* **	/əˈkaʊntənt/
actor *n C* ***	/ˈæktə(r)/
builder *n C* **	/ˈbɪldə(r)/
doctor *n C* ***	/ˈdɒktə(r)/
nurse *n C* ***	/nɜː(r)s/
secretary *n C* ***	/ˈsekrətri/
security guard *n C*	/sɪˈkjʊərəti gɑː(r)d/
vet *n C*	/vet/
waiter *n C* *	/ˈweɪtə(r)/

Describing work

badly-paid *adj*	/ˈbædli peɪd/
employed *adj*	/ɪmˈplɔɪd/
full-time *adj* **	/ˈfʊlˌtaɪm/
part-time *adj* **	/ˈpɑː(r)tˌtaɪm/
permanent *adj* ***	/ˈpɜː(r)mənənt/
temporary *adj* ***	/ˈtemp(ə)rəri/
unemployed *adj* ***	/ˌʌnɪmˈplɔɪd/
well-paid *adj*	/wel peɪd/

Collocations with *make* & *do*

do a good job	/duː ə ˈgʊd dʒɒb/
do homework	/duː ˈhəʊmˌwɜː(r)k/
make a friend	/meɪk ə frend/
make a mistake	/meɪk ə mɪˈsteɪk/
make coffee	/meɪk ˈkɒfi/
make plans	/meɪk plænz/

Phrasal verbs

clean up *v*	/kliːn ʌp/
log on *v*	/lɒg ɒn/
shut down *v*	/ʃʌt daʊn/
throw away *v*	/θrəʊ əˈweɪ/
turn off *v*	/tɜː(r)n ɒf/

Other words & phrases

chance *n C/U* ***	/tʃɑːns/
chapter *n C* ***	/ˈtʃæptə(r)/
invisible *adj* **	/ɪnˈvɪzəb(ə)l/
opportunity *n C/U* ***	/ˌɒpə(r)ˈtjuːnəti/
public *adj* ***	/ˈpʌblɪk/
quit *v* *	/kwɪt/
regret *v* **	/rɪˈgret/
save (money) *v* ***	/seɪv/
volunteer work *n C*	/ˌvɒlənˈtɪə(r) wɜː(r)k/

12A | Music fans

SPEAKING & VOCABULARY: music

1 Put the words into two groups.

singer	rock	pop	musician	songwriter
jazz	R&B	band	rap	folk	classical

People who make music	Kinds of music

2 How do you say these words in your language? Which ones are similar?

3 🔊 2.63 Listen to different kinds of music. What kind of music is each one? Do you like it?

4 Work in pairs. Discuss these questions.

- What kind of music do you listen to?
- Can you sing or play a musical instrument?
- Do you like going to concerts? What kind?

READING

1 You are going to read an article about music fans. What is a music fan?

1 a person who loves music
2 a person who hates music
3 a person who makes music

2 Read the article on page 123 and check your answer to exercise 1. What kinds of music fans are there in the article? What kind of music do they like?

3 Read the article again and answer the questions.

1 How long has the man liked rock music?
2 What bands has he seen?
3 What did the woman see with her parents?
4 Is the woman in the opera?
5 How does the girl know the band?
6 What have the girl and her friends done?

4 Work in pairs. Look at the first sentence of the article. Do you agree? Why or why not?

GRAMMAR: present perfect 1 – affirmative

> Use the present perfect to talk about general events or experiences in the past. When we use the present perfect, we don't talk about a specific time in the past.
>
> The present perfect uses *have/has* + past participle.
> We **have seen** them in concert three times!
> I**'ve taken** singing classes.
> I**'ve heard** of that group.

> ❯ SEE LANGUAGE REFERENCE PAGE 130

1 Underline all the examples of the present perfect affirmative in the article.

2 Make the past participles of these verbs.

make	say	write	stop	change	give	sing
have	win					

3 Complete the text about another music fan. Put the verbs in brackets into the present perfect.

The world music fan

In the past I liked pop music. One day, my friends took me to a world music concert. I loved it so I (1) _____ (change) my musical interests. I'm now a big fan of Tinariwen. I (2) _____ (see) them many times. They are from the Sahara Desert but they (3) _____ (play) concerts all over the world. They (4) _____ (write) some great songs and (5) _____ (won) international awards. I'm going to see them again next month.

PRONUNCIATION: contractions

1 🔊 2.64 Listen to these contractions.

I have seen her in concert.	I've seen her in concert.
He has not seen her in concert.	He hasn't seen her in concert.
They have seen her in concert.	They've seen her in concert.

2 Say the sentences below with contractions.

1 We have not seen her in concert.
2 He has written a song.
3 She has changed musical interests.
4 It has not been easy.
5 You have not changed.
6 I have started a fan club.

3 🔊 2.65 Listen to the recording to check your answers. Say the sentences.

The music fans

'Music is enough for a lifetime, but a lifetime is not enough for music,' said Sergei Rachmaninov, the famous Russian pianist and composer. Some people make music their whole life. This week we look at the world of the music fan. Why are they obsessed? What have they done?

The rocker

I've been a rock music fan since I was 12 years old. I went to my first concert when I was 18 years old. I've seen lots of new and classic rock bands: Linkin Park, Blink 182, U2 and even Bruce Springsteen. My favourite band is U2. I've seen them more than five times. I've gone to concerts in big sports stadiums and in small places too. I have more than one thousand rock songs on my mp3 player.

The opera fan

I'm a big opera fan. It started when my parents took me to see Verdi's *La Traviata* at the opera hall in our city. It was wonderful, and I knew opera was for me. I've seen many great operas. I've taken singing classes to join the opera. It didn't happen. I've even written an opera myself. One day, I'm going to go to Italy to see Puccini's *Madame Butterfly*, the greatest opera of all time.

The local fan

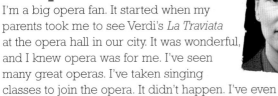

There's a group of boys from my school. They're in a pop band and I'm one of their biggest fans. People don't know them, but they are going to be very famous. I know it! I like lots of pop music, but this is better because I know them. My friends and I have seen them in concert three times! We've started a fan club and we've opened a Facebook fan group for them. It's so funny!

SPEAKING

1 🔵 2.66 Read and listen to two people talking about musicians they like a lot.

> I'm a fan of Gorillaz. They have made some great CDs. They've written lots of songs and they've given concerts all round the world.

> My sister plays the guitar. She has played a concert in our town and she's been on local radio. She hasn't made a CD, but I think she's great. I'm a fan.

2 Think of a musician or band that you like. Prepare a similar text about him, her or them. Look at exercise 1 for an example.

3 Work in pairs. Talk about the musician or group that you like.

12B | A public life

SPEAKING

1 Work in pairs, A and B.

A: Choose one of the photos. Describe it to your partner.
B: Guess the picture. Swap roles and repeat.

2 Have you been in one of these situations? How did you feel?

I was on television. I didn't like it. I was very nervous.

I spoke at a friend's wedding. It was great.

LISTENING

1 in 4 Americans have been on television, study says

Number 1 dream: to be on television, say young people

Psychologists say 'we are obsessed with public lives'

1 Look at the headlines. Do you think these statements are true for your country?

2 🔊 2.67 Listen to someone doing a survey in Britain. Complete the table.

	Speaker 1	Speaker 2	Speaker 3
been on TV	✗		
spoken on the radio	✗		
written to newspaper	?		

3 🔊 2.67 Listen again and decide if the sentences are true (T) or false (F). Correct the false sentences.

Dialogue 1
1 The man does not want to be on television.
2 The man has lots of time.

Dialogue 2
3 *The Big Award* is a television show on Channel 4.
4 The woman won a prize.

Dialogue 3
5 The man works on television.
6 The woman didn't recognize the man because she doesn't watch the news.

GRAMMAR: present perfect 2 – questions & negative

Use the present perfect to ask about experiences in the past.
In questions in the present perfect, we can use *ever*. *Ever* usually means 'in your life'.

*Have you **ever** been on television? Yes, I have.*
*Have you **ever** written to a newspaper? No, I haven't.*

We can use *never* in negatives. *Never* = not ever.
*I've **never** been on television.*

*Have you **ever** been in the newspaper? No, **never**.*

⊙ SEE LANGUAGE REFERENCE PAGE 130

1 Complete the past participles. Then match them to the infinitives in the box.

be write have hear call speak see

1 b _ _ n   4 h _ d   7 h _ _ rd
2 sp _ k _ n   5 s _ _ n
3 c _ ll _ d   6 wr _ tt _ n

2 Complete the dialogue. Put the words in brackets into the present perfect.

Journalist: (1) _____ (*you ever be*) on television?
Martin: No, I haven't.
Journalist: (2) _____ (*you ever speak*) on the radio?
Martin: What do you mean?
Journalist: Well, (3) _____ (*you call*) a radio station?
Martin: Yes, I have.
Journalist: (4) _____ (*you ever have*) your photo in the newspaper?
Martin: Yes, I have. I (5) _____ (*write*) several letters to the newspaper. One time my photo was next to my letter. (6) _____ (*you hear*) of the *Daily Star*?
Journalist: No, I haven't. I (7) _____ (*never hear*) of it. I work for the *Weekly Times*.
Martin: I (8) _____ (*never see*) your newspaper.

3 🔘 **2.68** Work in pairs. Listen to the recording to check your answers. Practise the dialogue with a partner.

PRONUNCIATION: irregular past participles

1 🔘 **2.69** Listen to the past participles.

/əʊ/	/ɪ/	/ʌ/	/eɪ/	/e/
known spoken	given driven	won done	made paid	read met

2 Put the words in the correct column in exercise 1.

> broken   slept   come   written   taken

3 🔘 **2.70** Listen to the recording to check your answers. Say the words.

SPEAKING

1 Read the *A Public Life* questionnaire. Make the questions.

A Public Life
Are you a public person or a private person?

Have you ever ...

be on television?	When?
speak in public?	Where?
call a radio programme?	When?
have your photo in the newspaper?	When?
write a letter to the newspaper?	When?
receive an award in public?	When?
sing in public?	When? What song?

2 Work in pairs. Ask and answer the questions from exercise 1. Answer *Yes, I have* or *No, I haven't*. If your partner answers *Yes, I have*, ask the next question (*Where? When?* etc).

A: *Have you ever been on television?*
B: *No, I haven't.*
A: *Have you ever spoken in public?*
B: *Yes, I have.*
A: *Where?*
B: *At school.*

3 Tell the rest of the class about the person you interviewed. Who has the most public life in the class?

DID YOU KNOW?

1 Work in pairs. Read about *Time* magazine and discuss the questions.

The American magazine *Time* has a special issue every year called Person of the Year. *Time* chooses the Person of the Year as the individual or group of individuals who have had the biggest effect on the year's news. They have had very public lives.

Some of the people of the year for *Time* magazine have been:

Mohandas Gandhi, Indian leader (1930)

Elizabeth II, Queen of England (1952)

Martin Luther King, American Civil Rights leader (1963)

Vladimir Putin, Russian leader (2007)

Barack Obama, American president (2008)

Mark Zuckerberg, founder of Facebook (2010)

- Do you know the magazine *Time*? Is there a similar news magazine in your country?
- Think of some people who are on television or in the news a lot at the moment. Why are they in the news? Do they have a very public life?

12c | English in your life

SPEAKING

1 Work in pairs. When you are learning English, what is important? Read the sentences and choose three things that are very important and three that aren't very important to you.

1 A good relationship with other people in the class
2 A small class (not many students)
3 A comfortable classroom, with good chairs and desks for the students
4 Interesting lessons
5 A CD player and television in the classroom
6 A good teacher
7 A computer with internet for every student
8 Lots of homework

2 Compare your answers with another pair. What other things are important when you are learning English?

READING

1 Read the text. What kind of text is it?

1 An advertisement brochure for a language school
2 A newspaper article about a language school
3 A story about people at a language school

2 Read the text again and answer the questions.

1 Who didn't feel relaxed when she came to the school?
2 Who likes speaking in class?
3 Who is going to take an important exam?
4 Who didn't learn English when he was younger?
5 Who says there aren't many students in the class?
6 Who comes to the school because it isn't expensive?
7 Who thought that English was difficult, but liked it?
8 Who makes a prediction about English in his country?

3 Work in pairs. Are you similar to one of these students? Discuss with a partner.

WHY LEARN ENGLISH WITH US?
BECAUSE WE'RE THE BEST.

If you don't believe us, read what our students say.

I came to your school because I wanted to learn English. I thought English was difficult and boring work, only grammar, lots of vocabulary to memorize, etc. But then I saw that here you can also learn English with films, or songs. We also had computer classes on the internet. I didn't know any English when I started at your school, but one year later I knew a lot of English.
Doris

I have been at the International School of English for two years. I'm studying now for an important exam. I like this school because there are not many students in the class and the teacher gives us a lot of personal attention.
Kanda

I'm a student at your school. I speak a lot of English, but I don't practise outside of class, so I come here to the conversation classes. I'm learning lots of English expressions. The teachers at your school have helped me a lot. The classes are good, and they are cheaper than other schools. That's why I'm with the International School.
Monica

I haven't studied English before. When I was a child, we didn't study English at school. Now all the children in my country are learning English when they are very young. I'm studying English because I need it for my work. In the future, everybody in my country will speak English.
Constantine

When I had my first lesson at the International School of English, I was very nervous because I could not speak English very well. But I liked studying English because all the teachers were very friendly, and they always made students relax so we could understand the lessons. I'm going to come back next year.
Renata

If you want
✔ English for school
✔ English for work
✔ English for fun
Come to
International
School of English.
English ... in your life.

Glossary
nervous *adj* anxious

GRAMMAR: verb forms (review)

SEE LANGUAGE REFERENCE PAGE 130

1 Find examples of the following verb forms in the text.

1 two different future verb forms
2 a present continuous
3 a present simple
4 a present simple in the negative

5 a past simple in the negative
6 an irregular past simple verb form
7 a regular past simple verb form
8 a present perfect

2 Complete the *English in Your Life* questionnaire. Put the words in brackets into the correct form of the verb.

English in your life

1 Why are you learning (*you learn*) English now?
2 How often _____ (*you have*) English classes?
3 How often _____ (*you do*) English homework?
4 Who _____ (*be*) your first English teacher?
5 When _____ (*you start*) studying English?
6 _____ (*you ever see*) a film in English?
7 _____ (*you ever speak*) on the phone in English?
8 _____ (*you study*) English next year?
9 _____ (*you visit*) an English-speaking country in the future?

3 Work in pairs. Ask and answer the questions in exercise 2.

SPEAKING

1 🔊 2.71 Listen to someone give a one-minute presentation in English. Tick (✓) the topic they are talking about.

Foods I like and don't like
Where I live
The capital city of my country
A typical day
A person that should win an award
A favourite thing
Learning a language

2 Now you are going to prepare a one-minute presentation in English. Choose a topic.

3 Prepare your presentation. Make notes of what you want to say in English.

4 Work in small groups. One person presents his/her topic.

- You must talk about your topic for one minute.
- You must talk only in English.
- You can look at your notes, but you mustn't read them.
- If you are not talking, you must listen to the speaker and think of one question to ask him/her after the presentation. Use the question words and phrases to help you.

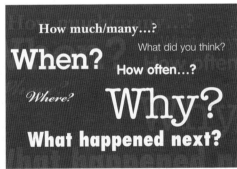

How much/many…?
What did you think?
When?
How often…?
Where?
Why?
What happened next?

5 The others in the group ask the speaker one question. Answer the questions. Swap roles.

12D | The end

All good things must come to an end.
Every end is a new beginning.

SPEAKING

1 Translate the proverbs above into your own language. Are there any similar expressions in your language? How do you say them in English?

2 Work in pairs. Ask and answer these questions.

- How do you feel at the end of an exam?
- How do you feel at the end of the school year?
- How do you feel at the end of the weekend?
- How do you feel at the end of a holiday?

LISTENING

1 🔘 **2.72** Listen to four short dialogues. Match the dialogues 1–4 to the situations a–d.

a the end of a language course
b the end of a guided tour
c the end of a dinner party
d a sports match

2 🔘 **2.72** Listen again and answer the questions.

Dialogue 1
1 What did they have for dinner?
2 What did the man like?

Dialogue 2
3 Where is Brian going to take people?
4 What does the man want the people to write on the paper?

Dialogue 3
5 Where can the students see their results?
6 What did the woman give the man?

Dialogue 4
7 Are the men on the same sports team?
8 When are they going to meet?

FUNCTIONAL LANGUAGE: thanking

Thanking	Responses
Thank you.	*You're w _ _ _ _ _ _.*
Thank you v _ _ _ much.	*Don't mention it.*
Thanks a l _ _.	*That's alr _ _ _ _.*
That's very kind of you.	*Not at all.*

1 Look at audioscript 2.72 on page 146. Find all the examples of thanking and the responses. Complete the functional language box above.

2 Choose the correct response.

1 We've bought you a little gift.
a) Oh, thank you.   b) You're welcome.

2 Thank you very much for dinner.
a) You're welcome.   b) You're alright.

3 Here, you can have my pen.
a) You're welcome.   b) Thanks.

4 Thank you very much for everything you've done.
a) Sorry.   b) Don't mention it.

5 Excuse me. You left your wallet in the shop.
a) Thank you very much.   b) Not at all.

3 🔘 **2.73** Listen to the recording to check your answers. Practise the dialogues.

4 Work in pairs. Prepare two similar dialogues and practise them with your partner.

SPEAKING

1 Work in groups of three or four. Turn to page 139. Read the instructions and play the *Travel With English* game on page 129.

Self-assessment (✓)
☐ I can use words related to music and talk about the music I like.
☐ I can give a very short presentation about a topic that interests me.
☐ I can thank someone and respond to thanks.

Travel with English

Rooms in a house

C

1 Arrival

B

3

4

Things to take on holiday

Food & drink

Furniture

A

2

D

5

Jobs

Transport

8

Music

G

E

9

6

7

Places in a city

F

H

SUBWAY

MUSEUM

12

Clothes

I

10

11

32 Departure

Body

GRAMMAR
Present perfect

Use the present perfect to talk about events that happened in the past when we don't say a specific time.

The present perfect is formed with the auxiliary *have/has* + past participle.

> He **has won** an award.
> They **have made** 35 albums.

He's been to London.

There are two kinds of past participle in English:

- regular (ends in *–ed*) *visited, received, opened*
- irregular (different form) *spoken, eaten, met*

See page 159 for a list of irregular past participles.

Affirmative

Full form		Contraction	
I have		I've	
You have		You've	
He has		He's	
She has	been to London.	She's	been to London.
It has		It's	
We have		We've	
They have		They've	

Negative

I haven't		
You haven't		
He hasn't		
She hasn't	(ever)	won an award.
It hasn't		
We haven't		
They haven't		

In the negative, we can use *not* + *ever*.

> I **haven't ever won** an award.

We can also use *never* to make a negative sentence. *Never = not ever.*

> I **have never won** an award.
> I **have never heard** him speak.

Use the present perfect to ask about experiences in the past. We can use *ever* in questions. *Ever* usually means 'in your life'.

Question

Have I		
Have you		
Has he		
Has she	(ever)	spoken in public?
Have we		
Have they		

Short answer

Yes,	I have.
	you have.
	he/she/it has.
	we have.
	they have.
No,	I haven't.
	you haven't.
	he/she/it hasn't.
	we haven't.
	they haven't.

Verb forms review

Tense	Affirmative	Negative	Question	Short answer	Use
Present simple	I live in Spain.	He doesn't work here.	Do you like chocolate?	Yes, I do. No, they don't.	routines habits facts
Past simple	They took the bus.	We didn't go to class.	Did you study for the exam?	Yes, he did. No, I didn't.	events in the past
Present continuous	He is working at home.	I'm not working at the moment.	Are they playing football?	Yes, they are. No, he isn't.	actions happening now
Future (going to)	We are going to see a film.	He isn't going to have a holiday.	Are you going to stop?	Yes, I am. No, they aren't.	future plans
Future (will)	He will get married.	They won't have a job.	Will I work at home?	Yes, you will. No, we won't.	future predictions
Present perfect	They've sung in many countries.	She hasn't made a CD.	Have you ever spoken in public?	Yes, I have. No, I haven't.	experiences unspecified past

FUNCTIONAL LANGUAGE
Thanking

Thank you.
Thank you very much.
Thanks a lot.
That's very kind of you.

Responses

You're welcome.
Don't mention it.
That's alright.
Not at all.

WORD LIST

Music

band *n C* ***	/bænd/
classical (music) *n U* *	/ˈklæsɪk(ə)l/
folk (music) *n U*	/fəʊk/
jazz *n U* *	/dʒæz/
musician *n C* **	/mjuˈzɪʃ(ə)n/
pop (music) *n U* **	/pɒp/
R&B *n U*	/ɑː(r) ˈn biː/
rap *n C/U*	/ræp/
rock (music) *n U* ***	/rɒk/
singer *n C* **	/ˈsɪŋə(r)/
song *n C* ***	/sɒŋ/
songwriter *n C*	/ˈsɒŋˌraɪtə(r)/

Media

camera *n C* ***	/ˈkæm(ə)rə/
game show *n C*	/ɡeɪm ʃəʊ/
journalist *n C* **	/ˈdʒɜː(r)nəlɪst/
newspaper *n C* ***	/ˈnjuːzˌpeɪpə(r)/
radio *n C* ***	/ˈreɪdiəʊ/
the (morning/evening) news *n U* ***	/ðə njuːz/

Other words & phrases

achievement *n C /U* ***	/əˈtʃiːvmənt/
award *n C* ***	/əˈwɔː(r)d/
beginning *n C* ***	/bɪˈɡɪnɪŋ/
brochure *n C* *	/ˈbrəʊʃə(r)/
choose *v* ***	/tʃuːz/
fan *n C* **	/fæn/
founder *n C* *	/ˈfaʊndə(r)/
lifetime *n C* **	/ˈlaɪfˌtaɪm/
memorize *v* *	/ˈmeməraɪz/

Communication activities

2D Speaking exercise 1 page 29

Student A

Describe your photos to your partner. Decide if the photos are the same or different.

In my picture 1, Elvis is young. He is thin and has short hair.

Elvis

Penélope Cruz

Diego Maradona

Halle Berry

3C Speaking exercise 1 page 37

Student A

Look at the picture of the room. Find six differences with your partner's picture.

Ask questions.

Are there any …?
How many … are there?
Is there a …?

5D Functional language exercise 3 page 59

Student A

You are a guest at the Chicago Sky Central Hotel. You are at reception. You want:

- to connect your laptop computer to the internet in your room
- to leave your passport and money at reception
- to change rooms (you want a room with a view)
- to pay the bill with your Visa card

Ask your partner.

4A Speaking exercise 1 page 43

Student A

Interview your partner. Ask questions about these activities.

What time / get up? *What time do you get up?*
have breakfast? *Do you have breakfast?*
What time / go to work or classes?
get the bus or train?
have coffee?
What time / have lunch?
have a nap?
What time / get home?

Answer your partner's questions. Ask: *What about you?*

10B Speaking exercise 1 page 105

Student A

You have a new job. You can live in the capital city or a smaller city. Discuss your choice with Students B and C.

At the end of the roleplay, choose which city you would like to live in.

9B Speaking exercise 3 page 95

Student A

Teach your partner how to do this exercise.

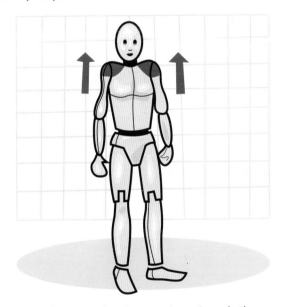

Hold: five seconds   Repeat: three times (x 3)

Do you know any other exercises like this? What are they? Tell your partner.

7B Speaking exercise 1 page 75

Student A

Look at the photo. Find six differences with your partner's photo. Ask questions.
Do you have any rice? How much rice do you have?

8C Speaking exercise 1 page 87

Student B

Listen to what Phil usually does. Answer your partner's questions about what Phil is doing today.

Phil's having cake for breakfast.

Today
(*have*) cake for breakfast
(*take*) a taxi
(*go*) to the cinema
(*eat*) in a restaurant
(*go*) to a birthday party

Tell your partner what Sarah does every Saturday. Find out what Sarah is doing today.

Sarah wakes up early on Saturday. What is she doing today?

Every Saturday
(*wake up*) late
(*have*) breakfast
(*do*) the shopping
(*go*) for a walk in the park
(*watch*) TV in the afternoon
Guess why Sarah is doing different things.

5A Grammar exercise 2 page 53

Student A

Read the example and then use the pictures to interview your partner.

swim
cook
drive
play tennis

Can you play football?   *Yes, I can. / No, I can't.*
How well?   *Very well.*

> ### Useful language
>
> *Very well.* 😊 😊
> *Quite well.* 😐
> *Not very well.* 😞

8A Grammar exercise 4 page 83

Student A

Read the example and use the pictures to interview your partner.

Do you like doing the dishes?
Yes, I do. I love it. / No, I don't. I hate it.

2c Vocabulary exercise 2 page 27

Student A

Look at Emily's family tree.
Ask questions about the people.
Who is Ian?
He's Emily's grandfather.

Answer B's questions.
Who is Liz?
She's Emily's grandmother.

7B Speaking exercise 1 page 75

Student B

Look at the photo. Find six differences with your partner's photo. Ask questions.

Do you have any eggs? How many eggs do you have?

9c Speaking exercise 1 page 97

Ask questions about the objects and their owners.

Whose dog is this?   *It's theirs.*
Whose sunglasses are these?   *They're his.*

Who has the better memory?

Ian (_____) = Liz (grandmother)

Laura (aunt) = Roger (_____)   Jack (father) = Doris (_____)

Nathan (_____) = *Emily*   Andy (_____)

Robbie (son)   Kylie (_____)

2D Speaking exercise 1 page 29

Student B

Describe your photos to your partner. Decide if the pictures are the same or different.

In my picture 1, Elvis is middle-aged. He is fat and has long hair.

Elvis

Penélope Cruz

Halle Berry

Diego Maradona

6B Vocabulary & speaking exercise 4 page 64

Student B

Interview your partner about books and reading. Ask these questions.

Do you read a lot?
What was the last book you read? What was it about?
How many books do you read every year?
Who are the most famous authors from your country?

9B Speaking exercise 3 page 95

Student B

Teach your partner how to do this exercise.

Hold: five seconds.   Repeat: twice (x 2)

Do you know any other exercises like this? What are they? Tell your partner.

10B Speaking exercise 1 page 105

Student C

Student A has a new job. He/She can live in the capital city or a smaller city. You think Student A should live in a smaller city, not the capital. Here are some reasons why you think the smaller city is a better choice:

- it's safer in a smaller city
- traffic in the capital is worse
- people in the smaller cities are friendlier

Think of other reasons.

I think you should choose … because …

2c Vocabulary exercise 2 page 27

Student B

Look at Emily's family tree.
Ask questions about the people.
Who is Liz?
She's Emily's grandmother.

Answer A's questions.
Who is Ian?
He's Emily's grandfather.

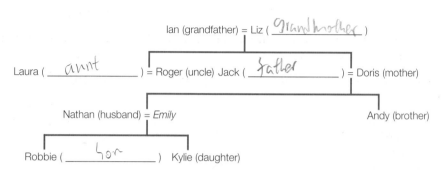

Ian (grandfather) = Liz (*Grandmother*)

Laura (*aunt*) = Roger (uncle) Jack (*father*) = Doris (mother)

Nathan (husband) = *Emily*

Andy (brother)

Robbie (*son*) Kylie (daughter)

3c Speaking exercise 1 page 37

Student B

Look at the picture of the room. Find six differences with your partner's picture.

Ask questions.

Are there any …?
How many … are there?
Is there a …?

4A Speaking exercise 1 page 43

Student B

Answer your partner's questions. Ask: *What about you?*

Interview your partner. Ask questions about these activities.

What time / wake up? *What time do you wake up?*
have a shower in the morning? *Do you have a shower in the morning?*
What time / get to work or classes?
have a break?
have meetings?
What time / go home?
What time / have dinner?
What time / go to sleep?

5A Grammar exercise 2 page 53

Student B

Read the example and then use the pictures to interview your partner.

type draw

play chess sing

Can you play football? *Yes, I can. / No, I can't.*
How well? *Very well.*

Useful language

Very well. ☺☺
Quite well. 😐
Not very well. ☹

8A Grammar exercise 4 page 83

Student B

Read the example and use the pictures to interview your partner.

Do you like doing the dishes?
Yes, I do. I love it. / No, I don't. I hate it.

8c Speaking exercise 1 page 87

Student A

Tell your partner what Phil usually does. Find out what Phil is doing today.

Phil usually takes the bus. What is he doing today?

Usually

(*have*) bread and coffee for breakfast
(*take*) the bus
(*go*) to work
(*eat*) at home
(*go*) to English class in the evening

Guess why Phil is doing different things.

Listen to what Sarah usually does. Answer your partner's questions about what Sarah is doing today.

Sarah's waking up early.

Today

(*wake up*) early
(*not have*) breakfast
(*go*) to the hairdresser
(*take*) a limousine
(*go*) to the church

BASICS 1 Numbers 1–10 exercise 4 page 6

Student A

Look at the numbers on the page. Say a number to your partner.

Student B

Listen to your partner. Point to the number your partner says.

5D Functional language exercise 3 page 59

Student B

You are the receptionist at the Chicago Sky Central Hotel. Here is information to help you with A's questions:

- the internet connection doesn't work at the moment
- there is a safe at reception for guests. It is £3 a day
- there are no rooms with a view available this week
- the hotel accepts all credit cards

10B Speaking exercise 1 page 105

Student B

Student A has a new job. He/She can live in the capital city or a smaller city. You think Student A should live in the capital city. Here are some reasons why you think the capital city is a better choice:

- the nightlife is more exciting
- the shops are better (there are more shops, and better quality)
- the people in the capital are more interesting

Think of other reasons.

I think you should choose …. because …

6B Vocabulary & speaking exercise 4 page 64

Student A

Interview your partner about the cinema. Ask these questions.

Do you often go to the cinema? How often do you go?
How often do you watch videos/DVDs?
What film would you like to see at the moment?
Who are your favourite actors/actresses?

INSTRUCTIONS

- Play the game in groups of three or four. You will need a dice and some counters.
- In the game, you are all on a tour. Decide what country you are touring and write it next to the plane.
- Place your counters on the circle marked ARRIVAL (circle 1).
- The first player to throw a six starts the game.
- The first player throws the dice and moves their counter according to the number on the dice.
- When a player lands on a letter circle, they must talk about the subject for 30 seconds. Look at the 'Talk about' subjects on this page.
- When a player lands on a number circle, they must roleplay the situation with other people in the group. Look at the roleplays on this page.
- When a player lands on a red circle, they must say as many English words in that category as they can in 30 seconds.
- The game continues until the first player reaches the circle marked DEPARTURE.

MINI ROLEPLAYS

1. You meet other tourists. Introduce yourself.
2. You are at a party. Offer the others food or drink.
3. Spell your first and last name for the hotel receptionist.
4. Give directions to the men's/women's toilets.
5. Phone the others in the group. Tell them that the museum visit is cancelled.
6. Ask permission to take a photograph.
7. Order something to eat.
8. You have the afternoon free. Make suggestions.
9. The bus is moving too quickly and you don't feel well. Tell the others.
10. Buy some souvenirs.
11. Thank the others for a nice tour.
12. Say goodbye.

TALK ABOUT

A. Talk about a friend or someone from your family.
B. Talk about an ugly/beautiful/interesting building that you know.
C. Talk about an important public holiday in your country.
D. Talk about the weather in the country you are visiting.
E. Talk about an actor/director/singer you like.
F. Talk about things to see in the country you are visiting.
G. Talk about the last time you went on a plane/train/boat.
H. Talk about the most interesting/ugliest/most expensive souvenir you have ever bought.
I. Talk about your job or school.

Audioscripts

BASICS 1 Introductions 1 exercise 3 🔘 1.06

1   **C = computer   A = astronaut**
C: Hello.
A: Hi.
C: What's your name?
A: My name's John.
C: Nice to meet you, John.
A: Nice to meet you.

2   **SC = ship's captain   C = castaway**
SC: Hello.
C: Hello.
SC: What's your name?
C: My name's Robinson.
SC: Nice to meet you.
C: Nice to meet you.

BASICS 1 Alphabet exercise 6 🔘 1.10

1   CNN   4   DVD
2   BBC   5   CD
3   USA

BASICS 2 Days of the week exercise 3 🔘 1.16

1
A: What day is it today?
B: It's Monday.
A: I thought so.
2
A: When is English class?
B: It's on Thursday this week.
A: OK.
3
A: Do you want to go out this Saturday?
B: This Saturday?
A: Yes.
4
A: So, what did you do last Saturday?
B: Nothing much. And you?
A: No. Nothing.
5
A: Hello, class. What day is it today?
B: It's Friday!
A: Yes, Friday.

1A Vocabulary exercise 3 🔘 1.24

A = Alyssa   M = Margaret
M: Hello.
A: Hi. My name's Alyssa.
M: Yes. I know. I'm Margaret.
A: Nice to meet you.
M: Umm. You're new, so I'll explain. This is our desk.
A: Great.
M: This is your computer.
A: Yes.
M: And this is my computer. Don't touch.
A: OK. I understand.
M: This is my phone. You don't have a phone.
A: And this?
M: Your paper. This is my paper. And this is my cup. And that's it.
A: OK. Thank you.

1B Listening exercise 2 🔘 1.26

R = receptionist   M = Mark
R: Good afternoon. The Social Language Network.
M: Hi. I would like to register for The Social Language Network, please.
R: Of course. What's your name?
M: My name's Mark.
R: What's your last name?

M: Richards.
R: How do you spell that?
M: R-I-C-H-A-R-D-S.
R: Thank you. Are you a language teacher?
M: No, I'm not.
R: Are you a language student?
M: Yes, I am.
R: What is your language of study?
M: I'm a German student.
R: German ...OK. We have lots of German students for you on The Social Language Network.
M: Great.
R: How old are you?
M: Um, I'm 26 years old.
R: Twenty … six. Good. Where are you from?
M: I'm from Sydney.
R: Are you Australian?
M: Yes, I am.
R: I love Australia. Nicole Kidman is my favourite actress.
M: Where are you from?
R: Me? I'm from London. OK, what's your email address?
M: Mark at mail dot com.
R: Thank you.

1C Vocabulary exercise 2 🔘 1.28

A   They're business cards.
B   They're glasses.
C   It's a camera.
D   It's a mobile phone.
E   It's a wallet.
F   It's an umbrella.
G   It's a bottle of water.
H   It's a memory stick.
I   It's a mirror.
J   It's an alarm clock.
K   They're earphones.
L   It's a newspaper.
M   It's a diary.

1C Listening exercise 1 🔘 1.29

M = man   W = woman
1
M: What's this?
W: It's my diary. My private diary.
M: OK. OK. Relax.
2
M: Wait a minute, is that a camera?
M2: Err … yes. Just one photo, please Mr Pott.
M: No cameras! No cameras!
3
M: Excuse me.
W: Yes?
M: I think these are your keys.
W: Yes, they are! Thank you.
M: You're welcome.
4
W: Is that the alarm clock, James?
M: No, that's my mobile phone. Hello?
W: Hello, Mr Pond.
5
W: Are those your glasses?
M: Huh? What? Where?
W: Oh, David! Those are your glasses.
M: Oh nooooo.

1D Listening exercise 1 🔘 1.31

1   **HR = hotel receptionist   R = Rob**
      M = Meg
HR: Good afternoon.
R: Good afternoon. We have a reservation.
HR: What are your names?
R: Rob and Meg Sherman.
HR: How do you spell that please?

R: S-H-E-R-M-A-N.
HR: Sherman, yes. Are you with the tour?
M: Yes we are.
HR: Room 34. These are your keys.
M/R: Thank you.

2   **He = Herb   Ha = Hannah**
      W = waiter
He: Is this the hotel restaurant?
Ha: Yes, sweetheart, I think it is.
He: It's very English!
Ha: I know!
W: Good afternoon. Would you like a drink?
He: Yes, please. A Coke for me.
Ha: Tea, please.
He: Well darling. We're here. We're in London. Listen to that. That's London.
Ha: Wonderful.
W: Tea?
Ha: Here.
He: Coke over here. Thanks.
W: You're welcome.

3   **S = Sam   V = Valerie**
      HR = hotel receptionist
HR: And these are your keys, Mr Moore.
S: Thank you.
V: Hello, are you Sam Moore?
S: Yes, I am.
V: Hi. My name's Valerie. I'm the tour guide for your tour.
S: Oh, hello. Nice to meet you.
V: Nice to meet you. Would you like a drink? Our welcome party is in the hotel restaurant over there.
S: Errr, no thank you. I'm tired, and I'll just go to my room.
V: Really? OK then. See you tomorrow then.
S: Thank you again. Goodbye.

4   **He = Herb   Ha = Hannah   V = Valerie**
      R = Rob   M = Meg
V: Hello! My name's Valerie.
He: Well, hi Valerie! I'm Herb. This is my wife, Hannah.
V: Nice to meet you.
Ha: Nice to meet you.
V: This is Rob, and Meg. They're on your tour.
He: Where are you from, Rob?
R: We're Australian.
Ha: Australia! Wow!
He: We're from Dallas, Texas.
V: Would you like a drink?
He: No, thanks.
V: Would you like a sandwich, Rob?
R: Yes, please.
V: Meg? Would you like a drink?
M: Yes, please. A mineral water, please. We had a terrible time at the airport … our bags were mixed up and all our things… Rob's mobile phone was just covered in water …

2A Vocabulary exercise 3 🔘 1.35

My name's Sabrina. I'm from Cardiff, Wales. I live in a flat. I don't have a cat or a dog. I go to school. I speak English and Italian. I drink coffee, lots of coffee.

2A Listening exercise 1 🔘 1.36

My name's David MacKinnon, that's M-A-C-K-I-N-N-O-N. I'm from Scotland but now I live in Istanbul. My life is very different here. I live in a flat, not a house. I only eat Turkish food now. I still read English newspapers, and I have the BBC on the internet in my flat. Oh yeah, I go to football matches here in Istanbul. That's different, because in Scotland I don't like football! I work at a university. I'm an English teacher. I speak Turkish, because I have a Turkish wife! I really like it here, it's great.

2B Listening exercise 2 1.37

I = interviewer P = Dr Palmer

I: What about women? Do women talk about sports?
P: No, no, they don't. Not like men. Women friends are more personal. They talk more about personal things. They talk about their feelings.
I: What other things are different?
P: Well, women listen to their friends a lot more.
I: Really?
P: Yes. That's why women know more about their friends.
I: Do men know a lot about their friends?
P: No, they don't. Ask a man what he knows about his friends and he can say 'My friend likes this music, and this sport, and this football team, and this kind of woman …' but after that, not much.
I: Very interesting. What about you, Doctor? Do you have a lot of friends?
P: No, I don't. I have one or two friends.
I: Do you play sports with your friends?
P: No, no, I don't. I'm seventy years old. But we talk about movies, and politics …
I: Thank you, Dr Palmer.
P: You're welcome.

2B Grammar exercise 2 1.38

I = interviewer   T = Tom   J = Jane

I: Do you have a lot of friends?
T: No, I don't. Not really. I have one good friend at the sports club, Tony.
I: The article says men do activities together. Do you play sports with your friends?
T: Yes, I do. Tony and I play tennis. Sometimes we watch the football together, but that's always at the sports club.
I: Do you talk about personal things, feelings, with your friends?
T: No, I don't. We don't talk a lot. If we do, we talk about sports.
I: Do you have women friends?
T: No, I don't. My wife wouldn't like it I think, if I had women friends.
I: Do you have a lot of friends?
J: Yes, I do. I have a lot of friends, yes.
I: Do you talk about personal things?
J: Yes, we do. We talk about problems, love life, things like that.
I: Do you do things together?
J: Yes, we do. Of course. But not typical things like shopping, if that's what you mean. We go out for a drink, or to a disco.
I: Do you have men friends?
J: Yes, I do! A lot of my friends are men friends. They talk about all their problems to me.

2D Listening exercise 2 1.44

W = woman B = Brian D = Dave

B: Hello?
W: Hi Brian? Are you at the airport?
B: Yes, I am.
W: Is the plane from New Zealand there?
B: Yes, it is. Who's on the plane?
W: You have to meet two girls, Delilah Williams and Patti Owen.
B: Fine. Delilah and Patti. What do they look like?
W: Hold on, I have their photos here. Yes, Delilah is short and pretty. She has long dark hair.
B: How old is she?
W: Around 30.
B: OK. And Patti?
W: Patti's also around 30 years old. They're friends. Patti's tall. She has fair hair.
B: Hello? Hello?

W: Yes?
B: Hi, it's Brian again. Sorry about that, my mobile phone. OK, Patti and Delilah. Who else?
W: There's also Dave.
B: Dave?
W: Yes, Dave Matthews. He's on the plane from Canada.
B: OK, what does he look like?
W: He's around 25. He's a little fat, he has dark hair. Oh, he has glasses.
B: OK. Wait a minute. I think I see Dave now.
W: Great. Call me when you meet everyone.
B: Sure. Bye. Excuse me. Are you Dave Matthews?
D: Yes, I am. Hi!

3B Listening exercise 2 1.47

V = visitor O = official

V: What is the name of the house?
O: There are at least four names for the house at 1600 Pennsylvania Avenue, including the President's Palace, the President's House and the Executive Mansion. But this famous building's common name is the White House.
V: Where is it?
O: The White House is in the centre of Washington, DC, the capital of the United States of America.
V: Who lives there?
O: The President of the United States and his family officially live in the White House. But there are hundreds of people who work there, and there are thousands of visitors every day.
V: How old is it?
O: The White House was built in 1800. It's now more than 200 years old.
V: How many rooms are there?
O: There are 132 rooms in the White House. There are 16 family bedrooms, 3 kitchens and 32 bathrooms. There are also 6 floors, 7 staircases, 3 elevators, 147 windows and 412 doors. There is a games room, a mini golf course, a tennis court, two swimming pools, a bowling alley and even a small cinema.
V: Are there public visits?
O: Yes, there are. Public visits are available for groups of 10 people or more from Tuesday to Saturday, from 7:30 am to 12:30 pm. Please note that there aren't any public telephones or public bathrooms on the tour of the White House.

3B Vocabulary exercise 2 1.49

M = man   W = woman

1
M: So, come in, come in.
W: Wow. So this is your new flat.
M: Yeah. Look, this is the hall. These are my pictures, here and here.
W: Mmm.

2
M: The bedroom.
W: Nice and big.
M: Yes. Look out the window. You can see the park …
W: Ooohh.

3
W: What's this room?
M: It's the dining room. I don't go in here really, there's only me.

4
W: Is this living room?
M: Yes, I'm here a lot of the time.
W: I like your TV.
M: Thanks.

5
M: Would you like a drink?
W: Umm, yes please. What do you have?
M: Come into the kitchen. Let's see.

6
W: Where's the bathroom?
M: Next to you. Right there.
W: I see.

7
W: Look at this balcony. You have a nice flat.
M: Thanks, it's not exactly the White House, but it's home.

3C Vocabulary exercise 4 1.51

L = landlord   S = Shelly   C = Claudia

L: OK, this is the flat. Bedroom here … and here. The beds are a little old.
S/C: Oh.
L: Here's the living room. You have a window, a sofa and a TV. The TV's Japanese. It's in good condition. It's my mother's TV.
S: That TV isn't new.
L: The kitchen. I know it's dirty, but look – the cooker works perfectly, and the fridge too. Look, oh … a sandwich. What's that doing there?
C: Yuk.
L: Anyway, it's 50 pounds per week. Do you want it or not?
C: Umm.
S: Yes, we do, thank you.

3D Listening exercise 3 1.55

I = information desk assistant
V = Valerie   D = Dave   S = Sam
W = woman

I: Can I help you?
V: Yes, where is the café please?
I: It's on the second floor. Go up the stairs and turn right.
V: Is there a lift?
I: Yes, there is. It's behind you.
V: Oh, yes. Thank you.
D: Excuse me, where are the toilets?
I: Sorry?
D: The men's toilets?
I: The toilets? They're over there. They're on the left, next to the lift.
D: Where?
I: Look, the brown doors.
D: Great.
S: Is there a public telephone near here?
I: Yes, there is. It's next to the stairs. It's on the right.
S: Thank you.
I: You need a card.
S: What?
I: You need a card. It doesn't accept coins.
W: Is there a baby changing room?
I: Sorry?
W: A baby changing room. I need to change the baby.
I: Yes, go down these stairs here. Then turn left and go along the hall. It's next to the women's toilets.
W: Thank you. Shhh shh.

3D Functional language exercise 2 1.56

1 Where is the café?
2 It's on the second floor. Go up the stairs and turn right.
3 Where are the men's toilets?
4 They're over there. They're on the left, next to the lift.
5 It's next to the stairs. It's on the right.
6 Go down these stairs here. Then turn left and go along the hall.

4A Functional language exercise 2 1.57

W = Will   M = man   Wo = woman

1
W: Excuse me, what time is it please?
M: It's five past twelve.
W: Thanks.

2
Wo: Excuse me, hello? What's the time, please?
W: I'm sorry, I don't know. I don't have a watch.
Wo: Oh, OK.

3
M: What time is your class?
M2: It's at eight thirty pm.
M: That's late.

4
M: I'm tired. What's the time?
Wo: It's half past one.
M: Half past one? Time for bed!

4B Listening exercise 1 1.62

1
This day is on May 15. We don't have this day in Britain, but I live in Mexico and it's great. That's because I'm a teacher. All the teachers take the day off and have a nice lunch together. On the next day, my students give me things: a bottle of wine, a book. I love it.

2
I don't work on this day, nobody works. It's a day to celebrate workers. My friends and I play a big game of football in the park. We have a meal together after the game too, of course. Then I go to the May Fair with my family and we watch the children dancing around the May pole.

3
While everybody is at a party or a restaurant or disco, I spend December 31 in my taxi. It's a very busy night, but I get a lot of money. There are lots of taxi drivers on the streets, and they all have customers. I get home early in the morning on January 1st and go to bed. In the afternoon, my family and I go to a good restaurant for lunch.

4
This is a very important day, I think. It is a day for us to remember some of the important things that have happened for women in the past. It's on March 8, which is in winter for me. It's not an official bank holiday, so I go to work. But I go on the Women's Day march every year, and then have a hot cup of tea with friends and talk

4C Listening exercise 2 1.64

H = host   R = Ralph   T = Tom   A = Anne
H: Hello, and welcome to our morning programme: *Phone In*. A new survey today says that 60% of men in this country never do the housework. That's the topic for our phone in today. Is that true for you? Please ring 01925 607607. Are you a man who does the housework? Please ring 01925 607607. Who does the housework in your house? We have several callers on the line – let's go to the first one. What's your name?
R: Ralph.
H: Where are you from, Ralph?
R: I'm from Scotland.
H: How often do you do the housework, Ralph?
R: I sometimes do the shopping.
H: What does 'sometimes' mean for you, Ralph?
R: Well, every Saturday.
H: Alright, that's normal. What other housework do you do?
R: Nothing.
H: Nothing?
R: My mother always does all the housework.

H: Lucky you. Do you want to say something to your mother on the radio?
R: Yeah, thanks, Mum!
H: That's nice. OK, who's the next caller?
T: Tom, from Liverpool.
H: Good morning, Tom. How are you?
T: Fine, thanks.
H: That's good. Here's our question of the day: how often do you do the housework?
T: Every day.
H: That's interesting. What housework do you do?
T: I make the bed every morning.
H: Excellent, Tom!
T: And I wash the clothes.
H: Great.
T: Thank you very much.
H: Next caller. Who is this?
A: I'm Anne, from Liverpool. I'm Tom's wife.
H: Hello, Anne. You have a very nice husband.
A: But it isn't true. Tom hardly ever does the housework. I do it!
H: Oh dear.
A: He never makes the bed. And the clothes? Ha! He washes them once a year.
H: What does he do?
A: He works in an office. He's always on the phone to silly radio shows!
H: Thank you very much for your call.

4D Listening exercise 1 1.70

V = Valerie   D = Dave   S = Sam
A = Angie   W = woman   M = man
T = teacher

1
D: Oh no, that's my phone. Just a minute… Hello?
A: Dave, it's Angie.
D: Hi, listen, I'm a bit busy right now …
A: I want to talk.
D: Now's not a good time. I'm in class. Can I call you back?
A: No, I want to talk now!
T: Is everything OK?
D: Fine. Everything is fine.

2
W: Hello?
S: Hello, I'd like to speak to Mr Green, please.
W: Sorry, he isn't here at the moment.
S: Where is he?
W: He's at the airport. Who's calling, please?
S: It's Sam Moore.
W: Would you like to leave a message?
S: Yes. Please tell him to call me.

3
V: Hello?
M: Is Simon there, please?
V: Sorry, you have the wrong number.
M: Oh, sorry. Goodbye.
V: Bye.

4D Listening exercise 3 1.71

Sh = Sharon   R = Rob   He = Herb
TA = travel agent

1
Sh: Hello, National History Society. Can I help you?
R: Sharon, hi. It's Rob.
Sh: Hello, Rob. How's the tour?
R: Fine, fine. The museum was very interesting. Are there any messages for me?
Sh: Yes, a woman called. Colleen Kerr.
R: OK. Meg, give me a pen. How do you spell that?
Sh: C-O-L-L-E-E-N Kerr K-E-R-R.
R: Yes. And what's her phone number?
Sh: 0865 455 901.
R: 0865 455 901. OK. Thanks, Sharon.
Sh: No problem. Bye.
R: Goodbye.

2
He: Come on, pick up the phone.
TA: Hello, Basic Airways?
He: Hello, I'd like to confirm a flight, please.
TA: Of course. Where to?
He: It's to Dallas, Texas.
TA: Flight number?
He: Just a minute … here it is – BAW 288.
TA: Date?
He: June 20.
TA: And your name?
He: Herb Curtis.
TA: Just a minute, please.
He: OK.
TA: Mr Curtis?
He: Yes?
TA: Your flight is confirmed. Flight BAW 288 to Dallas on Thursday June 20th at 8:45 am. Terminal 2.
He: Thank you very much.
TA: Thank you for calling. Have a nice day.

5A Speaking exercise 1 1.75

W = woman   M = man   T = teacher

1
W: Travellers from Europe go to desk A, travellers from outside Europe go to desk B.
M: Excuse me, can you repeat that, please?
W: Yes, if you are from Europe, go to desk A.

2
T: So, today in class we're going to do some vocabulary, vocabulary of tourism. You know tourism? Hotels, airports, visits to other countries … tourism. Open your books on page 80.
M: Excuse me, can you speak more slowly please?
T: Of course. I'm sorry. Open your books on page 80 please.

5B Listening exercise 1 1.77

L = Lara   T = Tom
L: Our holiday in Canada was lovely. It was a cross Canada trip. This is a photo of our train. We were on the train for ten days. The scenery in Canada is beautiful. This photo … oh, where was this one, Tom?
T: This photo was in Halifax. I remember it. Too bad about the weather. It wasn't very good.
L: That's right, it wasn't. It was rainy all the time there. The houses were lovely though, and the people were very nice.
T: Look at this one. This was amazing.
L: Yeah, yeah. Where was this? Was it in Quebec?
T: No it wasn't. It was Montreal. We were there for two days. This city has great jazz concerts.
L: Who was this musician?
T: I don't know. I can't remember his name. He was good though.
T: I remember this photo.
L: This is Toronto. You can see the CN Tower there. The shops weren't open that day. So we were in the park … doing nothing. I wasn't very happy.
T: No, you weren't. You were miserable.
L: It was cold!
T: Alright. Next photo?
L: Hmm.
L: I love this hotel.
T: This was in a big natural park. The park is called Banff. It was a perfect place to go skiing. Unfortunately, I can't ski. But Lara's right, the hotel was very good.
L: There was a Jacuzzi in our room!
T: Yep, good hotel. How many days were we in this park?
L: Three days, I think.

5C Reading & listening exercise 4
 1.79

W = Walter   T = Thelma   Wo = woman

Wo: Good morning, tickets and passports, please.
W: Here you are, tickets and … oh, wait a minute, where did you put the passports?
T: The passports? That was your job.
W: Was it?
T: Yes, it was. Do you have them?
W: Wait a minute.
T: Did you look in the black bag?
W: Yes, I did. Oh no …
T: Oh, Walter!

5D Listening exercise 1   1.82

J = Jane   G = George   C = Cathy

C: Oh George, is this our hotel?
G: I think so, dear. Isn't it beautiful?
C: Yes. What does the book say?
G: 'A happy, friendly 18th-century guest house, with gardens and barbecue …' This is good, darling.
C: So English! I love it.
J: Is this your first time in an English bed and breakfast?
C: Yes, it is. We don't have things like this in Texas. Did Shakespeare live here?
J: Umm, this guest house is only 200 years old, so no, I don't think so.
G: Too bad. Maybe he lived close to here.

5D Listening exercise 2   1.83

J = Jane   G = George   C = Cathy
O = owner

1
C: Darling, look. A dog.
O: Oi! Excuse me! You can't go there!
C: I'm sorry. I was only looking. What's his name?
O: Rex.
C: Can I touch him?
O: I'm afraid you can't. He's very dangerous.

2
O: Hello.
G: Hi. Excuse me, but could I use your phone? My mobile phone doesn't work here.
O: I'm afraid we don't have a phone for the public.
G: What do you mean, no phone? What about that phone?
O: Sorry, it's private.
J: Hi, is there a problem?
G: Yes, my phone doesn't work. He says this phone is not for guests. May I use your phone, please?
J: Of course. Here you are.
G: Thank you.

3
G: I'd like to pay the bill. Can I pay by credit card?
O: Of course. Visa? Mastercard?
G: American Express.
O: Oh no, I'm sorry, but we don't take American Express.
G: Fine. Visa then.

4
G: Oh, one more thing. Our bus leaves at a quarter past four. Is it OK to leave our bags here, please?
O: Certainly. It's £2 an hour.
G: But it's only for fifteen minutes!
O: I'm sorry, it's £2 minimum to keep bags.
G: I can't believe this.
C: George, what's wrong?
G: Happy, friendly hotel? I don't think so.

6B Listening exercise 1   2.1

J = Jim   S = Steph   M = Mike

J: Hello everybody and welcome to a new episode of *Actor! Author!* My name's Jim and today we have two new contestants: Mike from London.
M: Hello, Jim.
J: And Steph, from Birmingham.
S: Hi!
J: Now remember the rules. Each person takes a turn and chooses a category: Actor or Author. I give you four clues about the person, and you guess who it is. OK?
M/S: Yes.

6B Listening exercise 2   2.2

J = Jim   S = Steph   M = Mike

J: Mike, we'll start with you. When was the last time you saw a film?
M: Well Jim, I saw *Iron Man 2* last night.
J: Great film. Now, what category would you like?
M: Actor.
J: Alright, here we go. He was born in Kentucky, USA in 1963. He acted in many films by director Tim Burton, and is one of Hollywood's most popular male actors. His most famous role was as Captain Jack Sparrow in the *Pirates of the Caribbean* series of films.
M: Johnny Depp!
J: Yes!
J: OK Steph, now it's your turn. What category would you like?
S: Author, please.
J: Do you read a lot, Steph?
S: Yes, I do.
J: What was the last book you read?
S: Umm. I finished a book two weeks ago, but I can't remember the name. I'm a bit nervous.
J: That's alright. Right then, here we go. He is American. His books are translated into more than 40 languages. He wrote a very famous thriller. The book is in Paris, it starts in the Louvre Museum. The main character is an art professor called Robert Langdon. It's about symbols in the art of a famous Italian painter … Leonardo da Vinci.
S: Oh, wait … I read that book last year. Oh no …
J: Almost time …
S: David … Dan …
J: Yes?
S: Dan Brown.
J: Well done!
J: Back to you Mike. What category would you like?
M: Author this time, please.
J: She's from England and she taught English in Portugal about twenty years ago. She is now very, very rich. Her books are also movies. She wrote about a boy called Harry Potter. There are seven books in the series.
M: Umm … I know Harry Potter, but the author … ?
J: Time, Mike.
M: I don't know!
J: Steph?
S: JK Rowling!
J: Co-rrect!
J: Right, Steph you can win this. What category would you like?
S: Actor.
J: OK, this time it's an actress.
S: That's fine.
J: She was born in 1974. She's from Madrid, Spain. She got married to another famous Spanish actor in Hollywood, Javier Bardem. She won an Oscar® for the film *Vicky Cristina Barcelona* by Woody Allen.

S: Penélope Cruz! Penélope Cruz!
J: Co-rrect! Steph, you're the winner.

6C Pronunciation exercise 2
 2.7

1   M = man   W = woman
M: Come here, I want to tell you something.
W: What is it?
M: I love you.

2   M = man   W = woman   W2 = woman 2
W: What's that?
W2: Where?
W: I think there's a man at the window.

3   W = woman   C = child
W: Now listen to me, because I don't want to repeat this.
C: OK.

4   M = man   W = woman
M: Did you remember my book?
W: No, I didn't.
M: Doh!

6D Listening exercise 1   2.9

T = Tom   K = Karen   M = Mary
J = Janet   L = Lewis   P = Pete

M: So, what did you do yesterday?
P: I went to a football match.
M: Oh really? What did you think of it?
P: It was alright.
M: I love football. It's my favourite sport. Come on you Reds!
P: Oh.
M: What? You don't like football?
P: I'm not crazy about it.
M: Why did you go then?
P: I don't know. I went shopping yesterday too. That was good.
T: Wasn't that awful?
K: Sorry?
T: It was AWFUL.
K: I liked it.
T: I'm sorry, did we see the same film? It was awful. The actors were bad, the music was bad, everything was bad. I can't say a good word about that film.
K: I don't mind the actor. I think he's OK. He's very handsome.
T: Films were great before 1975. The last great film was *The Godfather*. Make him an offer he can't refuse. Fantastic film. Films today … humph. Rubbish.
K: OK then, can we go shopping now?
T: OK.
J: Hi there, where were you?
L: I was in the shops for a few minutes. I wanted something for my parents.
J: Oh. Anyway, what did you think of the boat ride?
L: What boat ride?
J: On the river Thames, silly! The boat ride we were on fifteen minutes ago!
L: Oh yes. I really liked it.
J: Really?
L: Yes. Usually I can't stand boats. I don't feel well. But that was wonderful.
J: Really?
L: Yes, really. You could see everything, and the light was perfect for photographs. What did you think of it?
J: It was good. Good.

7A Listening exercise 2   2.11

D = Daniel Barber   M = Martha Jones
A = Alex Willis

D: Good evening. I'm speaking to Martha Jones, famous for the *Two Fs diet: Fruit and Fish*. Martha, tell me about your diet.

M: Sure. It's simple. On our diet you can only eat fruit and fish. For example, have some fruit for breakfast. Don't eat any bread or drink any coffee in the morning. For lunch, eat fish and some tomatoes.

D: Tomatoes?

M: Yes, tomatoes are a fruit.

D: OK. What can I drink?

M: Water and fruit juice. You can't drink any wine, or beer or anything like that.

D: And what does this diet do for me?

M: You can see results very fast. Two or three kilos in a week. You feel good, too. Fish and fruit are a very good combination.

D: Thank you.

D: Our second diet is a Low C diet – that's C for carbohydrates. I asked Alex Willis about this diet. Alex, what can I eat on the Low C diet?

A: First, let me say it's a variation of the No C diet. So, eat lots of meat, chicken and fish.

D: Meat and chicken and fish?

A: Well, not at the same time. Eggs are good, too.

D: So, if I have eggs for breakfast, with some bread …

A: No, no, no, no, no! Bread, no.

D: No bread?

A: Bread is a carbohydrate. Don't eat any bread or pasta. And don't eat any fruit either. This is the key to this diet.

D: What about vegetables?

A: You can eat some lettuce for example, but don't eat any potatoes or carrots.

D: And what does this diet do for me?

A: Amazing results, fast! Many famous people follow this diet and it works, I guarantee you. Here, look at our list of celebrities …

D: Thank you.

D: Our third diet was the Soup diet. I couldn't speak to a representative of the Soup diet, but this is what their website says: 'In our amazing Soup diet, you can eat anything you want, but it has to be in soup form. This is because the human body digests soups very easily'. They have a list of soups you can buy from their website: fish soup, pasta soup and my favourite, banana and chocolate soup. Their website says that you can lose five kilos in a week with their diet.

7C Speaking & vocabulary exercise 2 2.16

1
A: What's this?
B: Sushi.
A: Sushi?
B: Yes, it's Japanese. It's raw fish. It's cold.

2
A: Would you like any salt with your chips?
B: No, thanks. These chips are very salty already.
A: Oh, I always put extra salt on.

3
A: How's your curry?
B: Excellent. It's very spicy. Can you give me some water, please?

4
A: Oh no. I can't stand spinach.
B: You can't?
A: No, not cooked spinach anyway. Horrible.

5
A: Brownies à la mode.
B: What does brownies 'à la mode' mean?
A: Well, the brownies are like a nice hot chocolate cake, and then you add a spoonful of cold ice cream. That's à la mode.
B: It looks very sweet to me.
A: I know.

7C Listening exercise 2 2.17

1 **M = man   W = woman**
W: I'm not a fussy eater. But my brother is. He's a very fussy eater. It's terrible. He only eats hamburgers, and he drinks lots of Coke.
M: How old is your brother?
W: He's twenty-six years old! That's why it's terrible!

2 **M = man   W = woman**
M: This red wine is very good.
W: I don't know. I think it's too young.
M: What year is it?
W: Just a minute. 2010. Yes, definitely too young.
M: I think it's good.

3 **M = man   W = woman**
W: How can you eat that?
M: What?
W: That cake!
M: Do you want some?
W: Good Lord, no. It's too sweet.
M: You're too fussy. Relax a little.

4 **M = man   W = woman**
W: And so we didn't eat it. Is there a fussy eater in your family?
M: Oh, yes. We invited my daughter and her boyfriend for dinner. It was awful. My wife made a delicious steak, and my daughter's boyfriend didn't eat anything. He said it was too salty. He was on a special diet. He's a swimmer and he can only eat rice.
W: What did you do?
M: My wife made him a very big plate of rice.

7D Listening exercise 1 2.21

M = Mr Owen   W = Mrs Owen
Wr = waiter
M: Bella Pizza. This looks nice. Let's eat here.
W: Good idea!
Wr: Hello sir, madam. Can I help you?
M: Table for two, please.
Wr: This way, please.

Wr: Would you like a drink?
M: Yes, please. A Cola.
W: And a mineral water for me, please.
Wr: Sparkling or still?
W: Err … sparkling please.
M: Could we have the menu too, please?
Wr: Of course.

Wr: Here you are. A Cola and a sparkling mineral water.
M/W: Thank you.
Wr: Are you ready to order?
M: Yes, we are. Ceri?
W: Can I have the seafood risotto?
Wr: I'm sorry. We don't have any seafood risotto today.
W: Oh, alright then. Just a minute.
M: Can I have the Mexican spicy pizza?
Wr: Yes.
W: Do you have a different risotto? Not the seafood?
Wr: Yes, we do. We have a vegetable risotto and a lovely cheese risotto.
W: The cheese risotto then, please.
Wr: Anything to drink?
M: Yes, some red wine please.

Wr: Here you are. Cheese risotto, Mexican spicy pizza, and red wine.
M: Do you have any salt?
Wr: Here you are.
M: Thank you.
Wr: You're welcome.

M: Well, that was delicious! Not too spicy.
W: I loved my risotto.
M: Waiter!
Wr: Yes?
M: Can we have the bill please?
Wr: Would you like a dessert? Coffee?
M: No, thanks. You?
W: No coffee for me, thank you. Just the bill.
Wr: Of course. Here you are. That's 15 pounds, please.

7D Pronunciation exercise 1 2.22

1   Can I help you?
2   Are you ready to order?
3   Could we have the menu, please?
4   I'd like a pizza, please.
5   Would you like a drink?
6   Can I have the bill?

8B Listening exercise 2 2.26

K = Kate   J = John
K: Yes, that was Aretha Franklin, another classic tune. Coming up we have lots more music and news, but first here's the traffic news. And it's a busy day out on the roads, isn't it, John?
J: Yes, it is, Kate. Good morning. We have an accident in Regent Street. There's a bus on fire. Everybody is OK, but traffic is moving very slowly. A large group of people are standing in the middle of Oxford Street. I can't hear them, but I think they are standing in front of the cars and singing! So, traffic isn't moving. The police are talking to them at the moment.
K: Can you tell us anything about the incident on Euston Road?
J: Yes, Kate. There's a lion – yes, I said a lion – on Euston Road. I'm looking at the camera now. A lot of cars are moving slowly around it. It's sitting in the middle of the road and looking at the cars …
K: Where did it come from! Do you have any more news?
J: Well, the police say that they think it escaped from the zoo. I'm waiting for more information on that. We have a report coming in now from East London. There's a big traffic problem. Someone is driving on the wrong side of the road.
K: It's another crazy day for drivers, then. Next traffic update at half past ten. Thanks, John.

8C Reading & listening exercise 5 2.28

J = Jack   T = Tracy
J: So, what do you do?
T: I'm a private detective.
J: That's interesting. Are you working now?
T: Yes, I am. At the moment, I'm following a man.
J: How exciting! Is he in this café?
T: Yes, he is. Right now he's talking with a woman.
J: So … who asked you to follow this man?
T: I can't tell you. He's waiting for me to call him now.
J: Well, my friends and I are having a little party. Would you like to join us?
T: No, thank you. I'm leaving.

8D Listening exercise 1 2.30

M = Man   W = Woman   M2 = Man 2
M: Right, let's go to that concert. I have my map …
W: OK. Where is it?
M: At the … Waterfront Hall.
W: Let's take a taxi.
M: A taxi? No, no, no. Taxis here are too expensive. We can take the metro.
W: Where are we?
M: We're … just a moment, we need to change here for another train. I think we're at this stop here …
W: Let's ask the man over there.
M: No, no. It's OK. Look, metro line 1, then change to the … line 3 … wait a minute, where am I?
W: Excuse me, we're going to the Waterfront Hall, and er …?

M2: Easy. Take the number 1 Line three stops, change there and onto the number 3 Line, then get off at the last station. Go upstairs and take the 232 bus going away from the town centre. It will take you 30 minutes.
W: Er, thank you. Did you understand that?
M: No.
W: Why don't we take that taxi now?
M: Wait. He said metro Line 1! Let's go on that.
M: I think we took the wrong train.
W: What do we do now?
M: Let's go up to the street and take a bus. At least we can see the city that way. And we can take photographs.
W: Uhhh, OK then.
W: I'm tired of buses.
M: We're nearly there. We can walk now. It takes 15 minutes to the Waterfront Hall.
W: I don't think that's a good idea. I don't want to walk. It's raining. I didn't bring an umbrella!
M: Wait … It's not far.
W: TAXI! TAXI!

9B Listening & speaking exercise 1
 2.37

Stand up. Move your fingers. At the same time you're moving your fingers, move your arms. Now move your shoulders and arms. Stop moving your arms. Move one leg and then the other leg. Sit down again.

9C Listening exercise 2 **2.39**

I = interviewer   D = David
I: Good afternoon. In the studio with us today we have David Barker. David works for the Exploratorium museum in San Francisco and is going to talk to us about memory and the human face. Hello, David.
D: Hello.
I: Now, my memory isn't very good. How's yours?
D: It's OK.
I: There's an expression in English, 'I never forget a face'. Is that true for you?
D: Well, it depends really. I'm interested in how we remember a human face. Many experts now believe that the top part of the face is more important than the bottom part.
I: What do you mean?
D: OK. For example, look at this picture.
I: This one here, with all the boys?
D: Yes. What do you notice about it?
I: I think this is an old picture. They're young, on a sports team. That's all.
D: Interesting. Because in this picture, if you look closely, all the boys have exactly the same face.
I: Really?! Oh, yes, you're right!
D: Hair is very important for memory. In fact, hair is the most important factor, then the eyes, then the nose.
I: This is the top part of the face.
D: Yes, the bottom part of the face, the mouth and err … chin are not so important. Look at this photo.
I: It looks very funny!
D: Yes. It's a combination of two faces, but with different hair again. Whose face is it, do you think?
I: Hmm … very difficult. Is that … is that the Mona Lisa's face?
D: Yes, it's hers.
I: Why is this difficult?
D: Because we've put Elvis' hair on her face.
I: Whose hair is it?
D: Elvis. The King of Rock and Roll.
I: Oh, yes. Now I can see it.
D: Yes. So you see how the hair makes it difficult. This is why famous people wear hats when they don't want people to know who they are.
I: They also wear sunglasses.
D: Yes, that's right.

9D Listening exercise 2 2.42

S = Sergio   J = Jackie   W = woman
D = doctor   Ma = Mark
S: Hello, Jackie. Are you alright?
J: Hi, Sergio. I don't know, I don't feel well.
S: Here, sit down. Sit down.
J: Oh, OK.
S: What's wrong?
J: I've got a headache. I feel cold. Oh, and my stomach.
S: Here, put on my jacket.
J: Thank you.
W: What's the matter?
J: I don't feel well.
W: Oh no.
J: It's alright. I'm fine, really.
W: Are you hungry?
J: No, no. I can't eat right now.
W: Was it something you ate last night?
J: I don't know. Maybe …
W: Here, take off that jacket.
J: Errr … OK.
J: Oh no.
Several voices: What's wrong?
J: I think … I think I'm going to be sick.
W: Do you want to go to the toilet?
J: Yes, sorry, oh … oh …
W: Is there a doctor here? Somebody call a doctor!
J: Hello. Are you a doctor?
D: Hello, I'm a doctor. How do you feel?
J: I feel alright now, thanks.
D: Good, good. Stand up. How's your stomach?
J: Not very good, but better now.
D: What did you eat for dinner last night?
J: I think … I think I had fish. Yes, it was Richard's retirement party at the restaurant. Was that the problem?
D: I'm sorry, but it probably was. Here, take two aspirin and lie down. You should sleep.
J: Thank you doctor.
W: Is she alright, doctor?
D: She'll be fine. Did anyone else eat fish at the office party last night?
Several voices: No, no …
W: Mark, didn't you …?
Ma: Wait a minute. You're right. Oh …
W: Are you OK, Mark?
Ma: Oh, no. I don't think so. I feel sick …

10B Vocabulary exercise 2 2.44

I = interviewer   G = Giovanni
I: So, tell me about Rome. Are the people friendly?
G: Yes, they are. They're very friendly.
I: Is it an expensive place?
G: Yes, it is. That's the problem with life in the capital.
I: Is it dangerous to walk on the streets at night?
G: It depends where you are. In some areas yes, it can be dangerous.
I: Can you visit interesting things in your city?
G: Yes, you can. Of course! There are lots of museums, art galleries, monuments …
I: Is it very noisy?
G: Yes, it is. Very noisy. Rome is famous for noise.
I: Are there any beautiful or historical buildings?
G: Of course. It has the most beautiful buildings in Europe. The Colosseum, for example. There's also the Vatican.
I: Is the air polluted?
G: Yes, it is. Unfortunately.

10B Listening exercise 2 **2.46**

1
Sofia: Oh no, I don't live in the capital, Madrid. I live in Alicante with my husband and two sons. It's in the south of Spain, on the coast of the Mediterranean Sea. It's smaller than Madrid, but life is much better. Madrid is

too big. In the summer it's too hot, and in the winter it's too cold. That's why people from Madrid come here. And there are a lot more children here – at least you see more families with two or three children. Life is more expensive in Madrid, too expensive for many big families.

2
Nick: Life in the capital city, Athens, is faster than in other cities of Greece. I was born in Athens, I live in Athens, and it's true – life is very fast! Athens is noisier and dirtier – but it has more of everything: more money, opportunities, jobs, noise, pollution, entertainment … bigger and better stadiums and sports facilities … Many Greeks say that people in Athens aren't very friendly, they don't have time for you. This isn't true. I know lots of very friendly people here in Athens.

10D Listening exercise 1 **2.49**

W = woman   M = man   SA = shop assistant
W: Look, a souvenir shop.
M: Oh. We don't have time, really.
W: Come on, I need things for my family.
M: Alright, but hurry. I'm going to look at the books.
SA: Hello, can I help you?
M: No, I'm just looking, thank you.
W: Excuse me, hello?
SA: Yes?
W: Do you have any small London mugs?
SA: No, just these large ones.
W: Can I have two of the red mugs then, please?
SA: Of course.
W: These pens are pretty. How much are they?
SA: £1.50 each.
W: Can I have five pens too, please?
SA: Yes, here you are.
W: Thank you.
M: Are we OK now?
W: Yes, look. I've got two mugs for my parents and these tiny pens for the children. I need something for my sister. What do you think of these key rings?
M: No.
W: Why not?
M: They're rubbish. Look, it's not real silver! The mugs are nicer.
W: I don't want to give her a mug.
M: What then?
W: Maybe a book. Did you see any good books?
M: Yes, this one is all about St Paul's cathedral. And it's a bargain. It only costs two pounds!
W: Oh, well let's get one for my sister too then. She likes architecture.
M: Fine. Can we pay now?
W: Yes, we can. Relax.
SA: Hello.
W: Yes, these please.
SA: The pens, two mugs and two books. That's £24.90 please.
W: Here you are. Could I have two bags please?
SA: Here you are.
W: Thank you.
M: Hurry, it's time to go.
W: I'm coming!

11A Listening exercise 2 **2.56**

I = interviewer   J = Janet   M = Michael
I: Tell us about yourself.
J: OK, my name's Janet. I'm from Canada, and I work in the security office of a big hospital in London.
I: What do you do?
J: I'm a security guard. Er … most of the time I watch the security televisions. It's not a very difficult job.
I: Who do you work with?

J: I work with two other security guards in the office. They are both men.
I: When did you start here?
J: I started at this hospital two years ago.
I: Do you like your job?
J: Yeah, yeah, I do.
I: Why?
J: Well, I like working at night. I always like working at night. It's quiet. It's easy work. I have a nice boss.
I: What do other people think of your job?
J: I think my job is great, but my parents don't like it. My father is very traditional. He says that a security guard is a man's job. Yeah, well … what can you do?

I: Hello, what's your name?
M: Michael.
I: Where do you work in the hospital?
M: I work in the accounts department.
I: So you're an accountant?
M: Yes, I am.
I: Who do you work with?
M: There are three people in the office.
I: When did you start here?
M: I worked in London for ten years in a big company. But I didn't like it. I started at this hospital last year.
I: Do you like your job?
M: Yes, I do. Many people say 'Oh, accounts, that's boring'. But I like it.
I: Why do you like your job?
M: Because it's interesting, I like working with numbers.

11C Listening exercise 1 2.58

D = David   S = Sandra   W = Will
A = Ali   J = Jarvis   R = reporter
R: What about you, David?
D: Well, I'm already 64 years old. Next year I'm not going to work any more. So, number 1 is good for me. I'm going to go and live in France. I'd like to practise my French more. Let's see, what else … a good bed. Yes, that makes me think. I'm going to get a good bed. The bed we have is ten years old.
R: Sandra, what things are you going to do?
S: Oh yes, I read all about the benefits of water in a magazine once. That's my resolution. I'm going to drink more water. And I'm going to tell my husband about optimists living longer than pessimists do. He always sees the bad side of everything!
R: So Will, is there anything here for you?
W: Well, I already play football and do lots of sports, so number 3 isn't a new thing for me. I'm not going to live in another country, or stop work, either.
R: Well, are you going to do anything on the list?
W: OK, OK. Umm … Number 5. My desk, especially, which is terrible. I'm going to clean my desk.
R: Ali, what about you?
A: Every year I say I'm going to stop smoking, I'm going to stop smoking. But then I always find an excuse to start again. What else is on the list? Exercise is a good idea. Yes, I'm going to go to a gym, starting next year. And I'm going to quit smoking.
R: And what about you, Jarvis?
J: I only work here part time, I'm still at university. When I finish, in two years, I'm going to take a long break. I'm going to travel around China on a motorbike with a friend. I got the idea from a film. I'm also going to vote in the next election, but I always vote in elections because I think that's important.

11D Listening exercise 1 2.61

M = man   W = woman   W2 = woman 2
1
M: Good morning.
W: Hello! How are you?
M: Fine. A bit tired. Listen, are you going to George's retirement party tomorrow?
W: George's retirement party? I didn't know!
M: There was a sign …
W: Well … tomorrow? I don't know.
M: Would you like to go? A group of us are meeting at 5:30 in the café. I'm going to take us by car.
W: I'm sorry, I can't. I'm busy tomorrow.
M: Oh.
W: I'm really sorry. Please give my congratulations to George though.
M: Ok, I will.

2
W: My computer isn't working again. I can't log on to the system.
W2: Oh dear. Well, what time is it?
W: Umm, almost 11 o'clock.
W2: I think it's time for a break. Would you like to have a cup of tea?
W: I'd love to. Thanks.
W2: Great!

3
M: Hello?
W: Yes, I'm here for the job interview.
M: Do you have a letter? Can I see the letter please?
W: Yes. Well. That. I think I threw away the letter. By accident. Is it a big problem?
M: What's your name?
W: Cecilia Hannon.
M: And what time is your interview?
W: Quarter past eleven.
M: OK, you're here. Would you like to come with me, please?
W: Thanks.

12B Listening exercise 2 2.67

J = journalist   M1 = man 1   W = woman
M2 = man 2
1
J: Hi. Can I ask you some questions?
M1: I'm busy, but OK.
J: One survey says that one in four Americans have been on television. Have you ever been on television?
M1: No, I haven't. I've never been on television. And I don't want to be.
J: Have you ever spoken on the radio?
M1: No, never. Sorry, I'm very busy now.
J: OK, thank you.

2
J: Excuse me, have you ever been on television?
W: Yes, I have! I was on a game show once. Have you heard of *The Big Award*?
J: Yes, I have. It's on Channel 4. Did you win anything?
W: No, I was in the audience.
J: Great. One more question. Have you spoken on the radio?
W: No, I haven't.
J: Have you written a letter to a newspaper?
W: No, I haven't.
J: Thanks.

3
J: Hello.
M2: Hello.
J: I'm doing a survey. Can I ask you some questions?
M2: Sure.
J: Have you ever been on television?
M2: What do you think?
J: I'm sorry? I don't understand.
M2: I work on television. I announce the evening news. Have you seen me?

J: Oh, yes, I have! You're wearing a hat. I didn't recognize you.
M2: That's alright.
J: Well, thanks anyway.

12C Speaking exercise 1 2.71

In my country, English is an important language. It wasn't always important, but it is now. In the past, people learnt French or German at school. Now, everybody is learning English. For learning a language, I think it's important to learn new vocabulary and grammar, but it's also very important to practise speaking. For me, learning English is difficult, and I think speaking is the most difficult. I can understand English in books, and in magazines, but when I listen to English or American people I don't understand. In my classes, we practise speaking a lot. When I started the year, it was impossible. I couldn't pronounce any sentences in English. Now it's better.

12D Listening exercise 1 2.72

M = man   M2 = man 2   W = woman
W2 = woman 2
1
M: Thank you very much.
W: Yes, thank you. It was wonderful. Just wonderful.
W2: Don't mention it. We're happy you enjoyed it.
W: I loved the soup. Delicious.
M: You have a lovely house too. I liked your husband's book collection.
W2: Oh, thank you. You must come again.
W: No no no. You must come and visit us in the country. It's our turn.
W2: That would be great. Thank you.
W: No, thank you.
M: Anyway, good night then.
W: Good night!
W2: Good night!

2
TG = tour guide
TG: Well everyone, this is the end.
TG: Brian is going to take people to the airport. He's waiting outside. I also wanted to say thank you VERY much. It was really really nice to meet you. I mean that honestly! This was my first tour and I had a very nice time.
TG: There's a paper going round for you to put your email addresses on if you want to write to each other. My email address is at the top. You can write to me!

3
T = teacher   S = student spokesperson
T: OK, OK. Quiet please.
T: Thanks. Listen, today is the last class as you know. You can see your results at the school webpage. They will be online next week. But I would like to say thanks a lot for being a very very nice group to work with. I hope you have enjoyed this semester as much as I have.
S: We wanted to give you a little something. From the class.
T: Oh! Oh, thank you.
S: You're welcome. We hope you like it.
T: Oh wow. A watch! I needed a watch too!

4
TP = tennis player
TP: Well done.
TP2: Thanks, it was a difficult game this time.
TP: No, no. You played really well. It was impossible for me.
TP2: Thank you. Thank you. I still can't believe it. Really, thank you.
TP: That's fine. Enjoy the victory, and see you next Saturday.
TP2: Great. OK, yeah.

1 | Review

1 Match the words in the box to the parts of the picture A–F.

> a computer   a chair   a phone
> a bottle of water   a clock   a newspaper

2 Complete with *his/her/their*.

1 She's the tour guide. _____ name is Valerie.
2 Sam isn't at the party. He is in _____ room.
3 They are from America. _____ names are Herb and Hannah.
4 Meg and Rob are in London. This is _____ hotel.
5 She's new. It's _____ first day at work.
6 He's famous. _____ photo is in the newspaper.

3 Make questions and answers.

> Emily Pryde is a teacher in Rio de Janeiro, Brazil. She's 43 years old. She teaches English and French. She's from Dublin, Ireland.

1 / her name Emily? *Is her name Emily? Yes, it is.*
2 / Brazilian?
3 / her last name Janeiro?
4 / a language teacher?
5 / Irish?
6 / 21 years old?

4 In each of the short dialogues below, there is a word missing. Insert the missing word.

1 Julian, this Alyssa. She's new.
　Nice to meet you.
2 How you spell your name?
　A-L-Y-S-S-A.
3 Are you language teacher?
　Yes, I am.
4 Where is she from?
　She from Warsaw. She's Polish.
5 Are these your keys?
　No, aren't. My keys are here.
6 Would you like a drink?
　No, thank.

5 Complete the dialogues with the phrases in the box.

> Would you like   How are you   I'm fine
> Yes, please   No, it isn't

A: Good morning.
B: Oh, hi. (1) _____?
A: Fine, thanks. And you?
B: Oh, (2) _____.
A: There's a bar over there. (3) _____ a drink?
B: (4) _____. A coffee, please.

A: OK, two coffees.
B: Is this your coffee?
A: (5) _____. This is my coffee.

6 Work in pairs. Read the dialogue.

2 | Review

1 Complete the profile with verbs from the box.

eat   go   have   speak   live   work

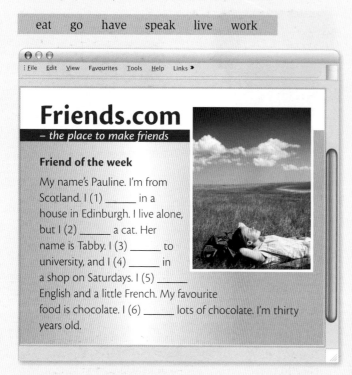

Friends.com
– the place to make friends

Friend of the week

My name's Pauline. I'm from Scotland. I (1) _____ in a house in Edinburgh. I live alone, but I (2) _____ a cat. Her name is Tabby. I (3) _____ to university, and I (4) _____ in a shop on Saturdays. I (5) _____ English and a little French. My favourite food is chocolate. I (6) _____ lots of chocolate. I'm thirty years old.

2 Make more sentences about Pauline. Use the words.

1 play football(✓) *She plays football.*
2 smoke (✗) *She doesn't smoke.*
3 drink coffee (✓)
4 speak Spanish (✗)
5 have lots of friends (✓)
6 have a boyfriend (✗)
7 go dancing (✓)
8 live with her parents (✗)

3 Complete the sentences with a word from the box.

aunt   brother   daughter   father
grandfather   mother   son   uncle   sisters

1 He is my mother's brother. He is my _____.
2 He's my father's father. He is my _____.
3 She's my father's wife. She is my _____.
4 She's my uncle's wife. She is my _____.
5 He's my father's son. He is my _____.
6 She's my sister. She is my parents' _____.

4 Make sentences for the other three words in the box in exercise 3.

5 There is a grammatical mistake in each sentence or question. Correct the mistakes.

1 We doesn't work.
2 No, he don't.
3 Do you has lots of friends?
4 She speak French and Spanish.
5 I don't lives in London.
6 Is you married?

6 Rearrange the words to make questions.

1 you of lot have friends a do ?
2 with you do your parents live ?
3 different is how life your ?
4 do do you what ?
5 name your what is ?
6 are from where you ?
7 you with who live do ?

7 Match the questions from exercise 6 with the answers in the article.

An interview with an expat

a _____ I'm Joe Matthews and I'm 28.
b _____ I'm from Dublin in Ireland.
c _____ No, I don't. I live in Paris now.
d _____ I'm a student. I study Art at The Sorbonne University.
e _____ I speak French every day and I eat lots of French bread.
f _____ Yes, I do.
g _____ I have a flat with friends.

8 Complete the sentences with the adjectives in the box.

beautiful   fair   tall   thin   young

1 She isn't old. She's _____.
2 She isn't fat. She's _____.
3 She isn't short. She's _____.
4 She isn't ugly. She's _____.
5 Her hair isn't dark. It's _____.

3 | Review

1 Complete the sentences. Write the words in brackets as an ordinal number.

1 This is my _____ (3) visit to Britain.
2 The toilets are on the _____ (4) floor.
3 Today is the _____ (1) day of school.
4 This wall is from the _____ (5) century.
5 Hannah is Herb's _____ (2) wife.

2 Look at the picture and make questions and answers.

1 a bed? *Is there a bed? Yes, there is.*
2 how many windows? *How many windows are there? There are two windows.*
3 how many chairs?
4 a desk?
5 a computer?
6 how many lamps?
7 any plants?
8 a television?
9 any curtains?

3 In the text below there are five grammatical mistakes. Underline and correct the mistakes.

The MoMA (Museum of Modern Art) is in New York near from Madison Avenue, between Fifth and Sixth Avenue. There are lots of differents types of art in the MoMA. There is paintings, sculptures, drawings and any photographs. There is an education centre on the one floor of the museum.

4 Underline the five adjectives in the text below and match them to their opposites 1–5.

This is my home. I live in a lovely cottage in a small village near to the mountains. The village is very old. It is beautiful here and very quiet.

1 big _____
2 ugly _____
3 horrible _____
4 noisy _____
5 new _____

5 Complete the phone conversation with *some, any, a, is* and *are*.

A: Good morning. Welcome to Houseswap USA. How can I help you?
B: Hi! I'd like a house for my holiday. Are there (1) _____ places in Florida?
A: Yes, there are (2) _____ houses near Miami. What kind of house do you want?
B: I'd like (3) _____ house with three bedrooms and a big garden.
A: OK, there (4) _____ three houses that match that description.
B: Do they have (5) _____ swimming pool?
A: Yes, they do.
B: Great. (6) _____ there a garage?
A: Yes, there (7) _____.

6 Complete the dialogue with phrases from the box.

The toilets. OK, go along the hall here and turn left
No, down the stairs
opposite the information desk
Then go down the stairs
Turn left
Yes, can I help you

Man: Excuse me!
Woman: (1) _____?
Man: Yes, where are the toilets please?
Woman: (2) _____.
Man: Sorry? Turn …?
Woman: (3) _____ …
Man: Left, OK.
Woman: (4) _____.
Man: Up the stairs.
Woman: (5) _____.
Man: Sorry! Down the stairs.
Woman: Yes, and the toilets are on the left (6) _____.
Man: Thank you.

4 | Review

1 Will Cotton's wife works as a nurse. Look at the pictures and complete the sentences with the correct verb.

1 She _____ breakfast with Will.

2 She _____ coffee.

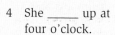

3 She _____ to bed.

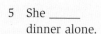

4 She _____ up at four o'clock.

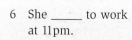

5 She _____ dinner alone.

6 She _____ to work at 11pm.

2 Work in pairs. Cover the sentences. Look at the pictures and say the sentences.

3 Complete the text about Nothing Day with the correct prepositions.

(1) _____ January 16, I celebrate Nothing Day. This year Nothing Day is (2) _____ Tuesday, so I don't go to work of course! I wake up (3) _____ 11 o'clock (4) _____ the morning. I read a newspaper and have a big breakfast. I watch television (5) _____ the afternoon. (6) _____ 6 o'clock, I go for a walk with a friend. I read a book (7) _____ the evening and I do nothing (8) _____ night. It's a boring day, but a good day.

4 Match the dates in the box to the special days in the United States for the year 2012. There are two extra dates you do not need.

Note: dates are Day/Month/Year

13/05/2012	14/06/2012	22/11/2012
12/01/2012	04/09/2012	30/03/2012
04/07/2012	~~19/02/2012~~	

1 The third Monday in February is Presidents' Day. *19/02/2012*
2 The second Sunday in May is Mother's Day.
3 July the fourth is Independence Day.
4 June the fourteenth is Flag Day.
5 The first Monday in September is Labor Day.
6 Thanksgiving Day is the fourth Thursday in November.

5 Rearrange the words to make questions and sentences.

1 dishes do do how often the you ?
2 do you what usually Saturdays on do ?
3 never Saturdays I on work .
4 make always the morning in the bed I .
5 up you often morning get in do early the ?
6 rubbish I the out rarely take .
7 Saturday the do on morning you shopping sometimes do ?

6 Choose the correct response, a or b.

1 Good morning, Explore London tours.
   a) Hello, I'm Valerie.
   b) Hello, it's Valerie.

2 Hello, I'd like to speak to Brian, please.
   a) I'm sorry, he isn't here.
   b) Please tell him to call me.

3 Hello, is that Michelle?
   a) I'm sorry, you have the wrong number.
   b) Is Michelle there please?

4 Dave can't answer the phone right now.
   a) Can I leave a message?
   b) Can I speak to Dave, please?

5 Would you like to leave a message?
   a) Yes, please. Please tell her to call me.
   b) You have the wrong number.

5 | Review

1 Make questions in the past from the prompts.

1 when / you on holiday?
2 where / you?
3 how many days/ you there?
4 who / you with?
5 what / the weather like?
6 the people nice?
7 what / the food like?
8 it a good holiday?

2 Match each answer to a question in exercise 1.

a   Five days.
b   Yes, it was a very good holiday.
c   I was in the south of France.
d   Yes, they were.
e   I was with my brother and his wife.
f   It was sunny and warm.
g   I was on holiday last summer.
h   The food was excellent.

3 Work in pairs. Think of your last holiday. Ask and answer the questions in exercise 1.

4 Complete the text with *was* or *were*.

Famous Canadians

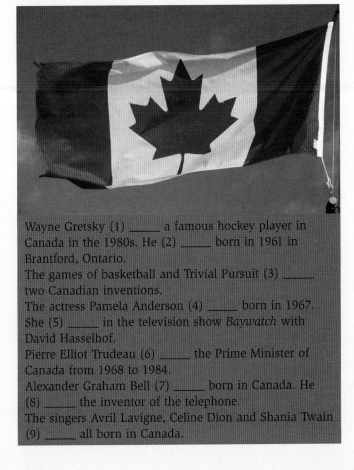

Wayne Gretsky (1) _____ a famous hockey player in Canada in the 1980s. He (2) _____ born in 1961 in Brantford, Ontario.
The games of basketball and Trivial Pursuit (3) _____ two Canadian inventions.
The actress Pamela Anderson (4) _____ born in 1967. She (5) _____ in the television show *Baywatch* with David Hasselhof.
Pierre Elliot Trudeau (6) _____ the Prime Minister of Canada from 1968 to 1984.
Alexander Graham Bell (7) _____ born in Canada. He (8) _____ the inventor of the telephone.
The singers Avril Lavigne, Celine Dion and Shania Twain (9) _____ all born in Canada.

5 In each of the sentences below, one word is not necessary. Cross out the unnecessary word in each sentence.

1 What's your favourite weather to like?
2 This new app can to translate lots of languages.
3 I can't not speak English very well.
4 The weather was lovely and was sunny.
5 Yes, I no agree. We can take lots of money.
6 I did remembered. Look! It's here.
7 Can I use your phone, please me?
8 Of course you can use.

6 Rewrite the sentences in the past tense.

1 Every night when I arrive home, I cook dinner.
  Last night when I arrived home …
2 I don't watch television.
3 I listen to music and study English for a couple of hours.
4 I use the internet to practise my English.
5 I look at English websites.
6 I don't go to bed late, around 11 o'clock.

7 Work in pairs. Which of the sentences in exercise 6 are true for you? What did you do last night?

8 Work in pairs, A and B.

A: Ask for permission using the pictures and words to help you.
B: Respond.

Swap roles and repeat.

pay?

use?

turn on?

use?

ask question?

6 | Review

1 There are five grammatical mistakes in the blog.
<u>Underline</u> and correct the mistakes.

Our new baby blog

Marcos is now one week old! We goed for a walk in the park with him yesterday. He opened his eyes and looked at his mother for five minutes! It was beautiful. I not go to work last week. I stayed at home and doed the housework. My parents saw Marcos on Saturday. They was very happy. My father sayed Marcos looks exactly like me! Here is a photo of Marcos with his grandparents.

2 Complete the text. Put the verbs in brackets into the past simple.

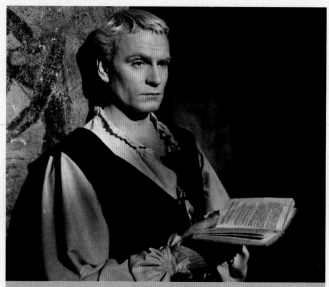

Laurence Olivier (1) _____ (*be*) born in England in 1907. He (2) _____ (*study*) acting in London, and (3) _____ (*start*) his career in 1926. He (4) _____ (*work*) in all the great Shakespeare plays when he (5) _____ (*be*) young, and (6) _____ (*make*) film versions of *Henry V*, *Hamlet* and *Richard III*. *Hamlet* (7) _____ (*win*) the Oscar® for best film in 1948. In 1947, he (8) _____ (*become*) a knight and his name (9) _____ (*change*) to Sir Laurence Olivier. He (10) _____ (*be*) married three times. Laurence Olivier (11) _____ (*die*) in 1989.

3 Complete the sentences with a verb from the box. Put the verbs into the past simple. There is one verb you don't need.

> write   win   die   read   make

1 John Wayne _____ in 1979. He was 72 years old.
2 The author Octavio Paz, from Mexico, _____ the Nobel Prize for Literature in 1990.
3 Frank Sinatra was a famous singer, but he also _____ more than 15 films.
4 JK Rowling _____ the first *Harry Potter* book at a time when she didn't have a job.
5 Clint Eastwood _____ an Oscar® for the films *Unforgiven* and *Million Dollar Baby*.
6 Agatha Christie _____ more than eighty novels and plays. She is one of the most famous authors in the English language.
7 Peter Jackson _____ the film version of *The Lord of the Rings* in 2000. The third film, *The Return of the King*, _____ many awards, including Best Picture Oscar®.

4 Change the adjectives in the brackets to adverbs and put the word in the correct position in the sentence.

1 Can you read this very please? (careful)
2 He cried really and we couldn't hear him. (quiet)
3 She speaks English. (good)
4 You sing very. Can you sing again, please? (beautiful)
5 Can you speak? I can't understand you. (slow)

5 Decide if the sentence is positive (☺), negative (☹) or neutral (☺).

1 I really like Chinese food.   ☺ ☹ ☺
2 I think the *Star Wars* movies are terrible.   ☺ ☹ ☺
3 I'm not crazy about holidays on the beach.   ☺ ☹ ☺
4 I can't stand football.   ☺ ☹ ☺
5 This food is awful!   ☺ ☹ ☺
6 I don't mind rainy weather.   ☺ ☹ ☺
7 I love old westerns.   ☺ ☹ ☺

6 Work in pairs. Change the sentences in exercise 5 so they are true for you.

7 | Review

1 <u>Underline</u> the word that doesn't belong.

1 bread   rice   pasta   fish
2 cheese   milk   carrots   eggs
3 tomatoes   lettuce   rice   carrots
4 eggs   oranges   apples   bananas
5 cake   chicken   chocolate ice cream

2 Tick (✓) *how much* or *how many*.

	How much …?	How many …?
apples		
chocolate		
milk		
oranges		
eggs		
sugar		
tomatoes		
juice		
chicken		

3 Make questions from the sentences. Use the chart in exercise 2 to help you.

1 We need some apples.   *How many apples do you need?*
2 We have chocolate.
3 I want some milk.
4 We need oranges.
5 I have eggs.
6 We need tomatoes.

4 Read the recipe for risotto and tick (✓) the photos A–I of the food you need.

This is a recipe for basic risotto. It's an Italian dish. An Italian friend taught me. You need special Arborio rice, butter, an onion, some white wine, water and Parmesan cheese. Oh, and some salt and pepper too. You can put fish, vegetables or chicken in the risotto.

5 Rearrange the words to make sentences or questions.

1 you week rice much how every eat do ?
2 have wine I some please can ?
3 a for I'd like please table two .
4 is this excuse too soup salty me !
5 any you German have do beer ?
6 vegetables raw eat I don't .

6 Choose the correct phrases to complete the sentences.

1 Can I have   a) that's twenty pounds?
                       b) the menu, please?

2 Do you have   a) any salt?
                       b) the bill, please?

3 We haven't   a) the four cheese pasta.
   got any   b) mineral water.

4 Would you like a   a) smoking or non-smoking table?
                       b) thank you.

5 Could we   a) look the menu, please?
                       b) have the menu, please?

7 Complete the dialogues with a word from the box. There is an extra word.

> tip   non-smoking   dessert   bill   main course
> menu

1 A table for two, please.
   Yes, of course. Smoking or _____?

2 What would you like for the _____?
   The steak, please.

3 What would you like for _____?
   Can I have chocolate ice cream, please?

4 How much is the _____?
   £12. That's cheap.

5 Did you leave a _____?
   Yes, I left £1 for the waiter.

8 | Review

1 Complete the sentences with a suitable word.

1 JFK International, Heathrow and Charles de Gaulle are very big a_____.
2 Ferrari, Volkswagen and Ford™ are different c_____.
3 Suzuki, Vespa and Honda are different m_____.
4 Paddington, Grand Central and Beloruskaya are important r_____ s_____.
5 Boeing, Airbus and Concorde are all names of p_____.

2 Complete the text with the correct form of the words in the box.

| drive stand take travel wait |

Every day I (1) _____ a bus to work. I can't stand (2) _____ by bus, but I live too far away to walk and I can't (3) _____ a car. I don't like (4) _____ at the bus stop and I hate (5) _____. I can never get a seat.

3 Choose the correct phrase to complete the dialogues.

1 a) What do you do?   I'm sitting in a restaurant.
  b) What are you doing?

2 Are you listening to me?   a) Yes, I am.
                             b) Yes, I do.

3 a) Do you often take taxis?   No, I don't.
  b) Are you often taking taxis?

4 Can you talk right now?   a) No, I'm driving.
                             b) No, I drive.

5 What does she do?   a) She's a teacher.
                             b) She's talking to the students.

6 What is he doing?   a) He works.
                             b) He's working.

4 Put the dialogue in the correct order.

☐1 Alan! What are you doing?
☐9 Indian.
☐ No, I don't want to see a film.
☐ Nothing at the moment. Why?
☐ That's a good idea. Where do you want to go?
☐ We could go to the cinema.
☐ If you don't want to see a film, let's go out for a meal.
☐ Why don't we go out?
☐ Yes, that sounds nice. Italian or Indian?

5 Complete the sentences with *love* or *hate* and the correct form of a word from the box.

| eat fly play watch |

Venus Williams (tennis star) (1) _____ horror movies. Sometimes she's frightened and wants to leave the cinema, but she still thinks they are great!

Jennifer Aniston (actress) really (2) _____ Mexican food. Her favourite is Tortilla chips with Salsa.

Dennis Bergkamp (football player – Arsenal & Holland) was on a plane to the USA and there was a storm. Now he really (3) _____.

Dan Brown (author – *The Da Vinci Code*) (4) _____ tennis. He plays every afternoon.

6 Look at the picture and make six sentences using the present continuous.

9 | Review

1 Look at the picture and label the clothes words A (for the top part of the body), B (for the bottom part of the body) or AB (for both).

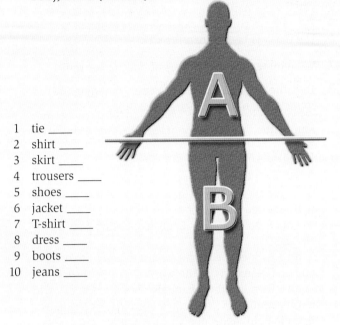

1 tie ____
2 shirt ____
3 skirt ____
4 trousers ____
5 shoes ____
6 jacket ____
7 T-shirt ____
8 dress ____
9 boots ____
10 jeans ____

2 Here is some advice for making a good impression at a job interview in Britain. Complete with *should/ shouldn't* + a verb from the box.

> wear   find out   be   answer   say

1 You ____ hello with confidence.
2 You ____ jeans or trainers.
3 You ____ information about the job and company first.
4 You ____ questions truthfully.
5 You ____ late.

3 Work in pairs. Choose a situation from the box below. Ask your partner for advice about the clothes you *should* or *shouldn't* wear.

> a party   a job interview   a walk in the mountains
> at the beach   going to the cinema   to school

4 Replace the underlined words in the dialogues with possessive pronouns.

1 **A:** I have brown eyes. What colour are <u>your eyes</u>?
   B: <u>My eyes</u> are green.
2 **A:** I know her name is Laura. What's <u>his name</u>?
   B: Michael. What about the baby? Is it <u>their baby</u>?
   A: It's <u>her son</u>, but not <u>his son</u>.
3 **A:** Mr Smith, please explain this money in your bag.
   B: It's not <u>my money</u>.
   A: Mr Smith, if the money isn't <u>your money</u>, whose money is it?
   B: I can't remember his name. I can only remember his face!
4 **A:** I have a terrible memory. Is this <u>your book</u>?
   B: No, it's not <u>my book</u>. It's <u>his book</u>.

5 In each sentence below there is a word missing. Insert the missing word.

☐ 1 What's matter?
☐ 2 Thank you much.
☐ 3 I've got stomach ache. And I'm cold.
☐ 4 Here, put my jacket.
☐ 5 Are alright?
☐ 6 I don't very well.

6 Put the lines in exercise 5 in the correct order to make a dialogue. Practise the dialogue with a partner.

10 | Review

1 Complete the sentences.

1 A library is *a place where you can look at books and CDs.*
2 A hotel is …
3 A bank is …
4 A town hall is …
5 A shop is …
6 A hospital is …
7 A stadium is …
8 A school is …

2 Each of these sentences has one extra word. Cross out the extra word.

1 You mustn't to take photographs in the airport.
2 Children mustn't not buy cigarettes.
3 You needn't to go to school after you are 16 years old.
4 You must to be 15 years old to get married.
5 You don't mustn't smoke in public buildings.
6 You must can have a licence to have a television.
7 You needn't not have a licence to buy a gun.

3 Work with a partner. Put a tick (✓) next to the laws in exercise 2 that are true for your country. Put a cross (✗) next to the laws that are not true.

4 Change the sentences with a cross so they are true.

5 Underline the word that has a different comparative form. Write the comparative form of the underlined word in the space.

1 nice   cheap   small   <u>interesting</u>   *more interesting*
2 easy   hot   happy   friendly   _____
3 safe   polluted   dangerous   beautiful   _____
4 big   nice   good   cold   _____
5 beautiful   modern   ugly   historical   _____
6 cheap   clean   safe   expensive   _____

6 Look at the photos of three different souvenirs from South Africa and decide if the sentences are true (T) or false (F). Correct the false sentences.

$150   mask
$15
$5

1 The keyring is bigger than the mask.
2 The keyring is the cheapest souvenir.
3 The CD is the most expensive souvenir.
4 The CD is smaller than the mask.
5 The mask is the most expensive souvenir.
6 The mask is bigger than the CD.

7 Make three other sentences about the souvenirs.

8 Read the facts about South Africa. Underline the correct form of the adjective.

1 South Africa is one of the *richest / richer* countries in Africa.
2 It is *biggest / bigger* than its neighbours Namibia, Botswana, Zimbabwe and Mozambique.
3 The weather is hot and dry, but it's *coldest / colder* at night than during the day.
4 It is the *biggest / bigger* English-speaking country in Africa.
5 South Africa is one of the *largest / larger* producers of gold and diamonds in the world.
6 South Africa has three capitals: Pretoria, Cape Town and Bloemfontein. Pretoria is *biggest / bigger* than Bloemfontein, and Cape Town is the *biggest / bigger*.

9 Put the dialogue in the correct order.

☐ Of course. What size?
☐ Yes, please. Do you have any other T-shirts?
☐ Medium, please.
☐ Yes, we do. We have the souvenir T-shirts over here.
☐ Good, can I have two, please?
[1] Hello, can I help you?
[7] Two medium souvenir T-shirts. That's twelve pounds.

10 Work in pairs. Practise the dialogue in exercise 9.

11 | Review

1 Complete the sentences.

1 My brother is going to work ___ a big company.
2 He's going to be in charge ___ lots of people.
3 It's going be a full-___ job.
4 He isn't going to work ___ the public.
5 It's a well-___ job.

2 Complete the questions.

1 _____ do?
I'm a shop assistant.

2 _____ work?
I work in a shoe shop.

3 _____ with?
I work with two other people. Janet is the other shop assistant and Kerry is the manager.

4 _____ start work?
The shop opens at nine o'clock, but I get to work at eight thirty.

5 _____ here?
I started here five years ago.

6 _____ your job?
Yes, I do. I like working with the public and I can get cheap shoes!

3 Rearrange the words to make predictions.

In fifty years …

1 work will people home from
2 colder than it much will be now .
3 and eat fresh fruit people vegetables won't .
4 speak everyone the language will same .
5 will travel everyone electric cars by .
6 in live people houses won't underground will live they .
7 cities people in live the countryside they will in live won't .

4 Work in pairs. Tick (✓) the predictions you agree with and compare.

5 Here are some phrasal verbs that are in *Straightforward Elementary*. Choose the correct preposition.

1 Take *off / on* your jacket if you feel hot.
2 Will Cotton gets *out / up* at six o'clock every morning.
3 Did you turn *off / in* the lights?
4 You look tired. Maybe you should sit *down / up*.
5 OK, everybody please stand *up / out* to do this exercise.
6 Did you take *off / out* the rubbish last night?
7 Can you turn *along / on* the radio please?

6 Work in pairs, A and B.

A: Invite B to one of these places.
B: Respond.

Swap roles and repeat.

7 Complete the sentences with a word from the box.

| shut throw turn log clean |

1 I'm sorry, we'll _____ up this mess right now.
2 I didn't _____ down the computer when I left work, and it was on all night.
3 First you _____ on with your username. Then enter your password.
4 Please don't _____ off the lights. I'm afraid of the dark.
5 They never _____ away anything. They keep it all.

12 Review

1 Complete the sentences with the present perfect of the verbs in the box.

> make   be   write   win   sing

1 We _____ in concerts around the world.
2 I _____ lots of books.
3 We _____ many CDs.
4 I _____ many sports competitions.
5 I _____ a singer for over 40 years.

2 Work in pairs. Look at the sentences in exercise 1. Think of a *living* famous person for each of the sentences.

We have sung in concerts around the world.
U2. Yes, or maybe Coldplay.

3 Make questions using the words in the box.

Have you ever	had	an English-speaking country?
	read	a book in English?
	cooked	diving in the sea?
	visited	breakfast in bed?
	gone	a meal for more than eight people?

4 Work in pairs. Ask the questions in exercise 3. Answer *Yes, I have* or *No, I haven't*.

5 Do the *Grammar Rules* quiz. For each definition, choose the correct verb form from the box.

6 Each dialogue below has one mistake. Correct the mistake.

Dialogue 1
A: What a beautiful gift! Thank you very much.
B: You welcome.

Dialogue 2
A: Excuse me. I could use your phone for a minute?
B: Sure. Here you are.
A: Thank you.

Dialogue 3
A: Why we don't ask the teacher?
B: Yes, that's a good idea.
A: OK then.

Dialogue 4
A: What does the matter?
B: Nothing. I'm fine.
A: You look tired.

Dialogue 5
A: What do you think of the *Star Wars*® films?
B: I think they great.
A: I don't like them.

7 Match the dialogues 1–5 in exercise 6 to the functions. There is one extra function.

a ___ suggesting   d ___ asking/saying how you feel
b ___ talking about   e ___ asking permission
     likes/dislikes
c ___ thanking   f ___ inviting someone

> present simple (x3)   present continuous (x2)   past simple (x3)
> future (*going* to) (x2)   future (*will*) (x2)   present perfect (x3)

GRAMMAR RULES

Part One
Rules of Form

1 There is no change to the infinitive EXCEPT third person (add 's'). _____
2 The form is *to be* + verb+ *-ing*. _____
3 For regular verbs, add *-ed* to the verb. There are irregular verbs, eg *went, saw, made*. _____
4 The form is the auxiliary *will* + infinitive. _____
5 For questions and negatives the form is the auxiliary verb *do/does* + infinitive. _____
6 The form is the auxiliary verb *have* + past participle. _____
7 The form for questions and negatives is the auxiliary verb *did* + infinitive. _____
8 The form is the auxiliary *to be* + *going to* + infinitive. _____

Part Two
Rules of Use

1 We use this verb form to talk about things we usually do. _____
2 We use this verb form to talk about things that happened at an unspecific time in the past. _____
3 We use this verb form to talk about things that happened at a specific time in the past. _____
4 We use this verb form to talk about things we are doing NOW. _____
5 We use this verb form to talk about predictions in the future. _____
6 We can use this verb form to ask about people's experiences. _____
7 We use this verb form to talk about plans for the future. _____

Irregular verb list

Infinitive	Past simple	Past participle
be	was / were	been
begin	began	begun
break	broke	broken
bring	brought	brought
buy	bought	bought
can	could	been able
choose	chose	chosen
come	came	come
cost	cost	cost
do	did	done
drink	drank	drunk
drive	drove	driven
eat	ate	eaten
feel	felt	felt
fly	flew	flown
forget	forgot	forgotten
get	got	got
give	gave	given
go	went	gone
have	had	had
hear	heard	heard
hurt	hurt	hurt
keep	kept	kept
know	knew	known
learn	learned / learnt	learned / learnt
leave	left	left
lose	lost	lost
make	made	made
mean	meant	meant
meet	met	met
pay	paid	paid
put	put	put
read	read	read
ride	rode	ridden
run	ran	run
say	said	said
see	saw	seen
sell	sold	sold
shine	shine	shone
show	showed	shown
shut	shut	shut
sing	sang	sung
sit	sat	sat
sleep	slept	slept
speak	spoke	spoken
spell	spelt / spelled	spelt / spelled
stand	stood	stood
swim	swam	swum
take	took	taken
teach	taught	taught
tell	told	told
think	thought	thought
throw	threw	thrown
understand	understood	understood
wake	woke	woken
wear	wore	worn
win	won	won
write	wrote	written

Macmillan Education
4 Crinan Street
London N1 9XW
A division of Macmillan Publishers Limited
Companies and representatives throughout the world

ISBN 978-0-230-42-305-3 Student's Book
ISBN 978-0-230-42-445-6 Student's Book & website access

This edition published 2012
First edition published 2005

Designed by eMC Design Ltd.
Original design by Newton Harris Design Partnership.
Illustrated by Rowan Barnes-Murphy p13; Mark Beech p17 (r); Paul Collicutt pp40, 89, 92, 97, 99, 134, 136, 150, 155, 157; Stephen Dew pp33, 38, 39, 47; Nigel Dobbyn pp 28, 29, 56, 86, 98; Mark Duffin pp20, 34, 39, 43, 50, 54, 95, 147, 149, 151; Geoff Jones pp36, 37, 53, 84, 112, 132, 133, 136, 137, 154; Joanna Kerr pp25, 28, 57, 72, 83, 85, 95, 107, 133, 135; Peter Lubach pp7, 8, 12, 24, 46, 63, 77, 102, 119, 154; Julian Mosedale pp17 (l), 66, 129; Peter Richardson p56; Laszlo Veres p18.
Cover design by eMC Design Ltd.
Cover photograph by Alamy/Robert Harding Picture Library Ltd, Getty Images/ Doug Chinnery, Corbis/Roger Tidman,Corbis/Lois Ellen Frank, Corbis/Gerolf Kalt, Alamy/Images & Stories
Picture research by Sally Cole

Author's acknowledgements
I would like to thank all the editors and representatives at Macmillan for their support for this project. I'd also like to thank my wife Sofia and my two children for putting up with all the time I spend in the office.
This book is for all the teachers who I've trained on Certificate and Diploma courses. I've learned as much from them as I hope they have from me.
Thanks to Philip Kerr for giving me a chance to join the *Straightforward* project all those years ago.

The publishers would like to thank all the teachers from around the world who provided invaluable comments, suggestions and feedback on the first edition. The publishers would also like to thank the following people for their help and contribution to the second edition:
Tatiana Baytimerova (Russia), Lenka Boehmová (Czech Republic), Dr. Manuel Padilla Cruz (Spain), Svetlana Elchaninova (Russia), Jennifer Díaz Green (Dublin), Elena Mokeeva (Romania), Lynn Thomson (freelance editor), Amany Shawkey (Macmillan Egypt), Maria Teresa Rius Villaplana (Spain), Natalia Vorobyeva (Russia).

The author(s) and publishers are grateful for permission to reprint the following copyright material:
Page 145: Extracted material from an interview by David Barker for an exhibit entitled 'If You're Going to Rob a Bank, Wear a Wig' copyright © David Barker 1998, as part of the Exploratorium's Memory Exhibition May 1998 – January 1999, reprinted by permission of the author.

The authors and publishers would like to thank the following for permission to reproduce their photographs:
Alamy/Aflo CoLtd p54(E), Alamy/Agefotostock p16(J), Alamy/D.Alexandre p33(D), Alamy/Antiques & Collectables p9(earring), Alamy/Bon Appetit p76(brownies), Alamy/V.Arcomano p6(taxi), Alamy/J.Arnold Images pp23(br), 52-53(b), Alamy/S.Belcher p16(G), Alamy/Bubbles p78(tl), Alamy/J.Blackler p6(hospital sign), Alamy/Blammo p9(sweets), Alamy/A.Burton pp32–33(A), Alamy/Colinspics p16(K), Alamy/T.Cordoza p151(bm), Alamy/D.Crausby p137(mr), Alamy/B.Crooks p6(police sign), Alamy/Cultura p151(bmr), Alamy/ Dinodia p9(identity card), Alamy/G.B.Evans p44(C), Alamy/Corbis Flirt p116(A), AlamyFoodfolio pp72(G),153(cheese), Alamy/C.Fichera p16(B), Alamy/a la France p52(insert), Alamy/P.Freels p33(F), Alamy/G.Gay p137(tr), Alamy/A. Ghazzel p6(football sign), Alamy/F1online digitale Bildagentur GmbH p108(mr), Alamy/D.Green p100(bear), Alamy/S.Hamblin p6(pizza sign), Alamy/M.

Harvey p156(tm), Alamy/P.Horree p103, Alamy/A.Hung p54(A), Alamy/ Ilian Studio p151(bml), Alamy/DW Images p108(taxi), Alamy/I Love Images p116(C), Alamy/Mode Images Ltd p108(keys), Alamy/RT Images p6(station sign), Alamy/T.Jackson p123(bmr), Alamy/R.Judges p137(ml), Alamy/N.van Kampenhout pp55, 151(ml), Alamy/A.Kowalsky pp84(tr), 104(A), Alamy/J. Palmer p151(m), Alamy/Golden Pixels LLC p62(b), Alamy/mediablitzimages(uk) Ltd, Alamy/MBI p96(bl), Alamy/B.Nicholson p153(bottle), Alamy/D.Pearson p38(tr), Alamy/C.Garnham Publishing p16(L), Alamy/Red Brick Stock p74(b), Alamy/J.Remisiewicz p16(M), Alamy/A.Rodriguez p119(ml), Alamy/A.Rome p104(E), Alamy/B.Schofield p38(tl), Alamy/Isifa Image Services s.r.o p54(D), Alamy/Photos 12 p64(B), Alamy/Stockfolio p72(H), Alamy/Studiomode p16(F), Alamy/Swedish & Swedish p6(hotel sign), Alamy/D.Green Technology p16(D), Alamy/H.Threlfall p151(mr), Alamy/P.Titmus p97(br), Alamy/Art Directors & Trip p108(shirt), Alamy/TTL Images p63(bl), Alamy/Eye Ubiquitous p16(H), Alamy/A.Weinbrecht p18(mr), Alamy/C.Howes/Wild Places Photography p6(bus sign), Alamy/Woodystock p137(b), Alamy/J.Woodworth p16(A), Alamy/G.Wrona p33(E), Alamy/J.Yeats p16(C); **Archive Photos** p132(tl); **Bananastock** pp98(A), 113(br), 126-127; **Blend Images** pp93(mt), 114, 118(br), 123(bl); **BrandX** p72(F); **Comstock Images** pp148, 153(onion), 153(salt), 153(garlic), 153(meat); **Corbis** pp94, 98(B), 98(D), 124(A), Corbis/D.Butow p18(br), Corbis/A.SkellyBlend Images p82(br), Corbis/Imane/BSIP p98(C), Corbis/J.Springer Collection p152(bl), Corbis/epa p66(bl), Corbis/M.Everton p6(airport sign), Corbis/R.Friedman p54(B), Corbis/M.Gareth p76(curry), Corbis/J.Hicks p106(B), Corbis/R.Jack p123(bml), Corbis/R.Koch p58(b), Corbis/ T.Laisne p123(tr), Corbis/G.Mendel p68(mr), Corbis/R.Nowitz p34(t), Corbis/The Food Passionates p153(rice), Corbis/Photoalto p27(br), Corbis/ Atlantide Phototravel p68(b), Corbis/ H.R.Abrams/Reuters p124(B), Corbis/ Rubberball p89(bl), Corbis/M.Kemp/In Pictures p68 (bmr), Corbis/S.Sonnet p68(br); **Exploratorium**, www.exploratorium.edu.(composites)/David Barker pp96(tr), 96(mr); **FoodPix** p72(B); **Gallo Images** p109(br); **Getty Images** pp19(C), 19(A), 72(A), 106(A), Getty/Bloomberg p125(mr), Getty/A.Crawford p153(jug), Getty/Fuse p147, Getty/A.Hall p49(br), Getty/G.Hall p82, Getty/AFP pp116(B), 124(D), 156(tr), Getty/ S.Simpson p62(ml), Getty/B.Thomas p135(b), Getty/Vetta p116(D); **Getty Images Entertainment** p66(br); **Getty Images News** p66(mr); **Glow Images**/Corbis p26, Glow Images/W.Schardt p76(spinach), Glow Images/Y.Tanaka p93(mb); **Harper Collins**/C.S.Lewis Estate, cover of The Lion, The Witch and The Wardrobe p65(tr); **Iconica** pp22(bl), 33(C), 54(C), 124(C); **ImageSource** p19(B), 19(F), 72(K), 123(tl), 153(butter); **Image100** p76 (sushi); **Macmillan Australia** p72(C); **Macmillan Publishers Ltd**/Haddon Davies p72(D), 72(J), Macmillan Publishers Ltd/Rob Judges pp133(tr), 134(tr), 137(mbr), 137(mbl), Macmillan Publishers Ltd/D.Tolley/D.Ryan p116(F); **MetroNaps Europe** p42(t); **Orkut** logo © Orkut/Google p9(mb); **Photoalto** pp9(pen), 62(mr); **Photographers Choice** pp9(keys), 19(G), 24(C), 48(t), 116(E); **Photolibrary**/P.Adams p78(br), Photolibrary/E.Audras p128(tr), Photolibrary/ Dr W.Bahnmuller p104(C), Photolibrary/Bowman p35(br), Photolibrary/ Corbis p24(B), Photolibrary/P.Desnerck p19(H), Photolibrary/E&E Image Library p33(B), Photolibrary/C.Ehlers p104(D), Photolibrary/Food Collection p72(E), Photolibrary/ S.Grandadam p104(F), Photolibrary/R.de la Harper p106(C), Photolibrary/HBSS p22(r), Photolibrary/J.Lee p72(I), Photolibrary/ Nicoloson p19(E), Photolibrary/C.Peterson p88,Photolibrary/J.Pigozne p58(t), Photolibrary/Radius Images p79(br), Photolibrary/Digital Light Source p104(B), Photolibrary/A.Sydenham p75(bl), Photolibrary/A.Watson p44(D), Photolibrary/M.Wordley p87; **Photonica** p108(t shirt); **Platform** p24(D); **Rex Features**/Action Press p132(ml), Rex Features/Broad Image p132(tr), 135(ml), Rex Features/Lions Gate/Everett p64(F), Rex Features/ Universal/Everett p64(E), Rex Features/Everett Collection p64(C), Rex Features/ Warner Brothers/Everett p64(D), Rex Features/Image Source p16(I), Rex Features/A.Hooper/Daily Mail p66(tr), Rex Features/B.J.Ritchie/Hotsauce p123(br), Rex Features/Paramount p64(A), 64(G), Rex Features/R.Sachs p34(tl), Rex Features/A.Segre p85(br), Rex Features/Startraks Photo pp132(br), 135(bmr), Rex Features/Sipa Press p44(A); **Riser** p44(B); **Stockbyte** pp7(br), 119(tl), 123(tm); **Stock Food Creative** p75(tr); **Stone** pp24(A), 115(tr); **Taxi** p76(chips); **Tuenti** logo © Tuenti 2011 p15(mt); **The Image Bank** p69(tl); **Up the Resolution** pp9(apple), 19(D); **Wire Image** p135(tl).

Printed and bound in Thailand
2017 2016 2015 2014
11 10 9 8 7 6 5